On the Holy Spirit Against th

It may indeed be undignified   statements that are foolish; w   pointed that way by Solomon's wise advice, *"not to answer a fool according to his folly."* But there is a danger lest through our silence error may prevail over the truth, and so the rotting sore of this heresy may invade it, and make havoc of the sound word of the faith. It has appeared to me, therefore, to be imperative to answer, not indeed according to the folly of these men who offer objections of such a description to our Religion, but for the correction of their depraved ideas. For that advice quoted above from the Proverbs gives, I think, the watchword not for silence, but for the correction of those who are displaying some act of folly; our answers, that is, are not to run on the level of their foolish conceptions, but rather to overturn those unthinking and deluded views as to doctrine.

What then is the charge they bring against us? They accuse us of profanity for entertaining lofty conceptions about the Holy Spirit. All that we, in following the teachings of the Fathers, confess as to the Spirit, they take in a sense of their own, and make it a handle against us, to denounce us for profanity. We, for instance, confess that the Holy Spirit is of the same rank as the Father and the Son, so that there is no difference between them in anything, to be thought or named, that devotion can ascribe to a Divine nature. We confess that, save His being contemplated as with peculiar attributes in regard of Person, the Holy Spirit is indeed from God, and of the Christ, according to Scripture , but that, while not to be confounded with the Father in being never originated, nor with the Son in being the Only-begotten, and while to be regarded separately in certain distinctive properties, He has in all else, as I have just said, an exact identity with them. But our opponents aver that He is a stranger to any vital communion with the Father and the Son; that by reason of an essential variation He is inferior to, and less than they in every point; in power, in glory, in dignity, in fine in everything that in word or thought we ascribe to Deity; that, in consequence, in their glory He has no share, to equal honour with them He has no claim; and that, as for power, He possesses only so much of it as is sufficient for the partial activities assigned to Him; that with the creative force He is quite disconnected.

Such is the conception of Him that possesses them; and the logical consequence of it is that the Spirit has in Himself none of those marks which our devotion, in word or thought, ascribes to a Divine nature. What then, shall be our way of arguing? We shall answer nothing new, nothing of our own invention, though they challenge us to it; we shall fall back upon the testimony in Holy Scripture about the Spirit, whence we learn that the Holy Spirit is Divine, and is to be called so. Now, if they allow this, and will not contradict the words of inspiration, then they, with all their eagerness to fight with us, must tell us why they are for contending with us, instead of with Scripture. We say nothing different from that which Scripture says.— But in a Divine nature, as such, when once we have believed in it, we can recognize no distinctions suggested either by the Scripture teaching or by our own common sense; distinctions, that is, that would divide that Divine and transcendent nature within itself by any degrees of intensity and remission, so as to be altered from itself by being more or less. Because we firmly believe that it is simple, uniform, incomposite, because we see in it no complicity or composition of dissimilars, therefore it is that, when once our minds have grasped the idea of Deity, we accept by the implication of that very name the perfection in it of every conceivable thing that befits the Deity. Deity, in fact, exhibits perfection in every line in which the good can be found. If it fails and comes short of perfection in any single point, in that point the conception of Deity will be impaired, so that it cannot, therein, be or be called Deity at all; for how could we apply that word to a thing that is imperfect and deficient, and requiring an addition external to itself?

We can confirm our argument by material instances. Fire naturally imparts the sense of heat to those who touch it, with all its component parts; one part of it does not have the heat more intense, the other less intense; but as long as it is fire at all, it exhibits an invariable oneness with itself in an absolutely complete sameness of activity; if in any part it gets cooled at all, in that part it can no longer be called fire; for, with the change of its heat-giving activity into the reverse, its name also is changed. It is the same with water, with air, with every element that underlies the universe; there is one and the same description of the element, in each case, admitting of no ideas of excess or defect; water, for instance, cannot be called more or less water; as long as it maintains an equal standard of wetness, so long

SELECTED WORKS
Gregory of Nyssa

Copyright © 2014 Beloved Publishing

All rights reserved. No part of this book may be reproduced, scanned, or distributed in any printed or electronic form without permission.

Printed in the United States of America

ISBN:1631740466

the term water will be realized by it; but when once it is changed in the direction of the opposite quality the name to be applied to it must be changed also. The yielding, buoyant, *"nimble"* nature of the air, too, is to be seen in every part of it; while what is dense, heavy, downward gravitating, sinks out of the connotation of the very term *"air."* So Deity, as long as it possesses perfection throughout all the properties that devotion may attach to it, by virtue of this perfection in everything good does not belie its name; but if any one of those things that contribute to this idea of perfection is subtracted from it, the name of Deity is falsified in that particular, and does not apply to the subject any longer. It is equally impossible to apply to a dry substance the name of water, to that whose quality is a state of coolness the name of fire, to stiff and hard things the name of air, and to call that thing Divine which does not at once imply the idea of perfection; or rather the impossibility is greater in this last case.

If, then, the Holy Spirit is truly, and not in name only, called Divine both by Scripture and by our Fathers, what ground is left for those who oppose the glory of the Spirit? He is Divine, and absolutely good, and Omnipotent, and wise, and glorious, and eternal; He is everything of this kind that can be named to raise our thoughts to the grandeur of His being. The singleness of the subject of these properties testifies that He does not possess them in a measure only, as if we could imagine that He was one thing in His very substance, but became another by the presence of the aforesaid qualities. That condition is peculiar to those beings who have been given a composite nature; whereas the Holy Spirit is single and simple in every respect equally. This is allowed by all; the man who denies it does not exist. If, then, there is but one simple and single definition of His being, the good which He possesses is not an acquired good; but, whatever He may be besides, He is Himself Goodness, and Wisdom, and Power, and Sanctification, and Righteousness, and Everlastingness, and Imperishability, and every name that is lofty, and elevating above other names. What, then, is the state of mind that leads these men, who do not fear the fearful sentence passed upon the blasphemy against the Holy Ghost, to maintain that such a Being does not possess glory? For they clearly put that statement forward; that we ought not to believe that He should be glorified: though I know not for what reason they judge it to be expedient not to confess the true nature of that which is essentially glorious.

For the plea will not avail them in their self-defence, that He is delivered by our Lord to His disciples third in order, and that therefore He is estranged from our ideal of Deity. Where in each case activity in working good shows no diminution or variation whatever, how unreasonable it is to suppose the numerical order to be a sign of any diminution or essential variation! It is as if a man were to see a separate flame burning on three torches (and we will suppose that the third flame is caused by that of the first being transmitted to the middle, and then kindling the end torch), and were to maintain that the heat in the first exceeded that of the others; that that next it showed a variation from it in the direction of the less; and that the third could not be called fire at all, though it burnt and shone just like fire, and did everything that fire does. But if there is really no hindrance to the third torch being fire, though it has been kindled from a previous flame, what is the philosophy of these men, who profanely think that they can slight the dignity of the Holy Spirit because He is named by the Divine lips after the Father and the Son? Certainly, if there is in our conceptions of the Substance of the Spirit anything that falls short of the Divine ideal, they do well in testifying to His not possessing glory; but if the highness of His dignity is to be perceived in every point, why do they grudge to make the confession of His glory? As if any one after describing some one as a man, were to consider it not safe to go on to say of him as well that he is reasoning, mortal, or anything else that can be predicated of a man, and so were to cancel what he had just allowed; for if he is not reasoning, he is not a man at all; but if the latter is granted, how can there be any hesitation about the conceptions already implied in *"man"*? So, with regard to the Spirit, if when one calls Him Divine one speaks the truth, neither when one defines Him to be worthy of honour, to be glorious, good, omnipotent, does one lie; for all such conceptions are at once admitted with the idea of Deity. So that they must accept one of two alternatives; either not to call Him Divine at all, or to refrain from subtracting from His Deity any one of those conceptions which are attributable to Deity. We must then, most surely, comprehend along with each other these two thoughts, viz. the Divine nature, and along with it a just idea, a devout intuition , of that Divine and transcendent nature.

Since, then, it has been affirmed, and truly affirmed, that the Spirit is of the Divine Essence, and since in that one word *"Divine"* every idea of greatness, as we have said, is involved, it follows that he who grants that Divinity has potentially granted all the rest—the gloriousness, the omnipotence, everything indicative of superiority. It is indeed a monstrous thing to refuse to confess this in the case of the Spirit; monstrous, because of the incongruity, as applied to Him, of the terms which in the list of opposites correspond to the above terms. I mean, if one does not grant gloriousness, one must grant the absence of gloriousness; if one sets aside His power, one must acquiesce in its opposite. So also with regard to honour, and goodness, and any other superiority, if they are not accepted, their opposites must be conceded.

But if all must shrink from that, as going even beyond the most revolting blasphemy, then a devout mind must accept the nobler names and conceptions of the Holy Spirit, and must pronounce concerning Him all that we have already named, that He has honour, power, glory, goodness, and everything else that inspires devotion. It must own, too, that these realities do not attach to Him in imperfection or with any limit to the quality of their brilliance, but that they correspond with their names to infinity. He is not to be regarded as possessing dignity up to a certain point, and then becoming different; but He is always such. If you begin to count behind the ages, or if you fix your gaze on the Hereafter , you will find no falling off whatever in dignity, or glory, or omnipotence, such as to constitute Him capable of increase by addition, or of diminution by subtraction. Being wholly and entirely perfect, He admits diminution in nothing. Whereinsoever, on such a supposition as theirs, He is lessened, therein He will be exposed to the inroad of ideas tending to dishonour Him. For that which is not absolutely perfect must be suspected on some one point of partaking of the opposite character. But if to entertain even the thought of this is a sign of extreme derangement of mind, it is well to confess our belief that His perfection in all that is good is altogether unlimited, uncircumscribed, in no particular diminished.

If such is the doctrine concerning Him when followed out , let the same inquiry be made concerning the Son and the Father as well. Do you not confess a perfection of glory in the case of the one as in the case of the other? I think that all who reflect will allow it. If, then, the honour of the Father is perfect, and the honour of the Son is perfect, and they have confessed as well the perfection of honour for the Holy

Spirit, wherefore do these new theorists dictate to us that we are not to allow in His case an equality of honour with the Father and the Son? As for ourselves, we follow out the above considerations and find ourselves unable to think, as well as to say, that that which requires no addition for its perfection is, as compared with something else, less dignified; for when we have something wherein, owing to its faultless perfection, reason can discover no possibility of increase, I do not see either wherein it can discover any possibility of diminution. But these men, in denying the equality of honour, really lay down the comparative absence of it; and so also when they follow out further this same line of thought, by a diminution arising from comparison they divert all the conceptions that devotion has formed of the Holy Spirit; they do not own His perfection either in goodness, or omnipotence, or in any such attribute. But if they shrink from such open profanity and allow His perfection in every attribute of good, then these clever people must tell us how one perfect thing can be more perfect or less perfect than another perfect thing; for so long as the definition of perfection applies to it, that thing can not admit of a greater and a less in the matter of perfection.

If, then, they agree that the Holy Spirit is perfect absolutely, and it has been admitted in addition that true reverence requires perfection in every good thing for the Father and the Son as well, what reasons can justify them in taking away the Father when once they have granted Him? For to take away *"equality of dignity"* with the Father is a sure proof that they do not think that the Spirit has a share in the perfection of the Father. And as regards the idea itself of this honour in the case of the Divine Being, from which they would exclude the Spirit, what do they mean by it? Do they mean that honour which men confer on men, when by word and gesture they pay respect to them, signifying their own deference in the form of precedence and all such-like practices, which in the foolish fashion of the day are kept up in the name of *"honour."* But all these things depend on the goodwill of those who perform them; and if we suppose a case in which they do not choose to perform them, then there is no one among mankind who has from mere nature any advantage, such that he should necessarily be more honoured than the rest; for all are marked alike with the same natural proportions. The truth of this is clear; it does not admit of any doubt. We see, for instance, the man who today, because of the office which he holds, is considered by the crowd an object of honour, becoming tomorrow himself one of those who pay honour, the office having been transferred to another. Do they, then, conceive of an honour such as that in the case of the Divine Being, so that, as long as we please to pay it, that Divine honour is retained, but when we cease to do so it ceases too at the dictate of our will? Absurd thought, and blasphemous as well! The Deity, being independent of us, does not grow in honour; He is evermore the same; He cannot pass into a better or a worse state; for He has no better, and admits no worse.

In what sort of manner, then, can you honour the Deity? How can you heighten the Highest? How can you give glory to that which is above all glory? How can you praise the Incomprehensible? If *"all the nations are as a drop of a bucket,"* as Isaiah says, if all living humanity were to send up one united note of praise in harmony together, what addition will this gift of a mere drop be to that which is glorious essentially? The heavens are telling the glory of God, and yet they are counted poor heralds of His worth; because His Majesty is exalted, not as far as the heavens, but high above those heavens, which are themselves included within a small fraction of the Deity called figuratively His *"span."* And shall a man, this frail and short-lived creature, so aptly likened to *"grass,"* who *"today is,"* and tomorrow is not, believe that he can worthily honour the Divine Being? It would be like some one lighting a thin fibre from some tow and fancying that by that spark he was making an addition to the dazzling rays of the sun. By what words, pray, will you honour the Holy Spirit, supposing you do wish to honour Him at all? By saying that He is absolutely immortal, without turning, or variableness, always beautiful, always independent of ascription from others, working as He wills all things in all, Holy, leading, direct, just, of true utterance, *"searching the deep things of God," "proceeding from the Father," "receiving from the Son,"* and all such-like things, what, after all, do you lend to Him by these and such-like terms? Do you mention what He has, or do you honour Him by what He has not? Well, if you attest what He has not, your ascription is meaningless and comes to nothing; for he who calls bitterness *"sweetness,"* while he lies himself, has failed to commend that which is blamable. Whereas, if you mention what He has, such and such a quality is essential, whether men recognize it or not; He remains the object of faith, says the Apostle, if we have not faith.

What means, then, this lowering and this expanding of their soul, on the part of these men who are enthusiastic for the Father's honour, and grant to the Son an equal share with Him, but in the case of the Spirit are for narrowing down their favours; seeing that it has been demonstrated that the intrinsic worth of the Divine Being does not depend for its contents upon any will of ours, but has been always inalienably inherent in Him? Their narrowness of mind, and unthankfulness, is exposed in this opinion of theirs, while the Holy Spirit is essentially honourable, glorious, almighty, and all that we can conceive of in the way of exaltation, in spite of them.

"Yes," replies one of them, *"but we have been taught by Scripture that the Father is the Creator, and in the same way that it was 'through the Son' that 'all things were made'; but God's word tells us nothing of this kind about the Spirit; and how, then, can it be right to place the Holy Spirit in a position of equal dignity with One Who has displayed such magnificence of power through the Creation?"*

What shall we answer to this? That the thoughts of their hearts are so much idle talk, when they imagine that the Spirit was not always with the Father and the Son, but that, as occasion varies, He is sometimes to be contemplated as alone, sometimes to be found in the closest union with Them. For if the heaven, and the earth, and all created things were really made through the Son and from the Father, but apart from the Spirit, what was the Holy Spirit doing at the time when the Father was at work with the Son upon the Creation? Was He employed upon some other works, and was this the reason that He had no hand in the building of the Universe? But, then, what special work of the Spirit have they to point to, at the time when the world was being made? Surely, it is senseless folly to conceive of a creation other than that which came into existence from the Father through the Son. Well, suppose that He was not employed at all, but dissociated Himself from the busy work of creating by reason of an inclination to ease and rest, which shrank from toil?

May the gracious Spirit Himself pardon this baseless supposition of ours! The blasphemy of these theorists, which we have had to follow out in every step it takes, has caused us unwittingly to soil our discussion with the mud of their own imaginings. The view which is consistent with all reverence is as follows. We are not to think of the Father as ever parted from the Son, nor to look for the Son as separate from the Holy Spirit. As it is impossible to mount to the

Father, unless our thoughts are exalted there through the Son, so it is impossible also to say that Jesus is Lord except by the Holy Spirit. Therefore, Father, Son, and Holy Spirit are to be known only in a perfect Trinity, in closest consequence and union with each other, before all creation, before all the ages, before anything whatever of which we can form an idea. The Father is always Father, and in Him the Son, and with the Son the Holy Spirit. If these Persons, then, are inseparate from each other, how great is the folly of these men who undertake to sunder this indivisibility by certain distinctions of time, and so far to divide the Inseparable as to assert confidently, *"the Father alone, through the Son alone, made all things"*; the Holy Spirit, that is, being not present at all on the occasion of this making, or else not working. Well, if He was not present, they must tell us where He was; and whether, while God embraces all things, they can imagine any separate standing-place for the Spirit, so that He could have remained in isolation during the time occupied by the process of creating. If, on the other hand, He was present, how was it that He was inactive? Because He could not, or because He would not, work? Did He abstain willingly, or because some strong necessity drove Him away? Now, if He deliberately embraced this inactivity, He must reject working in any other possible way either; and He Who affirmed that *"He works all things in all, as He wills 1 Corinthians 13:6,"* is according to them a liar. If, on the contrary, this Spirit has the impulse to work, but some overwhelming control hinders His design, they must tell us the wherefore of this hindrance. Was it owing to his being grudged a share in the glory of those operations, and in order to secure that the admiration at their success should not extend to a third person as its object; or to a distrust of His help, as if His co-operation would result in present mischief? These clever men most certainly furnish the grounds for our holding one of these two hypotheses; or else, if a grudging spirit has no connection with the Deity, any more than a failure can be conceived of in any relation to an Infallible Being, what meaning of any kind is there in these narrow views of theirs, which isolate the Spirit's power from all world-building efficiency? Their duty rather was to expel their low human way of thinking, by means of loftier ideas, and to make a calculation more worthy of the sublimity of the objects in question. For neither did the Universal God make the universe *"through the Son,"* as needing any help, nor does the Only-begotten God work all things *"by the Holy Spirit,"* as having a power that comes short of His design; but the fountain of power is the Father, and the power of the Father is the Son, and the spirit of that power is the Holy Spirit; and Creation entirely, in all its visible and spiritual extent, is the finished work of that Divine power. And seeing that no toil can be thought of in the composition of anything connected with the Divine Being (for performance being bound to the moment of willing, the Plan at once becomes a Reality), we should be justified in calling all that Nature which came into existence by creation a movement of Will, an impulse of Design, a transmission of Power, beginning from the Father, advancing through the Son, and completed in the Holy Spirit.

This is the view we take, after the unprofessional way usual with us; and we reject all these elaborate sophistries of our adversaries, believing and confessing as we do, that in every deed and thought, whether in this world, or beyond this world, whether in time or in eternity, the Holy Spirit is to be apprehended as joined to the Father and Son, and is wanting in no wish or energy, or anything else that is implied in a devout conception of Supreme Goodness ; and, therefore, that, except for the distinction of order and Person, no variation in any point is to be apprehended; but we assert that while His place is counted third in mere sequence after the Father and Son, third in the order of the transmission, in all other respects we acknowledge His inseparable union with them; both in nature, in honour, in godhead, and glory, and majesty, and almighty power, and in all devout belief.

But with regard to service and worship, and the other things which they so nicely calculate about, and bring into prominence, we say this; that the Holy Spirit is exalted above all that we can do for Him with our merely human purpose; our worship is far beneath the honour due; and anything else that in human customs is held as honourable is somewhere below the dignity of the Spirit; for that which in its essence is measureless surpasses those who offer their all with so slight and circumscribed and paltry a power of giving. This, then, we say to those of them who subscribe to the reverential conception of the Holy Spirit that He is Divine, and of the Divine nature. But if there is any of them who rejects this statement, and this idea involved in the very name of Divinity, and says that which, to the destruction of the Spirit's greatness, is in circulation among the many, namely, that He belongs, not to making, but to made, beings, that it is right to regard Him not as of a Divine, but as of a created nature, we answer to a proposition such as this, that we do not understand how we can count those who make it among the number of Christians at all. For just as it would not be possible to style the unformed embryo a human being, but only a potential one, assuming that it is completed so as to come forth to human birth, while as long as it is in this unformed state, it is something other than a human being; so our reason cannot recognize as a Christian one who has failed to receive, with regard to the entire mystery, the genuine form of our religion. We can hear Jews believing in God, and our God too: even our Lord reminds them in the Gospel that they recognize no other God than the Father of the Only-begotten, *"of Whom ye say that he is your God."* Are we, then, to call the Jews Christians because they too agree to worship the God Whom we adore? I am aware, too, that the Manichees go about vaunting the name of Christ. Because they hold revered the Name to which we bow the knee, shall we therefore number them among Christians? So, too, he who both believes in the Father and receives the Son, but sets aside the Majesty of the Spirit, has *"denied the faith, and is worse than an infidel,"* and belies the name of Christ which he bears. The Apostle bids the man of God to be *"perfect."* Now, to take only the *general* man, perfection must consist in completeness in every aspect of human nature, in having reason, capability of thought and knowledge, a share of animal life, an upright bearing, risibility, broadness of nail; and if any one were to term some individual a man, and yet were unable to produce evidence in his case of the foregoing signs of human nature, his terming him so would be a valueless honour. Thus, too, the Christian is marked by his Belief in Father, Son, and Holy Ghost; in this consists the form of him who is fashioned in accordance with the mystery of the truth. But if his form is arranged otherwise, I will not recognize the existence of anything whence the form is absent; there is a blurring out of the mark, and a loss of the essential form, and an alteration of the characteristic signs of our complete humanity, when the Holy Spirit is not included in the Belief. For indeed the word of Ecclesiastes says true; your heretic is no living man, but *"bones,"* he says, *"in the womb of her that is with child"*; for how can one who does not think of the unction along with the Anointed be said to believe in the Anointed? *"Him,"* says (Peter), *"did God anoint with the Holy Spirit."*

These destroyers of the Spirit's glory, who relegate Him to a subject world, must tell us of what thing that unction is the symbol. It not a symbol of the Kingship? And what? Do they not believe in the Only-begotten as in His very nature a King? Men who have not once for all enveloped their hearts with the Jewish *"veil 2 Corinthians 3:14-15 "* will not gainsay that He is this. If, then, the Son is in His very nature a king, and the unction is the symbol of His kingship, what, in the way of a consequence, does your reason demonstrate? Why, that the Unction is not a thing alien to that Kingship, and so that the Spirit is not to be ranked in the Trinity as anything strange and foreign either. For the Son is King, and His living, realized, and personified Kingship is found in the Holy Spirit, Who anoints the Only-begotten, and so makes Him the Anointed, and the King of all things that exist. If, then, the Father is King, and the Only-begotten is King, and the Holy Ghost is the Kingship, one and the same definition of Kingship must prevail throughout this Trinity, and the thought of *"unction"* conveys the hidden meaning that there is no interval of separation between the Son and the Holy Spirit. For as between the body's surface and the liquid of the oil nothing intervening can be detected, either in reason or in perception, so inseparable is the union of the Spirit with the Son; and the result is that whosoever is to touch the Son by faith must needs first encounter the oil in the very act of touching; there is not a part of Him devoid of the Holy Spirit. Therefore belief in the Lordship of the Son arises in those who entertain it, by means of the Holy Ghost; on all sides the Holy Ghost is met by those who by faith approach the Son. If, then, the Son is essentially a King, and the Holy Spirit is that dignity of Kingship which anoints the Son, what deprivation of this Kingship, in its essence and comparing it with itself, can be imagined?

Again, let us look at it in this way. Kingship is most assuredly shown in the rule over subjects. Now what is *"subject"* to this Kingly Being? The Word includes the ages certainly, and all that is in them; *"Your Kingdom,"* it says, *"is a Kingdom of ages,"* and, by ages, it means every substance in them created in infinite space , whether visible or invisible; for in them all things were created by the Maker of those ages. If, then, the Kingship must always be thought of along with the King, and the world of subjects is acknowledged to be something other than the world of rulers, what absurdity it is for these men to contradict themselves thus, attributing as they do the unction as an expression for the worth of Him Whose very nature it is to be a King, yet degrading that unction Itself to the rank of a subject, as if wanting in such worth! If It is a subject by virtue of its nature, then why is It made the unction of Kingship, and so associated with the Kingly dignity of the Only-begotten? If, on the other hand, the capacity to rule is shown by Its being included in the majesty of Kingship, where is the necessity of having everything dragged down to a plebeian and servile lower condition, and numbered with the subject creation? When we affirm of the Spirit the two conditions, we cannot be in both cases speaking the truth: *i.e.* that He is ruling, and that He is subject. If He rules, He is not under any lord, but if He is subject, then He cannot be comprehended with the Being who is a King. Men are recognized as among men, angels among angels, everything among its kind; and so the Holy Spirit must needs be believed to belong to one only of two worlds; to the ruling, or to the inferior world; for between these two our reason can recognize nothing; no new invention of any natural attribute on the borderland of the Created and the Uncreated can be thought of, such as would participate in both, yet be neither entirely; we cannot imagine such an amalgamation and welding together of opposites by anything being blended of the Created and the Uncreated, and two opposites thus coalescing into one person, in which case the result of that strange mixture would not only be a composite thing, but composed of elements that were unlike, and disagreeing as to time; for that which receives its personality from a creation is assuredly posterior to that which subsists without a creation.

If, then, they declare the Holy Ghost to be blended of both, they must consequently view that blending as of a prior with a posterior thing; and, according to them, He will be prior to Himself; and reversely, posterior to Himself; from the Uncreated He will get the seniority, and from the Created the juniority. But, in the nature of things, this cannot be; and so it must most certainly be true to affirm of the Holy Spirit one only of these alternatives, and that is, the attribute of being Uncreated; for notice the amount of absurdity involved in the other alternative; all things that we can think of in the actual creation have, by virtue of all having received their existence by an act of creation, a rank and value perfectly equal in all cases, and so what reason can there be for separating the Holy Spirit from the rest of the creation, and ranking Him with the Father and the Son? Logic, then, will discover this about Him; That which is contemplated as part of the Uncreated, does not exist by creation; or, if It does, then It has no more power than its kindred creation, It cannot associate itself with that Transcendent Nature; if, on the other hand, they declare that He is a created being, and at the same time has a power which is above the creation, then the creation will be found at variance with itself, divided into ruler and ruled, so that part of it is the benefactor, part the benefited, part the sanctifier, part the sanctified; and all that fund of blessings which we believe to be provided for the creation by the Holy Spirit are present in Him, welling up abundantly, and pouring forth upon others, while the creation remains in need of the thence-issuing help and grace, and receives, as a mere dole, those blessings which can be passed to it from a fellow-creature! That would be like favouritism and respecting of persons; when we know that there is no such partiality in the nature of things, as that those existences which differ in no way from each other on the score of substance should not have equal power; and I think that no one who reflects will admit such views. Either He imparts nothing to others, if He possesses nothing essentially; or, if we do believe that He does give, His possession beforehand of that gift must be granted; this capacity of giving blessings, while needing oneself no such extraneous help, is the peculiar and exquisite privilege of Deity, and of no other.

Then let us look to this too. In Holy Baptism, what is it that we secure thereby? Is it not a participation in a life no longer subject to death? I think that no one who can in any way be reckoned among Christians will deny that statement. What then? Is that life-giving power in the water itself which is employed to convey the grace of Baptism? Or is it not rather clear to every one that this element is only employed as a means in the external ministry, and of itself contributes nothing towards the sanctification, unless it be first transformed itself by the sanctification; and that what gives life to the baptized is the Spirit; as our Lord Himself says in respect to Him with His own lips, *"It is the Spirit that gives life;"* but for the completion of this grace He alone, received by faith, does not give life, but belief in our Lord must precede, in order that the lively gift may come upon the believer, as our Lord has spoken, *"He gives life to whom He wills."* But further still, seeing that this grace administered through the Son is dependent on the Ungenerate Source of all, Scripture accordingly teaches us that belief in the Father Who engenders all things is to come first; so that this life-giving grace should be completed, for those fit to receive it, after starting from that Source as from a spring pouring life abundantly, through the Only-begotten Who is the True life, by the operation of the Holy Spirit. If, then, life comes in baptism, and baptism receives its completion in the name of Father, Son, and Spirit, what do these men mean who count this Minister of life as nothing? If the gift is a slight one, they must tell us the thing that is more precious than this life. But if everything whatever that is precious is second to this life, I mean that higher and precious life in which the brute creation has no part, how can they dare to depreciate so great a favour, or rather the actual Being who grants the favour, and to degrade Him in their conceptions of Him to a subject world by disjoining Him from the higher world of deity. Finally, if they will have it that this bestowal of life is a small thing, and that it means nothing great and awful in the nature of the Bestower, how is it they do not draw the conclusion which this very view makes inevitable, namely, that we must suppose, even with regard to the Only-begotten and the Father Himself, nothing great in Their life, the same as that which we have through the Holy Spirit, supplied as it is from the Father through the Son?

So that if these despisers and impugners of their very own life conceive of the gift as a little one, and decree accordingly to slight the Being who imparts the gift, let them be made aware that they cannot limit to one Person only their ingratitude, but must extend its profanity beyond the Holy Spirit to the Holy Trinity Itself. For like as the grace flows down in an unbroken stream from the Father, through the Son and the Spirit, upon the persons worthy of it, so does this profanity return backward, and is transmitted from the Son to the God of all the world, passing from one to the other. If, when a man is slighted, He Who sent him is slighted (yet what a distance there was between the man and the Sender!), what criminality is thereby implied in those who thus defy the Holy Spirit! Perhaps this is the blasphemy against our Law-giver for which the judgment without remission has been decreed; since in Him the entire Being, Blessed and Divine, is insulted also. As the devout worshipper of the Spirit sees in Him the glory of the Only-begotten, and in that sight beholds the image of the Infinite God, and by means of that image makes an outline, upon his own cognition , of the Original, so most plainly does this contemner (of the Spirit), whenever he advances any of his bold statements against the glory of the Spirit, extend, by virtue of the same reasoning, his profanity to the Son, and beyond Him to the Father. Therefore, those who reflect must have fear lest they perpetrate an audacity the result of which will be the complete blotting out of the perpetrator of it; and while they exalt the Spirit in the naming, they will even before the naming exalt Him in their thought, it being impossible that words can mount along with thought; still when one shall have reached the highest limit of human faculties, the utmost height and magnificence of idea to which the mind can ever attain, even then one must believe it is far below the glory that belongs to Him, according to the words in the Psalms, that *"after exalting the Lord our God, even then ye scarcely worship the footstool beneath His feet"*: and the cause of this dignity being so incomprehensible is nothing else than that He is holy.

If, then, every height of man's ability falls below the grandeur of the Spirit (for that is what the Word means in the metaphor of *"footstool"*), what vanity is theirs who think that there is within themselves a power so great that it rests with them to define the amount of value to be attributed to a being who is invaluable! And so they pronounce the Holy Spirit unworthy of some things which are associated with the idea of value, as if their own abilities could do far more than the Spirit, as estimated by them, is capable of. What pitiable, what wretched madness! They understand not what they are themselves when they talk like this, and what the Holy Spirit against Whom they insolently range themselves. Who will tell these people that men are *"a spirit that goes forth and returns not again* Wisdom 16:14," built up in their mother's womb by means of a soiled conception, and returning all of them to a soiled earth; inheriting a life that is likened unto grass; blooming for a little during life's illusion , and then withering away, and all the bloom upon them being shed and vanishing; they themselves not knowing with certainty what they were before their birth, nor into what they will be changed, their soul being ignorant of her peculiar destiny as long as she tarries in the flesh? Such is man.

On the contrary the Holy Spirit is, to begin with, because of qualities that are essentially holy, that which the Father, essentially Holy, is; and such as the Only-begotten is, such is the Holy Spirit; then, again, He is so by virtue of life-giving, of imperishability, of unvariableness, of everlastingness, of justice, of wisdom, of rectitude, of sovereignty, of goodness, of power, of capacity to give all good things, and above them all life itself, and by being everywhere, being present in each, filling the earth, residing in the heavens, shed abroad upon supernatural Powers, filling all things according to the deserts of each, Himself remaining full, being with all who are worthy, and yet not parted from the Holy Trinity. He ever *"searches the deep things of God,"* ever *"receives"* from the Son, ever is being *"sent,"* and yet not separated, and being *"glorified,"* and yet He has always had glory. It is plain, indeed, that one who gives glory to another must be found himself in the possession of superabundant glory; for how could one devoid of glory glorify another? Unless a thing be itself light, how can it display the gracious gift of light? So the power to glorify could never be displayed by one who was not himself glory , and honour, and majesty, and greatness. Now the Spirit does glorify the Father and the Son. Neither does He lie Who says, *"Them that glorify Me I glorify"* 1 Samuel 2:30; and *"I have glorified You ,"* is said by our Lord to the Father; and again He says, *"Glorify Me with the glory which I had with You before the world was. "* The Divine Voice answers, *"I have both glorified, and will glorify again. "* You see the revolving circle of the glory moving from Like to Like. The Son is glorified by the Spirit; the Father is glorified by the Son; again the Son has His glory from the Father; and the Only-begotten thus becomes the glory of the Spirit. For with what shall the Father be glorified, but with the true glory of the Son: and with what again shall the Son be glorified, but with the majesty of the Spirit? In like manner, again, Faith completes the circle, and glorifies the Son by means of the Spirit, and the Father by means of the Son.

If such, then, is the greatness of the Spirit, and whatever is morally beautiful, whatever is good, coming from God as it does through the Son, is completed by the instrumentality of the Spirit that *"works all in all,"* why do they set themselves against their own life? Why do they alienate themselves from the hope belonging to *"such as are to be saved"*? Why do they sever themselves from their cleaving unto God? For how can any man cleave unto the Lord unless the Spirit operates within us that union of ourselves with Him? Why do they haggle with us about the amount of service and of worship? Why do they use that word *"worship"* in an ironical sense, derogatory to a Divine and entirely Independent Being, supposing that they desire their own salvation? We would say to them, Your supplication is the advantage of you who ask, and not the honouring of Him Who grants it. Why, then, do you approach your Benefactor as if you had something to give? Or rather, why do you refuse to name as a benefactor at all Him Who gives you your blessings, and slight the Life-giver while clinging to Life? Why, seeking for His sanctification, do you misconceive of the Dispenser of the Grace of sanctification; and as to the giving of those blessings, why, not denying that He has the power, do you deem Him not worthy to be asked to give, and fail to take this into consideration, viz. how much greater a thing it is to give some blessing than to be asked to give it? The asking does not unmistakably witness to greatness in him who is asked; for it is possible that one who does not have the thing to give might be asked for it, for the asking depends only on the will of the asker. But one who actually bestows some blessing has thereby given undoubted evidence of a power residing in him. Why then, while testifying to the greater thing in Him—I mean the power to bestow everything that is morally beautiful — do you deprive Him of the asking, as of something of importance; although his asking, as we have said, is often performed in the case of those who have nothing in their power, owing to the delusion of their devotees? For instance, the slaves of superstition ask the idols for the objects of their wishes; but the asking does not, in this instance of the idols, confer any glory; only people pay that attention to them owing to the deluded expectation that they will get some one of the things they ask for, and so they do not cease to ask. But you, persuaded as you are of what and how great things the Holy Spirit is the Giver, do you neglect the asking them from Him, taking refuge in the law which bids you 'worship God and serve Him only?' Well, how will you worship Him only, tell me, when you have severed Him from His intimate union with His own Only-begotten and His own Spirit? This worship is simply Jewish.

But you will say, *"When I think of the Father it is the Son (alone) that I have included as well in that term."* But tell me; when you have grasped the notion of the Son have you not admitted therein that of the Holy Spirit too? For how can you confess the Son except by the Holy Spirit? At what moment, then, is the Spirit in a state of separation from the Son, so that when the Father is being worshipped, the worship of the Spirit is not included along with that of the Son? And as regards their worship itself, what in the world do they reckon it to be? They bestow it, as some exquisite piece of honour, upon the God over all, and convey it over, sometimes, so as to reach the Only-begotten also; but the Holy Spirit they regard as unworthy of such a privilege. Now, in the common parlance of mankind, that self-prostration of inferiors upon the ground which they practise when they salute their betters is termed worship. Thus, it was by such a posture that the patriarch Jacob, in his self-humiliation, seems to have wished to show his inferiority when coming to meet his brother and to appease his wrath; for *"he bowed himself to the ground,"* says the Scripture, *"three times"*; and Joseph's brethren, as long as they knew him not, and he pretended before them that he knew them not, by reason of the exaltation of his rank reverenced his sovereignty with this worship; and even the great Abraham himself *"bowed himself" "to the children of Heth,"* a stranger among the natives of that land, showing, I opine, by that action, how far more powerful those natives were than sojourners. It is possible to speak of many such actions both in the ancient records, and from examples before our eyes in the world now.

Do they too, then, mean this by their worship? Well, is it anything but absurdity to think that it is wrong to honour the Holy Spirit with that with which the patriarch honoured even Canaanites? Or do they consider their *"worship"* something different to this, as if one sort were fitting for men, another sort for the Supreme Being? But then, how is it that they omit worship altogether in the instance of the Spirit, not even bestowing upon Him the worship conceded in the case of men? And what kind of worship do they imagine to be reserved especially for the Deity? Is it to be spoken word, or acted gesture? Well, but are not these marks of honour shared by men as well? In their case words are spoken and gestures acted. Is it not, then, plain to every one who possesses the least amount of reflection, that any gift worthy of the Deity mankind has not got to give; for the Author of all blessings has no need of us. But it is we men who have transferred these indications of respect and admiration, which we adopt towards each other, when we would show by the acknowledgment of a neighbour's superiority that one of us is in a humbler position than another, to our attendance upon a Higher Power; out of our possessions we make a gift of what is most precious to a priceless Nature. Therefore, since men, approaching emperors and potentates for the objects which they wish in some way to obtain from those rulers, do not bring to them their mere petition only, but employ every possible means to induce them to feel pity and favour towards themselves, adopting a humble voice, and a kneeling position , clasping their knees, prostrating themselves on the ground, and putting forward to plead for their petition all sorts of pathetic signs, to wake that pity—so it is that those who recognize the True Potentate, by Whom all things in existence are controlled, when they are supplicating for that which they have at heart, some lowly in spirit because of pitiable conditions in this world, some with their thoughts lifted up because of their eternal mysterious hopes, seeing that they know not how to ask, and that their humanity is not capable of displaying any reverence that can reach to the grandeur of that Glory, carry the ceremonial used in the case of men into the service of the Deity. And this is what *"worship"* is—that, I mean, which is offered for objects we have at heart along with supplication and humiliation. Therefore Daniel too bends the knees to the Lord, when asking His love for the captive people; and He Who *"bare our sicknesses,"* and intercedes for us, is recorded in the Gospel to have fallen on His face, because of the man that He had taken upon Him, at the hour of prayer, and in this posture to have made His petition, enjoining thereby, I think, that at the time of our petition our voice is not to be bold, but that we are to assume the attitude of the wretched; since the Lord *"resists the proud, but gives grace unto the humble;"* and somewhere else (He says), *"he that exalts himself shall be abased."* If, then, *"worship"* is a sort of suppliant state, or pleading put forward for the object of the petition, what is the intention of these new-fashioned regulations? These men do not even deign to ask of the Giver, nor to kneel to the Ruler, nor to attend upon the Potentate.

On the Holy Trinity

To Eustathius.

All you who study medicine have, one may say, humanity for your profession: and I think that one who preferred your science to all the serious pursuits of life would form the proper judgment, and not miss the right decision, if it be true that life, the most valued of all things, is a thing to be shunned, and full of pain, if it may not be had with health, and health your art supplies. But in your own case the science is in a notable degree of double efficacy; you enlarge for yourself the bounds of its humanity, since you do not limit the benefit of your art to men's bodies, but take thought also for the cure of troubles of the mind. I say this, not only following the common reports, but because I have learned it from experience, as in many other matters, so especially at this time in this indescribable malice of our enemies, which you skilfully dispersed when it swept like some evil flood over our life, dispelling this violent inflammation of our heart by your fomentation of soothing words. I thought it right, indeed, in view of the continuous and varied effort of our enemies against us, to keep silence, and to receive their attack quietly, rather than to speak against men armed with falsehood, that most mischievous weapon, which sometimes drives its point even through truth. But you did well in urging me not to betray the truth, but to refute the slanderers, lest, by a success of falsehood against truth, many might be injured.

I may say that those who conceived this causeless hatred for us seemed to be acting very much on the principle of Æsop's fable. For just as he makes his wolf bring some charges against the lamb (feeling ashamed, I suppose, of seeming to destroy, without just pretext, one who had done him no hurt), and then, when the lamb easily swept away all the slanderous charges brought against him, makes the wolf by no means slacken his attack, but carry the day with his teeth when he is vanquished by justice; so those who were as keen for hatred against us as if it were something good (feeling perhaps some shame of seeming to hate without cause), make up charges and complaints against us, while they do not abide consistently by any of the things they say, but allege, now that one thing, after a little while that another, and then again that something else is the cause of their hostility to us. Their malice does not take a stand on any ground, but when they are dislodged from one charge they cling to another, and from that again they seize upon a third, and if all their charges are refuted they do not give up their hate. They charge us with preaching three Gods, and din into the ears of the multitude this slander, which they never rest from maintaining persuasively. Then truth fights on our side, for we show both publicly to all men, and privately to those who converse with us, that we anathematize any man who says that there are three Gods, and hold him to be not even a Christian. Then, as soon as they hear this, they find Sabellius a handy weapon against us, and the plague that he spread is the subject of continual attacks upon us. Once more, we oppose to this assault our wonted armour of truth, and show that we abhor this form of heresy just as much as Judaism. What then? Are they weary after such efforts, and content to rest? Not at all. Now they charge us with innovation, and frame their complaint against us in this way:— They allege that while we confess three Persons we say that there is one goodness, and one power, and one Godhead. And in this assertion they do not go beyond the truth; for we do say so. But the ground of their complaint is that their custom does not admit this, and Scripture does not support it. What then is our reply? We do not think that it is right to make their prevailing custom the law and rule of sound doctrine. For if custom is to avail for proof of soundness, we too, surely, may advance our prevailing custom; and if they reject this, we are surely not bound to follow theirs. Let the inspired Scripture, then, be our umpire, and the vote of truth will surely be given to those whose dogmas are found to agree with the Divine words.

Well, what is their charge? There are two brought forward together in the accusation against us; one, that we divide the Persons; the other, that we do not employ any of the names which belong to God in the plural number, but (as I said already) speak of the goodness as one, and of the power, and the Godhead, and all such attributes in the singular. With regard to the dividing of the Persons, those cannot well object who hold the doctrine of the diversity of substances in the Divine nature. For it is not to be supposed that those who say that there are three substances do not also say that there are three Persons. So this point only is called in question: that those attributes which are ascribed to the Divine nature we employ in the singular.

But our argument in reply to this is ready and clear. For any one who condemns those who say that the Godhead is one, must necessarily support either those who say that there are more than one, or those who say that there is none. But the inspired teaching does not allow us to say that there are more than one, since, whenever it uses the term, it makes mention of the Godhead in the singular; as—*"In Him dwells all the fullness of the Godhead* Colossians 2:9 "; and, elsewhere —*"The invisible things of Him from the foundation of the world are clearly seen, being understood by the things that are made, even His eternal power and Godhead* Romans 1:20 ." If, then, to extend the number of the Godhead to a multitude belongs to those only who suffer from the plague of polytheistic error, and on the other hand utterly to deny the Godhead would be the doctrine of atheists, what doctrine is that which accuses us for saying that the Godhead is one? But they reveal more clearly the aim of their argument. As regards the Father, they admit the fact that He is God , and that the Son likewise is honoured with the attribute of Godhead; but the Spirit, Who is reckoned with the Father and the Son, they cannot include in their conception of Godhead, but hold that the power of the Godhead, issuing from the Father to the Son, and there halting, separates the nature of the Spirit from the Divine glory. And so, as far as we may in a short space, we have to answer this opinion also.

What, then, is our doctrine? The Lord, in delivering the saving Faith to those who become disciples of the word, joins with the Father and the Son the Holy Spirit also; and we affirm that the union of that which has once been joined is continual; for it is not joined in one thing, and separated in others. But the power of the Spirit, being included with the Father and the Son in the life-giving power, by which our nature is transferred from the corruptible life to immortality, and in many other cases also, as in the conception of *"Good,"* and *"Holy,"* and *"Eternal," "Wise," "Righteous," "Chief," "Mighty,"* and in fact everywhere, has an inseparable association with them in all the attributes ascribed in a sense of special excellence. And so we consider that it is right to think that that which is joined to the Father and the Son in such sublime and exalted conceptions is not separated from them in any. For we do not know of any differences by way of superiority and inferiority in attributes which express our conceptions of the Divine nature, so that we should suppose it an act of piety (while allowing to the Spirit community in the inferior attributes) to judge Him unworthy of those more exalted. For all the Divine attributes, whether named or conceived, are of like rank one with another, in that they are not distinguishable in respect of the signification of their subject. For the appellation of *"the Good"* does not lead our minds to one subject, and that of *"the Wise,"* or *"the Mighty,"* or *"the Righteous"* to another, but the thing to which all the attributes point is one; and, if you speak of God, you signify the same Whom you understood by the other attributes. If then all the attributes ascribed to the Divine nature are of equal force as regards their designation of the subject, leading our minds to the same subject in various aspects, what reason is there that one, while allowing to the Spirit community with the Father and the Son in the other attributes, should exclude Him from the Godhead alone? It is absolutely necessary either to allow to Him community in this also, or not to admit His community in the others. For if He is worthy in the case of those attributes, He is surely not less worthy in this. But if He is *"less,"* according to their phrase , so that He is excluded from community with the Father and the Son in the attribute of Godhead, neither is He worthy to share in any other of the attributes which belong to God. For the attributes, when rightly understood and mutually compared by that notion which we contemplate in each case, will be found to imply nothing less than the appellation of *"God."* And a proof of this is that many even of the inferior existences are called by this very name. Further, the Divine Scripture is not sparing in this use of the name even in the case of things incongruous, as when it names idols by the appellation of God. For it says, *"Let the gods that have not made the heavens and the earth perish, and be cast down beneath the earth "*; and, *"all the gods of the heathen are devils "*; and the witch in her incantations, when she brings up for Saul the spirits that he sought for, says that she *"saw gods 1 Samuel 28:13 ."* And again Balaam, being an augur and a seer, and engaging in divination, and having obtained for himself the instruction of devils and magical augury, is said in Scripture to receive counsel from God. Numbers xxii One may show by collecting many instances of the same kind from the Divine Scripture, that this attribute has no supremacy over the other attributes which are proper to God, seeing that, as has been said, we find it predicated, in an equivocal sense, even of things incongruous; but we are nowhere taught in Scripture that the names of *"the Holy,"* *"the Incorruptible,"* *"the Righteous,"* *"the Good,"* are made common to things unworthy. If, then, they do not deny that the Holy Spirit has community with the Father and the Son in those attributes which, in their sense of special excellence, are piously predicated only of the Divine nature, what reason is there to pretend that He is excluded from community in this only, wherein it was shown that, by an equivocal use, even devils and idols share?

But they say that this appellation is indicative of nature, and that, as the nature of the Spirit is not common to the Father and the Son, for this reason neither does he partake in the community of this attribute. Let them show, then, whereby they discern this diversity of nature. For if it were possible that the Divine nature should be contemplated in its absolute essence, and that we should find by appearances what is and what is not proper to it, we should surely have no need of other arguments or evidence for the comprehension of the question. But since it is exalted above the understanding of the questioners, and we have to argue from some particular evidence about those things which evade our knowledge , it is absolutely necessary for us to be guided to the investigation of the Divine nature by its operations. If, then, we see that the operations which are wrought by the Father and the Son and the Holy Spirit differ one from the other, we shall conjecture from the different character of the operations that the natures which operate are also different. For it cannot be that things which differ in their very nature should agree in the form of their operation: fire does not chill, nor ice give warmth, but their operations are distinguished together with the difference between their natures. If, on the other hand, we understand that the operation of the Father, the Son, and the Holy Spirit is one, differing or varying in nothing, the oneness of their nature must needs be inferred from the identity of their operation. The Father, the Son, and the Holy Spirit alike give sanctification, and life, and light, and comfort, and all similar graces. And let no one attribute the power of sanctification in a special sense to the Spirit, when he hears the Saviour in the Gospel saying to the Father concerning His disciples, *"Father, sanctify them in Your name."* So too all the other gifts are wrought in those who are worthy alike by the Father, the Son, and the Holy Spirit: every grace and power, guidance, life, comfort, the change to immortality, the passage to liberty, and every other boon that exists, which descends to us.

But the order of things which is above us, alike in the region of intelligence and in that of sense (if by what we know we may form conjectures about those things also which are above us), is itself established within the operation and power of the Holy Spirit, every man receiving the benefit according to his own desert and need. For although the arrangement and ordering of things above our nature is obscure to our sense, yet one may more reasonably infer, by the things which we know, that in them too the power of the Spirit works, than that it is banished from the order existing in the things above us. For he who asserts the latter view advances his blasphemy in a naked and unseemly shape, without being able to support his absurd opinion by any argument. But he who agrees that those things which are above us are also ordered by the power of the Spirit with the Father and the Son, makes his assertion on this point with the support of clear evidence from his own life. For as the nature of man is compounded of body and soul, and the angelic nature has for its portion life without a body, if the Holy Spirit worked only in the case of bodies, and the soul were not capable of receiving the grace that comes from Him, one might perhaps infer from this, if the intellectual and incorporeal nature which is in us were above the power of the Spirit, that the angelic life too was in no need of His grace. But if the gift of the Holy Spirit is principally a grace of the soul, and the constitution of the soul is linked by its intellectuality and invisibility to the angelic life, what person who knows how to see a consequence would not agree, that every intellectual nature is governed by the ordering of the Holy Spirit? For since it is said *"the angels do always behold the Face of My Father which is in heaven* Matthew 18:10,*"* and it is not possible to behold the person of the Father otherwise than by fixing the sight upon it through His image; and the image of the person of the Father is the Only-begotten, and to Him again no man can draw near whose mind has not been illumined by the Holy Spirit, what else is shown from this but that the Holy Spirit is not separated from any operation which is wrought by the Father and the Son? Thus the identity of operation in Father, Son, and Holy Spirit shows plainly the undistinguishable character of their substance. So that even if the name of Godhead does indicate nature, the community of substance shows that this appellation is properly applied also to the Holy Spirit. But I know not how these makers-up of all sorts of arguments bring the appellation of Godhead to be an indication of nature, as though they had not heard from the Scripture that it is a matter of appointment , in which way nature does not arise. For Moses was appointed as a god of the Egyptians, since He Who gave him the oracles, etc., spoke thus to him, *"I have given you as a god to Pharaoh* Exodus 7:1 *."* Thus the force of the appellation is the indication of some power, either of oversight or of operation. But the Divine nature itself, as it is, remains unexpressed by all the names that are conceived for it, as our doctrine declares. For in learning that He is beneficent, and a judge, good, and just, and all else of the same kind, we learn diversities of His operations, but we are none the more able to learn by our knowledge of His operations the nature of Him Who works. For when one gives a definition of any one of these attributes, and of the nature to which the names are applied, he will not give the same definition of both: and of things of which the definition is different, the nature also is distinct. Indeed the substance is one thing which no definition has been found to express, and the significance of the names employed concerning it varies, as the names are given from some operation or accident. Now the fact that there is no distinction in the operations we learn from the community of the attributes, but of the difference in respect of nature we find no clear proof, the identity of operations indicating rather, as we said, community of nature. If, then, Godhead is a name derived from operation, as we say that the operation of the Father, and the Son, and the Holy Spirit is one, so we say that the Godhead is one: or if, according to the view of the majority, Godhead is indicative of nature, since we cannot find any diversity in their nature, we not unreasonably define the Holy Trinity to be of one Godhead.

But if any one were to call this appellation indicative of dignity, I cannot tell by what reasoning he drags the word to this significance. Since however one may hear many saying things of this kind, in order that the zeal of its opponents may not find a ground for attacking the truth, we go out of our way with those who take this view, to consider such an opinion, and say that, even if the name does denote dignity, in this case too the appellation will properly befit the Holy Spirit. For the attribute of kingship denotes all dignity; and *"our God,"* it says, *"is King from everlasting."* But the Son, having all things which are the Father's, is Himself proclaimed a King by Holy Scripture. Now the Divine Scripture says that the Holy Spirit is the unction of the Only-Begotten Acts 10:38, interpreting the dignity of the Spirit by a transference of the terms commonly used in this world. For as, in ancient days, in those who were advanced to kingship, the token of this dignity was the unction which was applied to them, and when this took place there was thenceforth a change from private and humble estate to the superiority of rule, and he who was deemed worthy of this grace received after his anointing another name, being called, instead of an ordinary man, the Anointed of the Lord: for this reason, that the dignity of the Holy Spirit might be more clearly shown to men, He was called by the Scripture *"the sign of the Kingdom,"* and *"Unction,"* whereby we are taught that the Holy Spirit shares in the glory and kingdom of the Only-begotten Son of God. For as in Israel it was not permitted to enter upon the kingdom without the unction being previously given, so the word, by a transference of the terms in use among ourselves, indicates the equality of power, showing that not even the kingdom of the Son is received without the dignity of the Holy Spirit. And for this reason He is properly called Christ, since this name gives the proof of His inseparable and indivisible conjunction with the Holy Spirit. If, then, the Only-begotten God is the Anointed, and the Holy Spirit is His Unction, and the appellation of Anointed points to the Kingly authority, and the anointing is the token of His Kingship, then the Holy Spirit shares also in His dignity. If, therefore, they say that the attribute of Godhead is significative of dignity, and the Holy Spirit is shown to share in this last quality, it follows that He Who partakes in the dignity will also partake in the name which represents it.

On "Not Three Gods"
To Ablabius.

You that are strong with all might in the inner man ought by rights to carry on the struggle against the enemies of the truth, and not to shrink from the task, that we fathers may be gladdened by the noble toil of our sons; for this is the prompting of the law of nature: but as you turn your ranks, and send against us the assaults of those darts which are hurled by the opponents of the truth, and demand that their *"hot burning coals"* and their shafts sharpened by knowledge falsely so called should be quenched with the shield of faith by us old men, we accept your command, and make ourselves an example of obedience , in order that you may yourself give us the just requital on like commands, Ablabius, noble soldier of Christ, if we should ever summon you to such a contest.

In truth, the question you propound to us is no small one, nor such that but small harm will follow if it meets with insufficient treatment. For by the force of the question, we are at first sight compelled to accept one or other of two erroneous opinions, and either to say *"there are three Gods,"* which is unlawful, or not to acknowledge the Godhead of the Son and the Holy Spirit, which is impious and absurd.

The argument which you state is something like this:— Peter, James, and John, being in one human nature, are called three men: and there is no absurdity in describing those who are united in nature, if they are more than one, by the plural number of the name derived from their nature. If, then, in the above case, custom admits this, and no one forbids us to speak of those who are two as two, or those who are more than two as three, how is it that in the case of our statements of the mysteries of the Faith, though confessing the Three Persons, and acknowledging no difference of nature between them, we are in some sense at variance with our confession, when we say that the Godhead of the Father and of the Son and of the Holy Ghost is one, and yet forbid men to say *"there are three Gods"*? The question is, as I said, very difficult to deal with: yet, if we should be able to find anything that may give support to the uncertainty of our mind, so that it may no longer totter and waver in this monstrous dilemma, it would be well: on the other hand, even if our reasoning be found unequal to the problem, we must keep for ever, firm and unmoved, the tradition which we received by succession from the fathers, and seek from the Lord the reason which is the advocate of our faith: and if this be found by any of those endowed with grace, we must give thanks to Him who bestowed the grace; but if not, we shall none the less, on those points which have been determined, hold our faith unchangeably.

What, then, is the reason that when we count one by one those who are exhibited to us in one nature, we ordinarily name them in the plural and speak of *"so many men,"* instead of calling them all one: while in the case of the Divine nature our doctrinal definition rejects the plurality of Gods, at once enumerating the Persons, and at the same time not admitting the plural signification? Perhaps one might seem to touch the point if he were to say (speaking offhand to straightforward people), that the definition refused to reckon Gods in any number to avoid any resemblance to the polytheism of the heathen, lest, if we too were to enumerate the Deity, not in the singular, but in the plural, as they are accustomed to do, there might be supposed to be also some community of doctrine. This answer, I say, if made to people of a more guileless spirit, might seem to be of some weight: but in the case of the others who require that one of the alternatives they propose should be established (either that we should not acknowledge the Godhead in Three Persons, or that, if we do, we should speak of those who share in the same Godhead as three), this answer is not such as to furnish any solution of the difficulty. And hence we must needs make our reply at greater length, tracing out the truth as best we may; for the question is no ordinary one.

We say, then, to begin with, that the practice of calling those who are not divided in nature by the very name of their common nature in the plural, and saying they are *"many men,"* is a customary abuse of language, and that it would be much the same thing to say they are *"many human natures."* And the truth of this we may see from the following instance. When we address any one, we do not call him by the name of his nature, in order that no confusion may result from the community of the name, as would happen if every one of those who hear it were to think that he himself was the person addressed, because the call is made not by the proper appellation but by the common name of their nature: but we separate him from the multitude by using that name which belongs to him as his own—

that, I mean, which signifies the particular subject. Thus there are many who have shared in the nature— many disciples, say, or apostles, or martyrs— but the man in them all is one; since, as has been said, the term *"man"* does not belong to the nature of the individual as such, but to that which is common. For Luke is a man, or Stephen is a man; but it does not follow that if any one is a man he is therefore Luke or Stephen: but the idea of the persons admits of that separation which is made by the peculiar attributes considered in each severally, and when they are combined is presented to us by means of number; yet their nature is one, at union in itself, and an absolutely indivisible unit, not capable of increase by addition or of diminution by subtraction, but in its essence being and continually remaining one, inseparable even though it appear in plurality, continuous, complete, and not divided with the individuals who participate in it. And as we speak of a people, or a mob, or an army, or an assembly in the singular in every case, while each of these is conceived as being in plurality, so according to the more accurate expression, *"man"* would be said to be one, even though those who are exhibited to us in the same nature make up a plurality. Thus it would be much better to correct our erroneous habit, so as no longer to extend to a plurality the name of the nature, than by our bondage to habit to transfer to our statements concerning God the error which exists in the above case. But since the correction of the habit is impracticable (for how could you persuade any one not to speak of those who are exhibited in the same nature as *"many men"*?— indeed, in every case habit is a thing hard to change), we are not so far wrong in not going contrary to the prevailing habit in the case of the lower nature, since no harm results from the mistaken use of the name: but in the case of the statement concerning the Divine nature the various use of terms is no longer so free from danger: for that which is of small account is in these subjects no longer a small matter. Therefore we must confess one God, according to the testimony of Scripture, *"Hear, O Israel, the Lord your God is one Lord,"* even though the name of Godhead extends through the Holy Trinity. This I say according to the account we have given in the case of human nature, in which we have learned that it is improper to extend the name of the nature by the mark of plurality. We must, however, more carefully examine the name of *"Godhead,"* in order to obtain, by means of the significance involved in the word, some help towards clearing up the question before us.

Most men think that the word *"Godhead"* is used in a peculiar degree in respect of nature: and just as the heaven, or the sun, or any other of the constituent parts of the universe are denoted by proper names which are significant of the subjects, so they say that in the case of the Supreme and Divine nature, the word *"Godhead"* is fitly adapted to that which it represents to us, as a kind of special name. We, on the other hand, following the suggestions of Scripture, have learned that that nature is unnameable and unspeakable, and we say that every term either invented by the custom of men, or handed down to us by the Scriptures, is indeed explanatory of our conceptions of the Divine Nature , but does not include the signification of that nature itself. And it may be shown without much difficulty that this is the case. For all other terms which are used of the creation may be found, even without analysis of their origin, to be applied to the subjects accidentally, because we are content to denote the things in any way by the word applied to them so as to avoid confusion in our knowledge of the things signified. But all the terms that are employed to lead us to the knowledge of God have comprehended in them each its own meaning, and you cannot find any word among the terms especially applied to God which is without a distinct sense. Hence it is clear that by any of the terms we use the Divine nature itself is not signified, but some one of its surroundings is made known. For we say, it may be, that the Deity is incorruptible, or powerful, or whatever else we are accustomed to say of Him. But in each of these terms we find a peculiar sense, fit to be understood or asserted of the Divine nature, yet not expressing that which that nature is in its essence. For the subject, whatever it may be, is incorruptible: but our conception of incorruptibility is this—that that which is, is not resolved into decay: so, when we say that He is incorruptible, we declare what His nature does not suffer, but we do not express what that is which does not suffer corruption. Thus, again, if we say that He is the Giver of life, though we show by that appellation what He gives, we do not by that word declare what that is which gives it. And by the same reasoning we find that all else which results from the significance involved in the names expressing the Divine attributes either forbids us to conceive what we ought not to conceive of the Divine nature, or teaches us that which we ought to conceive of it, but does not include an explanation of the nature itself. Since, then, as we perceive the varied operations of the power above us, we fashion our appellations from the several operations that are known to us, and as we recognize as one of these that operation of surveying and inspection, or, as one might call it, beholding, whereby He surveys all things and overlooks them all, discerning our thoughts, and even entering by His power of contemplation into those things which are not visible, we suppose that Godhead, or θεότης, is so called from θέα, or beholding, and that He who is our θεατής or beholder, by customary use and by the instruction of the Scriptures, is called θεός, or God. Now if any one admits that to behold and to discern are the same thing, and that the God Who superintends all things, both is and is called the superintender of the universe, let him consider this operation, and judge whether it belongs to one of the Persons whom we believe in the Holy Trinity, or whether the power extends throughout the Three Persons. For if our interpretation of the term Godhead, or θεότης, is a true one, and the things which are seen are said to be beheld, or θεατά, and that which beholds them is called θεός, or God, no one of the Persons in the Trinity could reasonably be excluded from such an appellation on the ground of the sense involved in the word. For Scripture attributes the act of seeing equally to Father, Son, and Holy Spirit. David says, *"See, O God our defender "*: and from this we learn that sight is a proper operation of the idea of God, so far as God is conceived, since he says, *"See, O God."* But Jesus also sees the thoughts of those who condemn Him, and questions why by His own power He pardons the sins of men? For it says, *"Jesus, seeing their thoughts. "* And of the Holy Spirit also, Peter says to Ananias, *"Why has Satan filled your heart, to lie to the Holy Ghost?* Acts 5:3 " showing that the Holy Spirit was a true witness, aware of what Ananias had dared to do in secret, and by Whom the manifestation of the secret was made to Peter. For Ananias became a thief of his own goods, secretly, as he thought, from all men, and concealing his sin: but the Holy Spirit at the same moment was in Peter, and detected his intent, dragged down as it was to avarice, and gave to Peter from Himself the power of seeing the secret, while it is clear that He could not have done this had He not been able to behold hidden things.

But some one will say that the proof of our argument does not yet regard the question. For even if it were granted that the name of *"Godhead"* is a common name of the nature, it would not be established that we should not speak of *"Gods"*: but by these arguments, on the contrary, we are compelled to speak of *"Gods"*: for we find in the custom of mankind that not only those who are partakers in the same nature, but even any who may be of the same business, are not, when they are many, spoken of in the singular; as we speak of *"many orators,"* or *"surveyors,"* or *"farmers,"* or *"shoemakers,"* and so in all other cases. If, indeed, Godhead were an appellation of nature, it would be more proper, according to the argument laid down, to include the Three Persons in the singular number, and to speak of *"One God,"* by reason of the inseparability and indivisibility of the nature: but since it has been established by what has been said, that the term *"Godhead"* is significant of operation, and not of nature, the argument from what has been advanced seems to turn to the contrary conclusion, that we ought therefore all the more to call those *"three Gods"* who are contemplated in the same operation, as they say that one would speak of *"three philosophers"* or *"orators,"* or any other name derived from a business when those who take part in the same business are more than one.

I have taken some pains, in setting forth this view, to bring forward the reasoning on behalf of the adversaries, that our decision may be the more firmly fixed, being strengthened by the more elaborate contradictions. Let us now resume our argument.

As we have to a certain extent shown by our statement that the word *"Godhead"* is not significant of nature but of operation, perhaps one might reasonably allege as a cause why, in the case of men, those who share with one another in the same pursuits are enumerated and spoken of in the plural, while on the other hand the Deity is spoken of in the singular as one God and one Godhead, even though the Three Persons are not separated from the significance expressed by the term *"Godhead,"*— one might allege, I say, the fact that men, even if several are engaged in the same form of action, work separately each by himself at the task he has undertaken, having no participation in his individual action with others who are engaged in the same occupation. For instance, supposing the case of several rhetoricians, their pursuit, being one, has the same name in the numerous cases: but each of those who follow it works by himself, this one pleading on his own account, and that on his own account. Thus, since among men the action of each in the same pursuits is discriminated, they are properly called many, since each of them is separated from the others within his own environment, according to the special character of his operation. But in the case of the Divine nature we do not similarly learn that the Father does anything by Himself in which the Son does not work conjointly, or again that the Son has any special operation apart from the Holy Spirit; but every operation which extends from God to the Creation, and is named according to our variable conceptions of it, has its origin from the Father, and proceeds through the Son, and is perfected in the Holy Spirit. For this reason the name derived from the operation is not divided with regard to the number of those who fulfil it, because the action of each concerning anything is not separate and peculiar, but whatever comes to pass, in reference either to the acts of His providence for us, or to the government and constitution of the universe, comes to pass by the action of the Three, yet what does come to pass is not three things. We may understand the meaning of this from one single instance. From Him, I say, Who is the chief source of gifts, all things which have shared in this grace have obtained their life. When we inquire, then, whence this good gift came to us, we find by the guidance of the Scriptures that it was from the Father, Son, and Holy Spirit. Yet although we set forth Three Persons and three names, we do not consider that we have had bestowed upon us three lives, one from each Person separately; but the same life is wrought in us by the Father, and prepared by the Son, and depends on the will of the Holy Spirit. Since then the Holy Trinity fulfils every operation in a manner similar to that of which I have spoken, not by separate action according to the number of the Persons, but so that there is one motion and disposition of the good will which is communicated from the Father through the Son to the Spirit (for as we do not call those whose operation gives one life three Givers of life, neither do we call those who are contemplated in one goodness three Good beings, nor speak of them in the plural by any of their other attributes); so neither can we call those who exercise this Divine and superintending power and operation towards ourselves and all creation, conjointly and inseparably, by their mutual action, three Gods. For as when we learn concerning the God of the universe, from the words of Scripture, that He judges all the earth Romans 3:6, we say that He is the Judge of all things through the Son: and again, when we hear that the Father judges no man, we do not think that the Scripture is at variance with itself—(for He Who judges all the earth does this by His Son to Whom He has committed all judgment; and everything which is done by the Only-begotten has its reference to the Father, so that He Himself is at once the Judge of all things and judges no man, by reason of His having, as we said, committed all judgment to the Son, while all the judgment of the Son is conformable to the will of the Father; and one could not properly say either that They are two judges, or that one of Them is excluded from the authority and power implied in judgment);— so also in the case of the word *"Godhead,"* Christ is the power of God and the wisdom of God, and that very power of superintendence and beholding which we call Godhead, the Father exercises through the Only-begotten, while the Son perfects every power by the Holy Spirit, judging, as Isaiah says, by the Spirit of judgment and the Spirit of burning Isaiah 4:4, and acting by Him also, according to the saying in the Gospel which was spoken to the Jews. For He says, *"If I by the Spirit of God cast out devils* Matthew 12:28 "; where He includes every form of doing good in a partial description, by reason of the unity of action: for the name derived from operation cannot be divided among many where the result of their mutual operation is one.

Since, then, the character of the superintending and beholding power is one, in Father, Son, and Holy Spirit, as has been said in our previous argument, issuing from the Father as from a spring, brought into operation by the Son, and perfecting its grace by the power of the Spirit; and since no operation is separated in respect of the Persons, being fulfilled by each individually apart from that which is joined with Him in our contemplation, but all providence, care, and superintendence of all, alike of things in the sensible creation and of those of supramundane nature, and that power which preserves the things which are, and corrects those which are amiss, and instructs those which are ordered aright, is one, and not three, being, indeed, directed by the Holy Trinity, yet not severed by a threefold division according to the number of the Persons contemplated in the Faith, so that each of the acts, contemplated by itself, should be the work of the Father alone, or of the Son peculiarly, or of the Holy Spirit separately, but while, as the Apostle says, the one and the selfsame Spirit divides His good gifts to every man severally 1 Corinthians 12:11, the motion of good proceeding from the Spirit is not without beginning—we find that the power which we conceive as preceding this motion, which is the Only-begotten God, is the maker of all things; without Him no existent thing attains to the beginning of its being: and, again, this same source of good issues from the will of the Father.

If, then, every good thing and every good name, depending on that power and purpose which is without beginning, is brought to perfection in the power of the Spirit through the Only-begotten God, without mark of time or distinction (since there is no delay, existent or conceived, in the motion of the Divine will from the Father, through the Son, to the Spirit): and if Godhead also is one of the good names and concepts, it would not be proper to divide the name into a plurality, since the unity existing in the action prevents plural enumeration. And as the Saviour of all men, specially of them that believe 1 Timothy 4:10, is spoken of by the Apostle as one, and no one from this phrase argues either that the Son does not save them who believe, or that salvation is given to those who receive it without the intervention of the Spirit; but God who is over all, is the Saviour of all, while the Son works salvation by means of the grace of the Spirit, and yet they are not on this account called in Scripture three Saviours (although salvation is confessed to proceed from the Holy Trinity): so neither are they called three Gods, according to the signification assigned to the term *"Godhead,"* even though the aforesaid appellation attaches to the Holy Trinity.

It does not seem to me absolutely necessary, with a view to the present proof of our argument, to contend against those who oppose us with the assertion that we are not to conceive *"Godhead"* as an operation. For we, believing the Divine nature to be unlimited and incomprehensible, conceive no comprehension of it, but declare that the nature is to be conceived in all respects as infinite: and that which is absolutely infinite is not limited in one respect while it is left unlimited in another, but infinity is free from limitation altogether. That therefore which is without limit is surely not limited even by name. In order then to mark the constancy of our conception of infinity in the case of the Divine nature, we say that the Deity is above every name: and *"Godhead"* is a name. Now it cannot be that the same thing should at once be a name and be accounted as above every name.

But if it pleases our adversaries to say that the significance of the term is not operation, but nature, we shall fall back upon our original argument, that custom applies the name of a nature to denote multitude erroneously: since according to true reasoning neither diminution nor increase attaches to any nature, when it is contemplated in a larger or smaller number. For it is only those things which are contemplated in their individual circumscription which are enumerated by way of addition. Now this circumscription is noted by bodily appearance, and size, and place, and difference figure and colour, and that which is contemplated apart from these conditions is free from the circumscription which is formed by such categories. That which is not thus circumscribed is not enumerated, and that which is not enumerated cannot be contemplated in multitude. For we say that gold, even though it be cut into many figures, is one, and is so spoken of, but we speak of many coins or many staters, without finding any multiplication of the nature of gold by the number of staters; and for this reason we speak of gold, when it is contemplated in greater bulk, either in plate or in coin, as *"much,"* but we do not speak of it as *"many golds"* on account of the multitude of the material—except when one says there are *"many gold pieces"* (Darics, for instance, or staters), in which case it is not the material, but the pieces of money to which the significance of number applies: indeed, properly, we should not call them *"gold"* but *"golden."*

As, then, the golden staters are many, but the gold is one, so too those who are exhibited to us severally in the nature of man, as Peter, James, and John, are many, yet the man in them is one. And although Scripture extends the word according to the plural significance, where it says *"men swear by the greater* Hebrews 6:16,*"* and *"sons of men,"* and in other phrases of the like sort, we must recognize that in using the custom of the prevailing form of speech, it does not lay down a law as to the propriety of using the words in one way or another, nor does it say these things by way of giving us instruction about phrases, but uses the word according to the prevailing custom, with a view only to this, that the word may be profitable to those who receive it, taking no minute care in its manner of speech about points where no harm can result from the phrases in respect of the way they are understood.

Indeed, it would be a lengthy task to set out in detail from the Scriptures those constructions which are inexactly expressed, in order to prove the statement I have made; where, however, there is a risk of injury to any part of the truth, we no longer find in Scriptural phrases any indiscriminate or indifferent use of words. For this reason Scripture admits the naming of *"men"* in the plural, because no one is by such a figure of speech led astray in his conceptions to imagine a multitude of humanities, or supposes that many human natures are indicated by the fact that the name expressive of that nature is used in the plural. But the word *"God"* it employs studiously in the singular form only, guarding against introducing the idea of different natures in the Divine essence by the plural signification of *"Gods."* This is the cause why it says, *"the Lord our God is one Lord* Deuteronomy 6:4,*"* and also proclaims the Only-begotten God by the name of Godhead, without dividing the Unity into a dual signification, so as to call the Father and the Son two Gods, although each is proclaimed by the holy writers as God. The Father is God: the Son is God: and yet by the same proclamation God is One, because no difference either of nature or of operation is contemplated in the Godhead. For if (according to the idea of those who have been led astray) the nature of the Holy Trinity were diverse, the number would by consequence be extended to a plurality of Gods, being divided according to the diversity of essence in the subjects. But since the Divine, single, and unchanging nature, that it may be one, rejects all diversity in essence, it does not admit in its own case the signification of multitude; but as it is called one nature, so it is called in the singular by all its other names, *"God," "Good," "Holy," "Saviour," "Just," "Judge,"* and every other Divine name conceivable: whether one says that the names refer to nature or to operation, we shall not dispute the point.

If, however, any one cavils at our argument, on the ground that by not admitting the difference of nature it leads to a mixture and confusion of the Persons, we shall make to such a charge this answer —that while we confess the invariable character of the nature, we do not deny the difference in respect of cause, and that which is caused, by which alone we apprehend that one Person is distinguished from another—by our belief, that is, that one is the Cause, and another is of the Cause; and again in that which is of the Cause we recognize another distinction. For one is directly from the first Cause, and another by that which is directly from the first Cause; so that the attribute of being Only-begotten abides without doubt in the Son, and the interposition of the Son, while it guards His attribute of being Only-begotten, does not shut out the Spirit from His relation by way of nature to the Father.

But in speaking of *"cause,"* and *"of the cause,"* we do not by these words denote nature (for no one would give the same definition of *"cause"* and of *"nature"*), but we indicate the difference in manner of existence. For when we say that one is *"caused,"* and that the other is *"without cause,"* we do not divide the nature by the word *"cause"*, but only indicate the fact that the Son does not exist without generation, nor the Father by generation: but we must needs in the first place believe that something exists, and then scrutinize the manner of existence of the object of our belief: thus the question of existence is one, and that of the mode of existence is another. To say that anything exists without generation sets forth the mode of its existence, but what exists is not indicated by this phrase. If one were to ask a husbandman about a tree, whether it were planted or had grown of itself, and he were to answer either that the tree had not been planted or that it was the result of planting, would he by that answer declare the nature of the tree? Surely not; but while saying how it exists he would leave the question of its nature obscure and unexplained. So, in the other case, when we learn that He is unbegotten, we are taught in what mode He exists, and how it is fit that we should conceive Him as existing, but *what* He is we do not hear in that phrase. When, therefore, we acknowledge such a distinction in the case of the Holy Trinity, as to believe that one Person is the Cause, and another is of the Cause, we can no longer be accused of confounding the definition of the Persons by the community of nature.

Thus, since on the one hand the idea of cause differentiates the Persons of the Holy Trinity, declaring that one exists without a Cause, and another is of the Cause; and since on the one hand the Divine nature is apprehended by every conception as unchangeable and undivided, for these reasons we properly declare the Godhead to be one, and God to be one, and employ in the singular all other names which express Divine attributes.

On the Faith

To Simplicius.

God commands us by His prophet not to esteem any new God to be God, and not to worship any strange God. Now it is clear that that is called new which is not from everlasting, and on the contrary, that is called everlasting which is not new. He, then, who does not believe that the Only-begotten God is from everlasting of the Father does not deny that He is new, for that which is not everlasting is confessedly new; and that which is new is not God, according to the saying of Scripture, *"there shall not be in you any new God."* Therefore he who says that the Son *"once was not,"* denies His Godhead. Again, He Who says *"you shall never worship a strange God"* forbids us to worship another God; and the strange God is so called in contradistinction to our own God. Who, then, is our own God? Clearly, the true God. And who is the strange God? Surely, he who is alien from the nature of the true God. If, therefore, our own God is the true God, and if, as the heretics say, the Only-begotten God is not of the nature of the true God, He is a strange God, and not our God. But the Gospel says, the sheep *"will not follow a stranger."* He that says He is created will make Him alien from the nature of the true God. What then will they do, who say that He is created? Do they worship that same created being as God, or do they not? For if they do not worship Him, they follow the Jews in denying the worship of Christ: and if they do worship Him, they are idolaters, for they worship one alien from the true God. But surely it is equally impious not to worship the Son, and to worship the strange God. We must then say that the Son is the true Son of the true Father, that we may both worship Him, and avoid condemnation as worshipping a strange God. But to those who quote from the Proverbs the passage, *"the Lord created me* Proverbs 8:28,*"* and think that they hereby produce a strong argument that the Creator and Maker of all things was created, we must answer that the Only-begotten God was *made* for us many things. For He was the Word, and was made flesh; and He was God, and was made man; and He was without body, and was made a body; and besides, He was made *"sin,"* and *"a curse,"* and *"a stone,"* and *"an axe,"* and *"bread,"* and *"a lamb,"* and *"a way,"* and *"a door,"* and *"a rock,"* and many such things; not being by nature any of these, but being made these things for our sakes, by way of dispensation. As, therefore, being the Word, He was for our sakes made flesh, and as, being God, He was made man, so also, being the Creator, He was made for our sakes a creature; for the flesh is created. As, then, He said by the prophet, *"Thus says the Lord, He that formed me from the womb to be His servant* Isaiah 49:5;" so He said also by Solomon, *"The Lord created me as the beginning of His ways, for His works* Proverbs 8:28 ." For all creation, as the Apostle says, is in servitude. Therefore both He Who was formed in the Virgin's womb, according to the word of the prophet, is the servant, and not the Lord (that is to say, the man according to the flesh, in whom God was manifested), and also, in the other passage, He Who was created as the beginning of His ways is not God, but the man in whom God was manifested to us for the renewing again of the ruined way of man's salvation. So that, since we recognize two things in Christ, one Divine, the other human (the Divine by nature, but the human in the Incarnation), we accordingly claim for the Godhead that which is eternal, and that which is created we ascribe to His human nature. For as, according to the prophet, He was formed in the womb as a servant, so also, according to Solomon, He was manifested in the flesh by means of this servile creation. But when they say, *"if He was, He was not begotten, and if He was begotten He was not,"* let them learn that it is not fitting to ascribe to His Divine nature the attributes which belong to His fleshly origin. For bodies which do not exist, are generated, and God makes those things to be which are not, but does not Himself come into being from that which is not. And for this reason also Paul calls Him *"the brightness of glory* Hebrews 1:3,"* that we may learn that as the light from the lamp is of the nature of that which sheds the brightness, and is united with it (for as soon as the lamp appears the light that comes from it shines out simultaneously), so in this place the Apostle would have us consider both that the Son is of the Father, and that the Father is never without the Son; for it is impossible that glory should be without radiance, as it is impossible that the lamp should be without brightness. But it is clear that as His being brightness is a testimony to His being in relation with the glory (for if the glory did not exist, the brightness shed from it would not exist), so, to say that the brightness *"once was not"* is a declaration that the glory also was not, when the brightness was not; for it is impossible that the glory should be without the brightness. As therefore it is not possible to say in the case of the brightness, *"If it was, it did not come into being, and if it came into being it was not,"* so it is in vain to say this of the Son, seeing that the Son is the brightness. Let those also who speak of *"less"* and *"greater,"* in the case of the Father and the Son, learn from Paul not to measure things immeasurable. For the Apostle says that the Son is the express image of the Person of the Father. Hebrews 1:3 It is clear then that however great the Person of the Father is, so great also is the express image of that Person; for it is not possible that the express image should be less than the Person contemplated in it. And this the great John also teaches when he says, *"In the beginning was the Word, and the Word was with God."* For in saying that he was *"in the beginning"* and not *"after the beginning,"* he showed that the beginning was never without the Word; and in declaring that *"the Word was with God,"* he signified the absence of defect in the Son in relation to the Father; for the Word is contemplated as a whole together with the whole being of God. For if the Word were deficient in His own greatness so as not to be capable of relation with the whole being of God, we are compelled to suppose that that part of God which extends beyond the Word is without the Word. But in fact the whole magnitude of the Word is contemplated together with the whole magnitude of God: and consequently in statements concerning the Divine nature, it is not admissible to speak of *"greater"* and *"less."*

As for those who say that the begotten is in its nature unlike the unbegotten, let them learn from the example of Adam and Abel not to talk nonsense. For Adam himself was not begotten according to the natural generation of men; but Abel was begotten of Adam. Now, surely, he who was never begotten is called unbegotten, and he who came into being by generation is called begotten ; yet the fact that he was not begotten did not hinder Adam from being a man, nor did the generation of Abel make him at all different from man's nature, but both the one and the other were men, although the one existed by being begotten, and the other without generation. So in the case of our statements as to the Divine nature, the fact of not being begotten, and that of being begotten, produce no diversity of nature, but, just as in the case of Adam and Abel the manhood is one, so is the Godhead one in the case of the Father and the Son.

Now touching the Holy Spirit also the blasphemers make the same statement as they do concerning the Lord, saying that He too is created. But the Church believes, as concerning the Son, so equally concerning the Holy Spirit, that He is uncreated, and that the whole creation becomes good by participation in the good which is above it, while the Holy Spirit needs not any to make Him good (seeing that He is good by virtue of His nature, as the Scripture testifies) ; that the creation is guided by the Spirit, while the Spirit gives guidance; that the creation is governed, while the Spirit governs; that the creation is comforted, while the Spirit comforts; that the creation is in bondage, while the Spirit gives freedom; that the creation is made wise, while the Spirit gives the grace of wisdom; that the creation partakes of the gifts, while the Spirit bestows them at His pleasure: *"For all these works that one and the self-same Spirit, dividing to every man severally as He will* 1 Corinthians 12:11 *."* And one may find multitudes of other proofs from the Scriptures that all the supreme and Divine attributes which are applied by the Scriptures to the Father and the Son are also to be contemplated in the Holy Spirit:— immortality, blessedness, goodness, wisdom, power, justice, holiness— every excellent attribute is predicated of the Holy Spirit just as it is predicated of the Father and of the Son, with the exception of those by which the Persons are clearly and distinctly divided from each other; I mean, that the Holy Spirit is not called the Father, or the Son; but all other names by which the Father and the Son are named are applied by Scripture to the Holy Spirit also. By this, then, we apprehend that the Holy Spirit is above creation. Thus, where the Father and the Son are understood to be, there the Holy Spirit also is understood to be; for the Father and the Son are above creation, and this attribute the drift of our argument claims for the Holy Spirit. So it follows, that one who places the Holy Spirit above the creation has received the right and sound doctrine: for he will confess that uncreated nature which we behold in the Father and the Son and the Holy Spirit to be one.

But since they bring forward as a proof, according to their ideas, of the created nature of the Holy Spirit, that utterance of the prophet, which says, *"He that establishes the thunder and creates the spirit, and declares unto man His Christ,"* we must consider this, that the prophet speaks of the creation of another Spirit, in the establishing of the thunder, and not of the Holy Spirit. For the name of *"thunder"* is given in mystical language to the Gospel. Those, then, in whom arises firm and unshaken faith in the Gospel, pass from being flesh to become spirit, as the Lord says, *"That which is born of the flesh is flesh, and that which is born of the Spirit is spirit."* It is God, then, Who by establishing the voice of the Gospel makes the believer spirit: and he who is born of the Spirit and made spirit by such thunder, *"declares"* Christ; as the Apostle says, *"No man can say that Jesus Christ is Lord but by the Holy Spirit* 1 Corinthians 12:3 ."

On Virginity
Chapter 1

The holy look of virginity is precious indeed in the judgment of all who make purity the test of beauty; but it belongs to those alone whose struggles to gain this object of a noble love are favoured and helped by the grace of God. Its praise is heard at once in the very name which goes with it; *"Uncorrupted"* is the word commonly said of it, and this shows the kind of purity that is in it; thus we can measure by its equivalent term the height of this gift, seeing that among the many results of virtuous endeavour this alone has been honoured with the title of the thing that is uncorrupted. And if we must extol with laudations this gift from the great God, the words of His Apostle are sufficient in its praise; they are few, but they throw into the background all extravagant laudations; he only styles as *"holy and without blemish"* her who has this grace for her ornament. Now if the achievement of this saintly virtue consists in making one *"without blemish and holy,"* and these epithets are adopted in their first and fullest force to glorify the incorruptible Deity, what greater praise of virginity can there be than thus to be shown in a manner *deifying* those who share in her pure mysteries, so that they become partakers of His glory Who is in actual truth the only Holy and Blameless One; their purity and their incorruptibility being the means of bringing them into relationship with Him? Many who write lengthy laudations in detailed treatises, with the view of adding something to the wonder of this grace, unconsciously defeat, in my opinion, their own end; the fulsome manner in which they amplify their subject brings its credit into suspicion. Nature's greatnesses have their own way of striking with admiration; they do not need the pleading of words: the sky, for instance, or the sun, or any other wonder of the universe. In the business of this lower world words certainly act as a basement, and the skill of praise does impart a look of magnificence; so much so, that mankind are apt to suspect as the result of mere art the wonder produced by panegyric. So the one sufficient way of praising virginity will be to show that that virtue is above praise, and to evince our admiration of it by our lives rather than by our words. A man who takes this theme for ambitious praise has the appearance of supposing that one drop of his own perspiration will make an appreciable increase of the boundless ocean, if indeed he believes, as he does, that any human words can give more dignity to so rare a grace; he must be ignorant either of his own powers or of that which he attempts to praise.

Chapter 2

Deep indeed will be the thought necessary to understand the surpassing excellence of this grace. It is comprehended in the idea of the Father incorrupt; and here at the outset is a paradox, viz. that virginity is found in Him, Who has a Son and yet without passion has begotten Him. It is included too in the nature of this Only-begotten God, Who struck the first note of all this moral innocence; it shines forth equally in His pure and passionless generation. Again a paradox; that the Son should be known to us by virginity. It is seen, too, in the inherent and incorruptible purity of the Holy Spirit; for when you have named the pure and incorruptible you have named virginity. It accompanies the whole supramundane existence; because of its passionlessness it is always present with the powers above; never separated from anything that is Divine, it never touches the opposite of this. All whose instinct and will have found their level in virtue are beautified with this perfect purity of the uncorrupted state; all who are ranked in the opposite class of character are what they are, and are called so, by reason of their fall from purity. What force of expression, then, will be adequate to such a grace? How can there be no cause to fear lest the greatness of its intrinsic value should be impaired by the efforts of any one's eloquence? The estimate of it which he will create will be less than that which his hearers had before. It will be well, then, to omit all laudation in this case; we cannot lift words to the height of our theme. On the contrary, it is possible to be ever mindful of this gift of God; and our lips may always speak of this blessing; that, though it is the property of spiritual existence and of such singular excellence, yet by the love of God it has been bestowed on those who have received their life from the will of the flesh and from blood; that, when human nature has been based by passionate inclinations, it stretches out its offer of purity like a hand to raise it up again and make it look above. This, I think, was the reason why our Master, Jesus Christ Himself, the Fountain of all innocence, did not come into the world by wedlock. It was, to divulge by the manner of His Incarnation this great secret; that purity is the only complete indication of the presence of God and of His coming, and that no one can in reality secure this for himself, unless he has altogether estranged himself from the passions of the flesh. What happened in the stainless Mary when the fullness of the Godhead which was in Christ shone out through her, that happens in every soul that leads by rule the virgin life. No longer indeed does the Master come with bodily presence; *"we know Christ no longer according to the flesh* 2 Corinthians 5:16 *"*; but, spiritually, He dwells in us and brings His Father with Him, as the Gospel somewhere tells. Seeing, then, that virginity means so much as this, that while it remains in Heaven with the Father of spirits, and moves in the dance of the celestial powers, it nevertheless stretches out hands for man's salvation; that while it is the channel which draws down the Deity to share man's estate, it keeps wings for man's desires to rise to heavenly things, and is a bond of union between the Divine and human, by its mediation bringing into harmony these existences so widely divided— what words could be discovered powerful enough to reach this wondrous height? But still, it is monstrous to seem like creatures without expression and without feeling; and we must choose (if we are silent) one of two things; either to appear never to have felt the special beauty of virginity, or to exhibit ourselves as obstinately blind to all beauty: we have consented therefore to speak briefly about this virtue, according to the wish of him who has assigned us this task, and whom in all things we must obey. But let no one expect from us any display of style; even if we wished it, perhaps we could not produce it, for we are quite unversed in that kind of writing. Even if we possessed such power, we would not prefer the favour of the few to the edification of the many. A writer of sense should have, I take it, for his chiefest object not to be admired above all other writers, but to profit both himself and them, the many.

Chapter 3

Would indeed that some profit might come to myself from this effort! I should have undertaken this labour with the greater readiness, if I could have hope of sharing, according to the Scripture, in the fruits of the plough and the threshing-floor; the toil would then have been a pleasure. As it is, this my knowledge of the beauty of virginity is in some sort vain and useless to me, just as the grain is to the muzzled ox that treads the floor, or the water that streams from the precipice to a thirsty man when he cannot reach it. Happy they who have still the power of choosing the better way, and have not debarred themselves from it by engagements of the secular life, as we have, whom a gulf now divides from glorious virginity: no one can climb up to that who has once planted his foot upon the secular life. We are but spectators of others' blessings and witnesses to the happiness of another class. Even if we strike out some fitting thoughts about virginity, we shall not be better than the cooks and scullions who provide sweet luxuries for the tables of the rich, without having any portion themselves in what they prepare. What a blessing if it had been otherwise, if we had not to learn the good by after-regrets! Now *they* are the enviable ones, *they* succeed even beyond their prayers and their desires, who have not put out of their power the enjoyment of these delights. We are like those who have a wealthy society with which to compare their own poverty, and so are all the more vexed and discontented with their present lot. The more exactly we understand the riches of virginity, the more we must bewail the other life; for we realize by this contrast with better things, how poor it is. I do not speak only of the future rewards in store for those who have lived thus excellently, but those rewards also which they have while alive here; for if any one would make up his mind to measure exactly the difference between the two courses, he would find it nearly as great as that between heaven and earth. The truth of this statement may be known by looking at actual facts.

But in writing this sad tragedy what will be a fit beginning? How shall we really bring to view the evils common to life? All men know them by experience, but somehow nature has contrived to blind the actual sufferers so that they willingly ignore their condition. Shall we begin with its choicest sweets? Well then, is not the sum total of all that is hoped for in marriage to get delightful companionship? Grant this obtained; let us sketch a marriage in every way most happy; illustrious birth, competent means, suitable ages, the very flower of the prime of life, deep affection, the very best that each can think of the other , that sweet rivalry of each wishing to surpass the other in loving; in addition, popularity, power, wide reputation, and everything else. But observe that even beneath this array of blessings the fire of an inevitable pain is smouldering. I do not speak of the envy that is always springing up against those of distinguished rank, and the liability to attack which hangs over those who seem prosperous, and that natural hatred of superiors shown by those who do not share equally in the good fortune, which make these seemingly favoured ones pass an anxious time more full of pain than pleasure. I omit that from the picture, and will suppose that envy against them is asleep; although it would not be easy to find a single life in which both these blessings were joined, *i.e.* happiness above the common, and escape from envy. However, let us, if so it is to be, suppose a married life free from all such trials; and let us see if it is possible for those who live with such an amount of good fortune to enjoy it. Why, what kind of vexation is left, you will ask, when even envy of their happiness does not reach them? I affirm that this very thing, this sweetness that surrounds their lives, is the spark which kindles pain. They are human all the time, things weak and perishing; they have to look upon the tombs of their progenitors; and so pain is inseparably bound up with their existence, if they have the least power of reflection. This continued expectancy of death, realized by no sure tokens, but hanging over them the terrible uncertainty of the future, disturbs their present joy, clouding it over with the fear of what is coming. If only, before experience comes, the results of experience could be learned, or if, when one has entered on this course, it were possible by some other means of conjecture to survey the reality, then what a crowd of deserters would run from marriage into the virgin life; what care and eagerness never to be entangled in that retentive snare, where no one knows for certain how the net galls till they have actually entered it! You would see there, if only you could do it without danger, many contraries uniting; smiles melting into tears, pain mingled with pleasure, death always hanging by expectation over the children that are born, and putting a finger upon each of the sweetest joys. Whenever the husband looks at the beloved face, that moment the fear of separation accompanies the look. If he listens to the sweet voice, the thought comes into his mind that some day he will not hear it. Whenever he is glad with gazing on her beauty, then he shudders most with the presentiment of mourning her loss. When he marks all those charms which to youth are so precious and which the thoughtless seek for, the bright eyes beneath the lids, the arching eyebrows, the cheek with its sweet and dimpling smile, the natural red that blooms upon the lips, the gold-bound hair shining in many-twisted masses on the head, and all that transient grace, then, though he may be little given to reflection, he must have this thought also in his inmost soul that some day all this beauty will melt away and become as nothing, turned after all this show into noisome and unsightly bones, which wear no trace, no memorial, no remnant of that living bloom. Can he live delighted when he thinks of that? Can he trust in these treasures which he holds as if they would be always his? Nay, it is plain that he will stagger as if he were mocked by a dream, and will have his faith in life shaken, and will look upon what he sees as no longer his. You will understand, if you have a comprehensive view of things as they are, that nothing in this life looks that which it is. It shows to us by the illusions of our imagination one thing, instead of something else. Men gaze openmouthed at it, and it mocks them with hopes; for a while it hides itself beneath this deceitful show; then all of a sudden in the reverses of life it is revealed as something different from that which men's hopes, conceived by its fraud in foolish hearts, had pictured. Will life's sweetness seem worth taking delight in to him who reflects on this? Will he ever be able really to feel it, so as to have joy in the goods he holds? Will he not, disturbed by the constant fear of some reverse, have the use without the enjoyment? I will but mention the portents, dreams, omens, and such-like things which by a foolish habit of thought are taken notice of, and always make men fear the worst. But her time of labour comes upon the young wife; and the occasion is regarded not as the bringing of a child into the world, but as the approach of death; in bearing it is expected that she will die; and, indeed, often this sad presentiment is true, and before they spread the birthday feast, before they taste any of their expected joys, they have to change their rejoicing into lamentation. Still in love's fever, still at the height of their passionate affection, not yet having grasped life's sweetest gifts, as in the vision of a dream, they are suddenly torn away from all they possessed. But what comes next? Domestics, like conquering foes, dismantle the bridal chamber; they deck it for the funeral, but it is death's room now; they make the useless wailings and beatings of the hands. Then there is the memory of former days, curses on those who advised the marriage, recriminations against friends who did not stop it; blame thrown on parents whether they be alive or dead, bitter outbursts against human destiny, arraigning of the whole course of nature, complaints and accusations even against the Divine government; war within the man himself, and fighting with those who would admonish; no repugnance to the most shocking words and acts. In some this state of mind continues, and their reason is more completely swallowed up by grief; and *their* tragedy has a sadder ending, the victim not enduring to survive the calamity.

But rather than this let us suppose a happier case. The danger of childbirth is past; a child is born to them, the very image of its parents' beauty. Are the occasions for grief at all lessened thereby? Rather they are increased; for the parents retain all their former fears, and feel in addition those on behalf of the child, lest anything should happen to it in its bringing up; for instance a bad accident, or by some turn of misfortunes a sickness, a fever, any dangerous disease. Both parents share alike in these; but who could recount the special anxieties of the wife? We omit the most obvious, which all can understand, the weariness of pregnancy, the danger in childbirth, the cares of nursing, the tearing of her heart in two for her offspring, and, if she is the mother of many, the dividing of her soul into as many parts as she has children; the tenderness with which she herself feels all that is happening to them. That is well understood by every one. But the oracle of God tells us that she is not her own mistress, but finds her resources only in him whom wedlock has made her lord; and so, if she be for ever so short a time left alone, she feels as if she were separated from her head, and can ill bear it; she even takes this short absence of her husband to be the prelude to her widowhood; her fear makes her at once give up all hope; accordingly her eyes, filled with terrified suspense, are always fixed upon the door; her ears are always busied with what others are whispering; her heart, stung with her fears, is nearly bursting even before any bad news has arrived; a noise in the doorway, whether fancied or real, acts as a messenger of ill, and on a sudden shakes her very soul; most likely all outside is well, and there is no cause to fear at all; but her fainting spirit is quicker than any message, and turns her fancy from good tidings to despair. Thus even the most favoured live, and they are not altogether to be envied; their life is not to be compared to the freedom of virginity. Yet this hasty sketch has omitted many of the more distressing details. Often this young wife too, just wedded, still brilliant in bridal grace, still perhaps blushing when her bridegroom enters, and shyly stealing furtive glances at him, when passion is all the more intense because modesty prevents it being shown, suddenly has to take the name of a poor lonely widow and be called all that is pitiable. Death comes in an instant and changes that bright creature in her white and rich attire into a black-robed mourner. He takes off the bridal ornaments and clothes her with the colours of bereavement. There is darkness in the once cheerful room, and the waiting-women sing their long dirges. She hates her friends when they try to soften her grief; she will not take food, she wastes away, and in her soul's deep dejection has a strong longing only for her death, a longing which often lasts till it comes. Even supposing that time puts an end to this sorrow, still another comes, whether she has children or not. If she has, they are fatherless, and, as objects of pity themselves, renew the memory of her loss. If she is childless, then the name of her lost husband is rooted up, and this grief is greater than the seeming consolation. I will say little of the other special sorrows of widowhood; for who could enumerate them all exactly? She finds her enemies in her relatives. Some actually take advantage of her affliction. Others exult over her loss, and see with malignant joy the home falling to pieces, the insolence of the servants, and the other distresses visible in such a case, of which there are plenty. In consequence of these, many women are compelled to risk once more the trial of the same things, not being able to endure this bitter derision. As if they could revenge insults by increasing their own sufferings! Others, remembering the past, will put up with anything rather than plunge a second time into the like troubles. If you wish to learn all the trials of this married life, listen to those women who actually know it. How they congratulate those who have chosen from the first the virgin life, and have not had to learn by experience about the better way, that virginity is fortified against all these ills, that it has no orphan state, no widowhood to mourn; it is always in the presence of the undying Bridegroom; it has the offspring of devotion always to rejoice in; it sees continually a home that is truly its own, furnished with every treasure because the Master always dwells there; in this case death does not bring separation, but union with Him Who is longed for; for when (a soul) departs , then it is with Christ, as the Apostle says. But it is time, now that we have examined on the one side the feelings of those whose lot is happy, to make a revelation of other lives, where poverty and adversity and all the other evils which men have to suffer are a fixed condition; deformities, I mean, and diseases, and all other lifelong afflictions. He whose life is contained in himself either escapes them altogether or can bear them easily, possessing a collected mind which is not distracted from itself; while he who shares himself with wife and child often has not a moment to bestow even upon regrets for his own condition, because anxiety for his dear ones fills his heart. But it is superfluous to dwell upon that which every one knows. If to what seems prosperity such pain and weariness is bound, what may we not expect of the opposite condition? Every description which attempts to represent it to our view will fall short of the reality. Yet perhaps we may in a very few words declare the depths of its misery. Those whose lot is contrary to that which passes as prosperous receive their sorrows as well from causes contrary to that. Prosperous lives are marred by the expectancy, or the presence, of death; but the misery of these is that death delays his coming. These lives then are widely divided by opposite feelings; although equally without hope, they converge to the same end. So many-sided, then, so strangely different are the ills with which marriage supplies the world. There is pain always, whether children are born, or can never be expected, whether they live, or die. One abounds in them but has not enough means for their support; another feels the want of an heir to the great fortune he has toiled for, and regards as a blessing the other's misfortune; each of them, in fact, wishes for that very thing which he sees the other regretting. Again, one man loses by death a much-loved son; another has a reprobate son alive; both equally to be pitied, though the one mourns over the death, the other over the life, of his boy. Neither will I do more than mention how sadly and disastrously family jealousies and quarrels, arising from real or fancied causes, end. Who could go completely into all those details? If you would know what a network of these evils human life is, you need not go back again to those old stories which have furnished subjects to dramatic poets. *They* are regarded as myths on account of their shocking extravagance; there are in them murders and eating of children, husband-murders, murders of mothers and brothers, incestuous unions, and every sort of disturbance of nature; and yet the old chronicler begins the story which ends in such horrors with marriage. But turning from all that, gaze only upon the tragedies that are being enacted on this life's stage; it is marriage that supplies mankind with actors there. Go to the law-courts and read through the laws there; then you will know the shameful secrets of marriage. Just as when you hear a physician explaining various diseases, you understand the misery of the human frame by learning the number and the kind of sufferings it is liable to, so when you peruse the laws and read there the strange variety of crimes in marriage to which their penalties are attached, you will have a pretty accurate idea of its properties; for the law does not provide remedies for evils which do not exist, any more than a physician has a treatment for diseases which are never known.

Chapter 4

But we need no longer show in this narrow way the drawback of this life, as if the number of its ills was limited to adulteries, dissensions, and plots. I think we should take the higher and truer view, and say at once that none of that evil in life, which is visible in all its business and in all its pursuits, can have any hold over a man, if he will not put himself in the fetters of this course. The truth of what we say will be clear thus. A man who, seeing through the illusion with the eye of his spirit purged, lifts himself above the struggling world, and, to use the words of the Apostle, slights it all as but dung, in a way exiling himself altogether from human life by his abstinence from marriage, — that man has no fellowship whatever with the sins of mankind, such as avarice, envy, anger, hatred, and everything of the kind. He has an exemption from all this, and is in every way free and at peace; there is nothing in him to provoke his neighbours' envy, because he clutches none of those objects round which envy in this life gathers. He has raised his own life above the world, and prizing virtue as his only precious possession he will pass his days in painless peace and quiet. For virtue is a possession which, though all according to their capacity should share it, yet will be always in abundance for those who thirst after it; unlike the occupation of the lands on this earth, which men divide into sections, and the more they add to the one the more they take from the other, so that the one person's gain is his fellow's loss; whence arise the fights for the lion's share, from men's hatred of being cheated. But the larger owner of *this* possession is never envied; he who snatches the lion's share does no damage to him who claims equal participation; as each is capable each has this noble longing satisfied, while the wealth of virtues in those who are already occupiers is not exhausted. The man, then, who, with his eyes only on such a life, makes virtue, which has no limit that man can devise, his only treasure, will surely never brook to bend his soul to any of those low courses which multitudes tread. He will not admire earthly riches, or human power, or any of those things which folly seeks. If, indeed, his mind is still pitched so low, he is outside our band of novices, and our words do not apply to him. But if his thoughts are above, walking as it were with God, he will be lifted out of the maze of all these errors; for the predisposing cause of them all, marriage, has not touched him. Now the wish to be before others is the deadly sin of pride, and one would not be far wrong in saying that this is the seed-root of all the thorns of sin; but it is from reasons connected with marriage that this pride mostly begins. To show what I mean, we generally find the grasping man throwing the blame on his nearest kin; the man mad after notoriety and ambition generally makes his family responsible for this sin: *"he must not be thought inferior to his forefathers; he must be deemed a great man by the generation to come by leaving his children historic records of himself"*: so also the other maladies of the soul, envy, spite, hatred and such-like, are connected with this cause; they are to be found among those who are eager about the things of this life. He who has fled from it gazes as from some high watchtower on the prospect of humanity, and pities these slaves of vanity for their blindness in setting such a value on bodily well-being. He sees some distinguished person giving himself airs because of his public honours, and wealth, and power, and only laughs at the folly of being so puffed up. He gives to the years of human life the longest number, according to the Psalmist's computation, and then compares this atom-interval with the endless ages, and pities the vain glory of those who excite themselves for such low and petty and perishable things. What, indeed, among the things here is there enviable in that which so many strive for—honour? What is gained by those who win it? The mortal remains mortal whether he is honoured or not. What good does the possessor of many acres gain in the end? Except that the foolish man thinks his own that which never belongs to him, ignorant seemingly in his greed that *"the earth is the Lord's, and the fullness thereof,"* for *"God is king of all the earth."* It is the passion of having which gives men a false title of lordship over that which can never belong to them. *"The earth,"* says the wise Preacher, *"abides for ever* Ecclesiastes 1:4,*"* ministering to every generation, first one, then another, that is born upon it; but men, though they are so little even their own masters, that they are brought into life without knowing it by their Maker's will, and before they wish are withdrawn from it, nevertheless in their excessive vanity think that they are her lords; that they, now born, now dying, rule that which remains continually. One who reflecting on this holds cheaply all that mankind prizes, whose only love is the divine life, because *"all flesh is grass, and all the glory of man as the flower of grass* 1 Peter 1:24,*"* can never care for this grass which *"today is and tomorrow is not"*; studying the divine ways, he knows not only that human life has no fixity, but that the entire universe will not keep on its quiet course for ever; he neglects his existence here as an alien and a passing thing; for the Saviour said, *"Heaven and earth shall pass away* Matthew 24:35,*"* the whole of necessity awaits its refashioning. As long as he is *"in this tabernacle* 2 Corinthians 5:4,*"* exhibiting mortality, weighed down with this existence, he laments the lengthening of his sojourn in it; as the Psalmist-poet says in his heavenly songs. Truly, they live in darkness who sojourn in these living tabernacles; wherefore that preacher, groaning at the continuance of this sojourn, says, *"Woe is me that my sojourn is prolonged ,"* and he attributes the cause of his dejection to *"darkness"*; for we know that darkness is called in the Hebrew language *"kedar."* It is indeed a darkness as of the night which envelops mankind, and prevents them seeing this deceit and knowing that all which is most prized by the living, and moreover all which is the reverse, exists only in the conception of the unreflecting, and is in itself nothing; there is no such reality anywhere as obscurity of birth, or illustrious birth, or glory, or splendour, or ancient renown, or present elevation, or power over others, or subjection. Wealth and comfort, poverty and distress, and all the other inequalities of life, seem to the ignorant, applying the test of pleasure, vastly different from each other. But to the higher understanding they are all alike; one is not of greater value than the other; because life runs on to the finish with the same speed through all these opposites, and in the lots of either class there remains the same power of choice to live well or ill, *"through armour on the right hand and on the left, through evil report and good report* 2 Corinthians 6:7 *."* Therefore the clearseeing mind which measures reality will journey on its path without turning, accomplishing its appointed time from its birth to its exit; it is neither softened by the pleasures nor beaten down by the hardships; but, as is the way with travellers, it keeps advancing always, and takes but little notice of the views presented. It is the travellers way to press on to their journey's end, no matter whether they are passing through meadows and cultivated farms, or through wilder and more rugged spots; a smiling landscape does not detain them; nor a gloomy one check their speed. So, too, that lofty mind will press straight on to its self-imposed end, not turning aside to see anything on the way. It passes through life, but its gaze is fixed on heaven; it is the good steersman directing the bark to some landmark there. But the grosser mind looks down; it bends its energies to bodily pleasures as surely as the sheep stoop to their pasture; it lives for gorging and still lower pleasures ; it is alienated from the life of God , and a stranger to the promise of the

Covenants; it recognizes no good but the gratification of the body. It is a mind such as this that *"walks in darkness,"* and invents all the evil in this life of ours; avarice, passions unchecked, unbounded luxury, lust of power, vain-glory, the whole mob of moral diseases that invade men's homes. In these vices, one somehow holds closely to another; where one has entered all the rest seem to follow, dragging each other in a natural order, just as in a chain, when you have jerked the first link, the others cannot rest, and even the link at the other end feels the motion of the first, which passes thence by virtue of their contiguity through the intervening links; so firmly are men's vices linked together by their very nature; when one of them has gained the mastery of a soul, the rest of the train follow. If you want a graphic picture of this accursed chain, suppose a man who because of some special pleasure it gives him is a victim to his thirst for fame; then a desire to increase his fortune follows close upon this thirst for fame; he becomes grasping; but only because the first vice leads him on to this. Then this grasping after money and superiority engenders either anger with his kith and kin, or pride towards his inferiors, or envy of those above him; then hypocrisy comes in after this envy; a soured temper after that; a misanthropical spirit after that; and behind them all a state of condemnation which ends in the dark fires of hell. You see the chain; how all follows from one cherished passion. Seeing, then, that this inseparable train of moral diseases has entered once for all into the world, one single way of escape is pointed out to us in the exhortations of the inspired writings; and that is to separate ourselves from the life which involves this sequence of sufferings. If we haunt Sodom, we cannot escape the rain of fire; nor if one who has fled out of her looks back upon her desolation, can he fail to become a pillar of salt rooted to the spot. We cannot be rid of the Egyptian bondage, unless we leave Egypt, that is, this life that lies under water, and pass, not that Red Sea, but this black and gloomy Sea of life. But suppose we remain in this evil bondage, and, to use the Master's words, *"the truth shall not have made us free,"* how can one who seeks a lie and wanders in the maze of this world ever come to the truth? How can one who has surrendered his existence to be chained by nature run away from this captivity? An illustration will make our meaning clearer. A winter torrent, which, impetuous in itself, becomes swollen and carries down beneath its stream trees and boulders and anything that comes in its way, is death and danger to those alone who live along its course; for those who have got well out of its way it rages in vain. Just so, only the man who lives in the turmoil of life has to feel its force; only he has to receive those sufferings which nature's stream, descending in a flood of troubles, must, to be true to its kind, bring to those who journey on its banks. But if a man leaves this torrent, and these *"proud waters ,"* he will escape from being *"a prey to the teeth"* of this life, as the Psalm goes on to say, and, as *"a bird from the snare,"* on virtue's wings. This simile, then, of the torrent holds; human life *is* a tossing and tumultuous stream sweeping down to find its natural level; none of the objects sought for in it last till the seekers are satisfied; all that is carried to them by this stream comes near, just touches them, and passes on; so that the present moment in this impetuous flow eludes enjoyment, for the after-current snatches it from their view. It would be our interest therefore to keep far away from such a stream, lest, engaged on temporal things, we should neglect eternity. How can a man keep for ever anything here, be his love for it never so passionate? Which of life's most cherished objects endures always? What flower of prime? What gift of strength and beauty? What wealth, or fame, or power? They all have their transient bloom, and then melt away into their opposites. Who can continue in life's prime? Whose strength lasts for ever? Has not Nature made the bloom of beauty even more short-lived than the shows of spring? For they blossom in their season, and after withering for a while again revive; after another shedding they are again in leaf, and retain their beauty of today to a late prime. But Nature exhibits the human bloom only in the spring of early life; then she kills it; it is vanished in the frosts of age. All other delights also deceive the bodily eye for a time, and then pass behind the veil of oblivion. Nature's inevitable changes are many; they agonize him whose love is passionate. One way of escape is open: it is, to be attached to none of these things, and to get as far away as possible from the society of this emotional and sensual world; or rather, for a man to go outside the feelings which his own body gives rise to. Then, as he does not live for the flesh, he will not be subject to the troubles of the flesh. But this amounts to living for the spirit only, and imitating all we can the employment of the world of spirits. There they neither marry, nor are given in marriage. Their work and their excellence is to contemplate the Father of all purity, and to beautify the lines of their own character from the Source of all beauty, so far as imitation of It is possible.

Chapter 5

Now we declare that Virginity is man's *"fellow-worker"* and helper in achieving the aim of this lofty passion. In other sciences men have devised certain practical methods for cultivating the particular subject; and so, I take it, virginity is the practical method in the science of the Divine life, furnishing men with the power of assimilating themselves with spiritual natures. The constant endeavour in such a course is to prevent the nobility of the soul from being lowered by those sensual outbreaks, in which the mind no longer maintains its heavenly thoughts and upward gaze, but sinks down to the emotions belonging to the flesh and blood. How can the soul which is riveted to the pleasures of the flesh and busied with merely human longings turn a disengaged eye upon its kindred intellectual light? This evil, ignorant, and prejudiced bias towards material things will prevent it. The eyes of swine, turning naturally downward, have no glimpse of the wonders of the sky; no more can the soul whose body drags it down look any longer upon the beauty above; it must pore perforce upon things which though natural are low and animal. To look with a free devoted gaze upon heavenly delights, the soul will turn itself from earth; it will not even partake of the recognized indulgences of the secular life; it will transfer all its powers of affection from material objects to the intellectual contemplation of immaterial beauty. Virginity of the body is devised to further such a disposition of the soul; it aims at creating in it a complete forgetfulness of natural emotions; it would prevent the necessity of ever descending to the call of fleshly needs. Once freed from such, the soul runs no risk of becoming, through a growing habit of indulging in that which seems to a certain extent conceded by nature's law, inattentive and ignorant of Divine and undefiled delights. Purity of the heart, that master of our lives, alone can capture them.

Chapter 6

This, I believe, makes the greatness of the prophet Elias, and of him who afterwards appeared in the spirit and power of Elias, than whom *"of those that are born of women there was none greater* Matthew 12:11 ." If their history conveys any other mystic lesson, surely this above all is taught by their special mode of life, that the man whose thoughts are fixed upon the invisible is necessarily separated from all the ordinary events of life; his judgments as to the

Selected Works

True Good cannot be confused and led astray by the deceits arising from the senses. Both, from their youth upwards, exiled themselves from human society, and in a way from human nature, in their neglect of the usual kinds of meat and drink, and their sojourn in the desert. The wants of each were satisfied by the nourishment that came in their way, so that their taste might remain simple and unspoilt, as their ears were free from any distracting noise, and their eyes from any wandering look. Thus they attained a cloudless calm of soul, and were raised to that height of Divine favour which Scripture records of each. Elias, for instance, became the dispenser of God's earthly gifts; he had authority to close at will the uses of the sky against the sinners and to open them to the penitent. John is not said indeed to have done any miracle; but the gift in him was pronounced by Him Who sees the secrets of a man greater than any prophet's. This was so, we may presume, because both, from beginning to end, so dedicated their hearts to the Lord that they were unsullied by any earthly passion; because the love of wife or child, or any other human call, did not intrude upon them, and they did not even think their daily sustenance worthy of anxious thought; because they showed themselves to be above any magnificence of dress, and made shift with that which chance offered them, one clothing himself in goat-skins, the other with camel's hair. It is my belief that they would not have reached to this loftiness of spirit, if marriage had softened them. This is not simple history only; it is *"written for our admonition 1 Corinthians 10:11,"* that we might direct our lives by theirs. What, then, do we learn thereby? This: that the man who longs for union with God must, like those saints, detach his mind from all worldly business. It is impossible for the mind which is poured into many channels to win its way to the knowledge and the love of God.

Chapter 7

An illustration will make our teaching on this subject clearer. Imagine a stream flowing from a spring and dividing itself off into a number of accidental channels. As long as it proceeds so, it will be useless for any purpose of agriculture, the dissipation of its waters making each particular current small and feeble, and therefore slow. But if one were to mass these wandering and widely dispersed rivulets again into one single channel, he would have a full and collected stream for the supplies which life demands. Just so the human mind (so it seems to me), as long as its current spreads itself in all directions over the pleasures of the sense, has no power that is worth the naming of making its way towards the Real Good; but once call it back and collect it upon itself, so that it may begin to move without scattering and wandering towards the activity which is congenital and natural to it, it will find no obstacle in mounting to higher things, and in grasping realities. We often see water contained in a pipe bursting upwards through this constraining force, which will not let it leak; and this, in spite of its natural gravitation: in the same way, the mind of man, enclosed in the compact channel of an habitual continence, and not having any side issues, will be raised by virtue of its natural powers of motion to an exalted love. In fact, its Maker ordained that it should always move, and to stop is impossible to it; when therefore it is prevented employing this power upon trifles, it cannot be but that it will speed toward the truth, all improper exits being closed. In the case of many turnings we see travellers can keep to the direct route, when they have learned that the other roads are wrong, and so avoid them; the more they keep out of these wrong directions, the more they will preserve the straight course; in like manner the mind in turning from vanities will recognize the truth. The great prophets, then, whom we have mentioned seem to teach this lesson, viz. to entangle ourselves with none of the objects of this world's effort; marriage is one of these, or rather it is the primal root of all striving after vanities.

Chapter 8

Let no one think however that herein we depreciate marriage as an institution. We are well aware that it is not a stranger to God's blessing. But since the common instincts of mankind can plead sufficiently on its behalf, instincts which prompt by a spontaneous bias to take the high road of marriage for the procreation of children, whereas Virginity in a way thwarts this natural impulse, it is a superfluous task to compose formally an Exhortation to marriage. We put forward the pleasure of it instead, as a most doughty champion on its behalf. It may be however, notwithstanding this, that there *is* some need of such a treatise, occasioned by those who travesty the teaching of the Church. Such persons 1 Timothy 4:2 *"have their conscience seared with a hot iron,"* as the Apostle expresses it; and very truly too, considering that, deserting the guidance of the Holy Spirit for the *"doctrines of devils,"* they have some ulcers and blisters stamped upon their hearts, abominating God's creatures, and calling them *"foul," "seducing," "mischievous,"* and so on. *"But what have I to do to judge them that are without* 1 Corinthians 5:12*?"* asks the Apostle. Truly those persons are outside the Court in which the words of our mysteries are spoken; they are not installed under God's roof, but in the monastery of the Evil One. They *"are taken captive by him at his will* 2 Timothy 2:16 *."* They therefore do not understand that all virtue is found in moderation, and that any declension to either side of it becomes a vice. He, in fact, who grasps the middle point between doing too little and doing too much has hit the distinction between vice and virtue. Instances will make this clearer. Cowardice and audacity are two recognized vices opposed to each other; the one the defect, the other the excess of confidence; between them lies courage. Again, piety is neither atheism nor superstition; it is equally impious to deny a God and to believe in many gods. Is there need of more examples to bring this principle home? The man who avoids both meanness and prodigality will by this shunning of extremes form the moral habit of liberality; for liberality is the thing which is neither inclined to spend at random vast and useless sums, nor yet to be closely calculating in necessary expenses. We need not go into details in the case of all good qualities. Reason, in all of them, has established virtue to be a middle state between two extremes. Sobriety itself therefore is a middle state, and manifestly involves the two declensions on either side towards vice; he, that is, who is wanting in firmness of soul, and is so easily worsted in the combat with pleasure as never even to have approached the path of a virtuous and sober life, slides into shameful indulgence; while he who goes beyond the safe ground of sobriety and overshoots the moderation of this virtue, falls as it were from a precipice into the *"doctrines of devils," "having his conscience seared with a hot iron."* In declaring marriage abominable he brands himself with such reproaches; for *"if the tree is corrupt"* (as the Gospel says), *"the fruit also of the tree will be like it"*; if a man is the shoot and fruitage of the tree of marriage, reproaches cast on that turn upon him who casts them. These persons, then, are like branded criminals already; their conscience is covered with the stripes of this unnatural teaching. But our view of marriage is this; that, while the pursuit of heavenly things should be a man's first care, yet if he can use the advantages of marriage with sobriety and moderation, he need not despise this way of serving the state. An example might be found in the patriarch Isaac. He married Rebecca when he was past the flower of his age and his prime was nearly

spent, so that his marriage was not the deed of passion, but because of God's blessing that should be upon his seed. He cohabited with her till the birth of her only children, and then, closing the channels of the senses, lived wholly for the Unseen; for this is what seems to be meant by the mention in his history of the *dimness* of the Patriarch's eyes. But let that be as those think who are skilled in reading these meanings, and let us proceed with the continuity of our discourse. What then, were we saying? That in the cases where it is possible at once to be true to the diviner love, and to embrace wedlock, there is no reason for setting aside this dispensation of nature and misrepresenting as abominable that which is honourable. Let us take again our illustration of the water and the spring. Whenever the husbandman, in order to irrigate a particular spot, is bringing the stream there, but there is need before it gets there of a small outlet, he will allow only so much to escape into that outlet as is adequate to supply the demand, and can then easily be blended again with the main stream. If, as an inexperienced and easy-going steward, he opens too wide a channel, there will be danger of the whole stream quitting its direct bed and pouring itself sideways. In the same way, if (as life does need a mutual succession) a man so treats this need as to give spiritual things the first thought, and because of the shortness of the time indulges but sparingly the sexual passion and keeps it under restraint, that man would realize the character of the prudent husband man to which the Apostle exhorts us. About the details of paying these trifling debts of nature he will not be over-calculating, but the long hours of his prayers will secure the purity which is the key-note of his life. He will always fear lest by this kind of indulgence he may become nothing but flesh and blood; for in them God's Spirit does not dwell. He who is of so weak a character that he cannot make a manful stand against nature's impulse had better keep himself very far away from such temptations, rather than descend into a combat which is above his strength. There is no small danger for him lest, cajoled in the valuation of pleasure, he should think that there exists no other good but that which is enjoyed along with some sensual emotion, and, turning altogether from the love of immaterial delights, should become entirely of the flesh, seeking always his pleasure only there, so that his character will be a Pleasure-lover, not a God-lover. It is not every man's gift, owing to weakness of nature, to hit the due proportion in these matters; there is a danger of being carried far beyond it, and *"sticking fast in the deep mire,"* to use the

Psalmist's words. It would therefore be for our interest, as our discourse has been suggesting, to pass through life without a trial of these temptations, lest under cover of the excuse of lawful indulgence passion should gain an entrance into the citadel of the soul.

Chapter 9

Custom is indeed in everything hard to resist. It possesses an enormous power of attracting and seducing the soul. In the cases where a man has got into a fixed state of sentiment, a certain imagination of the good is created in him by this habit; and nothing is so naturally vile but it may come to be thought both desirable and laudable, once it has got into the fashion. Take mankind now living on the earth. There are many nations, and their ambitions are not all the same. The standard of beauty and of honour is different in each, the custom of each regulating their enthusiasm and their aims. This unlikeness is seen not only among nations where the pursuits of the one are in no repute with the other, but even in the same nation, and the same city, and the same family; we may see in those aggregates also much difference existing owing to customary feeling. Thus brothers born from the same throe are separated widely from each other in the aims of life. Nor is this to be wondered at, considering that each single man does not generally keep to the same opinion about the same thing, but alters it as fashion influences him. Not to go far from our present subject, we have known those who have shown themselves to be in love with chastity all through the early years of puberty; but in taking the pleasures which men think legitimate and allowable they make them the starting-point of an impure life, and when once they have admitted these temptations, all the forces of their feeling are turned in that direction, and, to take again our illustration of the stream, they let it rush from the diviner channel into low material channels, and make within themselves a broad path for passion; so that the stream of their love leaves dry the abandoned channel of the higher way and flows abroad in indulgence. It would be well then, we take it, for the weaker brethren to fly to virginity as into an impregnable fortress, rather than to descend into the career of life's consequences and invite temptations to do their worst upon them, entangling themselves in those things which through the lusts of the flesh war against the law of our mind; it would be well for them to consider that herein they risk not broad acres, or wealth, or any other of this life's prizes, but the hope which has been their guide. It is impossible that one who has turned to the world and feels its anxieties, and engages his heart in the wish to please men, can fulfil that first and great commandment of the Master, *"You shall love God with all your heart and with all your strength* Matthew 22:37 *."* How can he fulfil that, when he divides his heart between God and the world, and exhausts the love which he owes to Him alone in human affections? *"He that is unmarried cares for the things of the Lord; but he that is married cares for the things that are of the world. "* If the combat with pleasure seems wearisome, nevertheless let all take heart. Habit will not fail to produce, even in the seemingly most fretful , a feeling of pleasure through the very effort of their perseverance; and that pleasure will be of the noblest and purest kind; which the intelligent may well be enamoured of, rather than allow themselves, with aims narrowed by the lowness of their objects, to be estranged from the true greatness which goes beyond all thought.

Chapter 10

What words indeed could possibly express the greatness of that loss in falling away from the possession of real goodness? What consummate power of thought would have to be employed! Who could produce even in outline that which speech cannot tell, nor the mind grasp? On the one hand, if a man has kept the eye of his heart so clear that he can in a way behold the promise of our Lord's Beatitudes realized, he will condemn all human utterance as powerless to represent that which he has apprehended. On the other hand, if a man from the atmosphere of material indulgences has the weakness of passion spreading like a film over the keen vision of his soul, all force of expression will be wasted upon him; for it is all one whether you understate or whether you magnify a miracle to those who have no power whatever of perceiving it. Just as, in the case of the sunlight, on one who has never from the day of his birth seen it, all efforts at translating it into words are quite thrown away; you cannot make the splendour of the ray shine through his ears; in like manner, to see the beauty of the true and intellectual light, each man has need of eyes of his own; and he who by a gift of Divine inspiration can see it retains his ecstasy unexpressed in the depths of his consciousness; while he who sees it not cannot be made to know even the greatness of his loss. How should he? This good escapes his perception, and it cannot be represented to him; it is unspeakable, and cannot be delineated. We have not learned the peculiar language expressive of this beauty. An example of what we want to say does not exist in the world; a comparison for it would at least be very difficult to find. Who compares the Sun to a little spark? Or the vast Deep to a drop? And that tiny drop and that diminutive spark bear the same relation to the Deep and to the Sun, as any beautiful object of man's admiration does to that real beauty on the features of the First Good, of which we catch the glimpse beyond any other good. What words could be invented to show the greatness of this loss to him who suffers it? Well does the great David seem to me to express the impossibility of doing this. He has been lifted by the power of the Spirit out of himself, and sees in a blessed state of ecstacy the boundless and incomprehensible Beauty; he sees it as fully as a mortal can see who has quitted his fleshly envelopments and entered, by the mere power of thought, upon the contemplation of the spiritual and intellectual world, and in his longing to speak a word worthy of the spectacle he bursts forth with that cry, which all re-echo, *"Every man a liar!"* I take that to mean that any man who entrusts to language the task of presenting the ineffable Light is really and truly a liar; not because of any hatred on his part of the truth, but because of the feebleness of his instrument for expressing the thing thought of. The visible beauty to be met with in this life of ours, showing glimpses of itself, whether in inanimate objects or in animate organisms in a certain choiceness of colour, can be adequately admired by our power of aesthetic feeling. It can be illustrated and made known to others by description; it can be seen drawn in the language as in a picture. Even a perfect type of such beauty does not baffle our conception. But how can language illustrate when it finds no media for its sketch, no colour, no contour, no majestic size, no faultlessness of feature; nor any other commonplace of art? The Beauty which is invisible and formless, which is destitute of qualities and far removed from everything which we recognize in bodies by the eye, can never be made known by the traits which require nothing but the perceptions of our senses in order to be grasped. Not that we are to despair of winning this object of our love, though it does seem too high for our comprehension. The more reason shows the greatness of this thing which we are seeking, the higher we must lift our thoughts and excite them with the greatness of that object; and we must fear to lose our share in that transcendent Good. There is indeed no small amount of danger lest, as we can base the apprehension of it on no knowable qualities, we should slip away from it altogether because of its very height and mystery. We deem it necessary therefore, owing to this weakness of the thinking faculty, to lead it towards the Unseen by stages through the cognizances of the senses. Our conception of the case is as follows.

Chapter 11

Now those who take a superficial and unreflecting view of things observe the outward appearance of anything they meet, *e.g.* of a man, and then trouble themselves no more about him. The view they have taken of the bulk of his body is enough to make them think that they know all about him. But the penetrating and scientific mind will not trust to the eyes alone the task of taking the measure of reality; it will not stop at appearances, nor count that which is not seen among unrealities. It inquires into the qualities of the man's soul. It takes those of its characteristics which have been developed by his bodily constitution, both in combination and singly; first singly, by analysis, and then in that living combination which makes the personality of the subject. As regards the inquiry into the nature of beauty, we see, again, that the man of half-grown intelligence, when he observes an object which is bathed in the glow of a seeming beauty, thinks that that object is in its essence beautiful, no matter what it is that so prepossesses him with the pleasure of the eye. He will not go deeper into the subject. But the other, whose mind's eye is clear, and who can inspect such appearances, will neglect those elements which are the material only upon which the Form of Beauty works; to him they will be but the ladder by which he climbs to the prospect of that Intellectual Beauty, in accordance with their share in which all other beauties get their existence and their name. But for the majority, I take it, who live all their lives with such obtuse faculties of thinking, it is a difficult thing to perform this feat of mental analysis and of discriminating the material vehicle from the immanent beauty, and thereby of grasping the actual nature of the Beautiful; and if any one wants to know the exact source of all the false and pernicious conceptions of it, he would find it in nothing else but this, viz. the absence, in the soul's faculties of feeling, of that exact training which would enable them to distinguish between true Beauty and the reverse. Owing to this men give up all search after the true Beauty. Some slide into mere sensuality. Others incline in their desires to dead metallic coin. Others limit their imagination of the beautiful to worldly honours, fame, and power. There is another class which is enthusiastic about art and science. The most debased make their gluttony the test of what is good. But he who turns from all grosser thoughts and all passionate longings after what is seeming, and explores the nature of the beauty which is simple, immaterial, formless, would never make a mistake like that when he has to choose between all the objects of desire; he would never be so misled by these attractions as not to see the transient character of their pleasures and not to win his way to an utter contempt for every one of them. This, then, is the path to lead us to the discovery of the Beautiful. All other objects that attract men's love, be they never so fashionable, be they prized never so much and embraced never so eagerly, must be left below us, as too low, too fleeting, to employ the powers of loving which we possess; not indeed that those powers are to be locked up within us unused and motionless; but only that they must first be cleansed from all lower longings; then we must lift them to that height to which sense can never reach. Admiration even of the beauty of the heavens, and of the dazzling sunbeams, and, indeed, of any fair phenomenon, will then cease. The beauty noticed there will be but as the hand to lead us to the love of the supernal Beauty whose glory the heavens and the firmament declare, and whose secret the whole creation sings. The climbing soul, leaving all that she has grasped already as too narrow for her needs, will thus grasp the idea of that magnificence which is exalted far above the heavens. But how can any one reach to this, whose ambitions creep below? How can any one fly up into the heavens, who has not the wings of heaven and is not already buoyant and lofty-minded by reason of a heavenly calling? Few can be such strangers to evangelic mysteries as not to know that there is but one vehicle on which man's soul can mount into the heavens, viz. the self-made likeness in himself to the descending Dove, whose wings David the Prophet also longed for. This is the allegorical name used in Scripture for the power of the Holy Spirit; whether it be because not a drop of gall is found in that bird, or because it cannot bear any noisome smell, as close observers tell us. He therefore who keeps away from all bitterness and all the noisome effluvia of the flesh, and raises himself on the aforesaid wings above all low earthly ambitions, or, more than that, above the whole universe itself, will be the man to find that which is alone worth loving, and to become himself as beautiful as the Beauty which he has touched and entered, and to be made bright and luminous himself in the communion of the real Light. We are told by those who have studied the subject, that those gleams which follow each other so fast through the air at night and which some call shooting stars, are nothing but the air itself streaming into the upper regions of the sky under stress of some particular blasts. They say that the fiery track is traced along the sky when those blasts ignite in the ether. In like manner, then, as this air round the earth is forced upwards by some blast and changes into the pure splendour of the ether, so the mind of man leaves this murky miry world, and under the stress of the spirit becomes pure and luminous in contact with the true and supernal Purity; in such an atmosphere it even itself emits light, and is so filled with radiance, that it becomes itself a Light, according to the promise of our Lord that *"the righteous should shine forth as the sun* Matthew 13:43 ." We see this even here, in the case of a mirror, or a sheet of water, or any smooth surface that can reflect the light; when they receive the sunbeam they beam themselves; but they would not do this if any stain marred their pure and shining surface. We shall become then as the light, in our nearness to Christ's true light, if we leave this dark atmosphere of the earth and dwell above; and we shall be light, as our Lord says somewhere to His disciples, if the true Light that shines in the dark comes down even to us; unless, that is, any foulness of sin spreading over our hearts should dim the brightness of our light. Perhaps these examples have led us gradually on to the discovery that we can be changed into something better than ourselves; and it has been proved as well that this union of the soul with the incorruptible Deity can be accomplished in no other way but by herself attaining by her virgin state to the utmost purity possible—a state which, being like God, will enable her to grasp that to which it is like, while she places herself like a mirror beneath the purity of God, and moulds her own beauty at the touch and the sight of the Archetype of all beauty. Take a character strong enough to turn from all that is human, from persons, from wealth, from the pursuits of Art and Science, even from whatever in moral practice and in legislation is viewed as right (for still in all of them error in the apprehension of the Beautiful comes in, sense being the criterion); such a character will feel as a passionate lover only towards that Beauty which has no source but Itself, which is not such at one particular time or relatively only, which is Beautiful from, and through, and in itself, not such at one moment and in the next ceasing to be such, above all increase and addition, incapable of change and alteration. I venture to affirm that, to one who has cleansed all the powers of his being from every form of vice, the Beauty which is essential, the source of every beauty and every good, will become visible. The visual eye, purged from its blinding humour, can clearly discern objects even on the distant sky ; so to the soul by virtue of her innocence there comes the power of taking in that Light; and the real Virginity, the real zeal for chastity, ends in no other goal than this, viz. the power thereby of seeing God. No one in fact is so mentally blind as not to understand *that* without telling; viz. that the God of the Universe is the only absolute, and primal, and unrivalled Beauty and Goodness. All, maybe, know that; but there are those who, as might have been expected, wish besides this to discover, if possible, a process by which we may be actually guided to it. Well, the Divine books are full of such instruction for our guidance; and besides that many of the Saints cast the refulgence of their own lives, like lamps, upon the path for those who are *"walking with God."* But each may gather in abundance for himself suggestions towards this end out of either Covenant in the inspired writings; the Prophets and the Law are full of them; and also the Gospel and the Traditions of the Apostles. What we ourselves have conjectured in following out the thoughts of those inspired utterances is this.

Chapter 12

This reasoning and intelligent creature, man, at once the work and the likeness of the Divine and Imperishable Mind (for so in the Creation it is written of him that *"God made man in His image* Genesis 1:27 "), this creature, I say, did not in the course of his first production have united to the very essence of his nature the liability to passion and to death. Indeed, the truth about the image could never have been maintained if the beauty reflected in that image had been in the slightest degree opposed to the Archetypal Beauty. Passion was introduced afterwards, subsequent to man's first organization; and it was in this way. Being the image and the likeness, as has been said, of the Power which rules all things, man kept also in the matter of a Free-Will this likeness to Him whose Will is over all. He was enslaved to no outward necessity whatever; his feeling towards that which pleased him depended only on his own private judgment; he was free to choose whatever he liked; and so he was a free agent, though circumvented with cunning, when he drew upon himself that disaster which now overwhelms humanity. He became himself the discoverer of evil, but he did not therein discover what God had made; for God did not make death. Man became, in fact, himself the fabricator, to a certain extent, and the craftsman of evil. All who have the faculty of sight may enjoy equally the sunlight; and any one can if he likes put this enjoyment from him by shutting his eyes: in that case it is not that the sun retires and produces that darkness, but the man himself puts a barrier between his eye and the sunshine; the faculty of vision cannot indeed, even in the closing of the eyes, remain inactive , and so this operative sight necessarily becomes an operative darkness rising up in the man from his own free act in ceasing to see. Again, a man in building a house for himself may omit to make in it any way of entrance for the light; he will necessarily be in darkness, though he cuts himself off from the light voluntarily. So the first man on the earth, or rather he who generated evil in man, had for choice the Good and the Beautiful lying all around him in the very nature of things; yet he wilfully cut out a new way for himself against this nature, and in the act of turning away from virtue, which was his own free act, he created the usage of evil. For, be it observed, there is no such thing in the world as evil irrespective of a will, and discoverable in a substance apart from that. Every creature of God is good, and nothing of His *"to be rejected"*; all that God made was *"very good."* But the habit of sinning entered as we have described, and with fatal quickness, into the life of man; and from that small beginning spread into this infinitude of evil. Then that godly beauty of the soul which was an imitation of the Archetypal Beauty, like fine steel blackened with the vicious rust, preserved no longer the glory of its familiar essence, but was disfigured with the ugliness of sin. This thing so great and precious , as the Scripture calls him, this being man, has fallen from his proud birthright. As those who have slipped and fallen heavily into mud, and have all their features so besmeared with it, that their nearest friends do not recognize them, so this creature has fallen into the mire of sin and lost the blessing of being an image of the imperishable Deity; he has clothed himself instead with a perishable and foul resemblance to something else; and this Reason counsels him to put away again by washing it off in the cleansing water of this calling. The earthly envelopment once removed, the soul's beauty will again appear. Now the putting off of a strange accretion is equivalent to the return to that which is familiar and natural; yet such a return cannot be but by again becoming that which in the beginning we were created. In fact this likeness to the divine is not our work at all; it is not the achievement of any faculty of man; it is the great gift of God bestowed upon our nature at the very moment of our birth; human efforts can only go so far as to clear away the filth of sin, and so cause the buried beauty of the soul to shine forth again. This truth is, I think, taught in the Gospel, when our Lord says, to those who can hear what Wisdom speaks beneath a mystery, that *"the Kingdom of God is within you* Luke 17:21 *."* That word points out the fact that the Divine good is not something apart from our nature, and is not removed far away from those who have the will to seek it; it is in fact within each of us, ignored indeed, and unnoticed while it is stifled beneath the cares and pleasures of life, but found again whenever we can turn our power of conscious thinking towards it. If further confirmation of what we say is required, I think it will be found in what is suggested by our Lord in the searching for the Lost Drachma. The thought, there, is that the widowed soul reaps no benefit from the other virtues (called drachmas in the Parable) being all of them found safe, if that one other is not among them. The Parable therefore suggests that a candle should first be lit, signifying doubtless our reason which throws light on hidden principles; then that in one's own house, that is, within oneself, we should search for that lost coin; and by that coin the Parable doubtless hints at the image of our King, not yet hopelessly lost, but hidden beneath the dirt; and by this last we must understand the impurities of the flesh, which, being swept and purged away by carefulness of life, leave clear to the view the object of our search. Then it is meant that the soul herself who finds this rejoices over it, and with her the neighbours, whom she calls in to share with her in this delight. Verily, all those powers which are the housemates of the soul, and which the Parable names her neighbours for this occasion , when so be that the image of the mighty King is revealed in all its brightness at last (that image which the Fashioner of each individual heart of us has stamped upon this our Drachma), will then be converted to that divine delight and festivity, and will gaze upon the ineffable beauty of the recovered one. *"Rejoice with me,"* she says, *"because I have found the Drachma which I had lost."* The neighbours, that is, the soul's familiar powers, both the reasoning and the appetitive, the affections of grief and of anger, and all the rest that are discerned in her, at that joyful feast which celebrates the finding of the heavenly Drachma are well called her friends also; and it is meet that they should all rejoice in the Lord when they all look towards the Beautiful and the Good, and do everything for the glory of God, no longer instruments of sin. Romans 6:13 If, then, such is the lesson of this Finding of the lost, viz. that we should restore the divine image from the foulness which the flesh wraps round it to its primitive state, let us become that which the First Man was at the moment when he first breathed. And what was that? Destitute he was then of his covering of dead skins, but he could gaze without shrinking upon God's countenance. He did not yet judge of what was lovely by taste or sight; he found in the Lord alone all that was sweet; and he used the helpmeet given him only for this delight, as Scripture signifies when it said that *"he knew her not* Genesis 4:1 " till he was driven forth from the garden, and till she, for the sin which she was decoyed into committing, was sentenced to the pangs of childbirth. We, then, who in our first ancestor were thus ejected, are allowed to return to our earliest state of blessedness by the very same stages by which we lost Paradise. What are they? Pleasure, craftily offered, began the Fall, and there followed after pleasure shame, and fear, even to remain longer in the sight of their Creator, so that they hid themselves in leaves and shade; and after that they covered themselves with the skins of dead animals; and then were sent forth into this pestilential and exacting land where, as the compensation for having to die, marriage was instituted. Genesis 3:16 Now if we are destined *"to depart hence, and be with Christ* Philippians 1:23," we must begin at the end of the route of departure (which lies nearest to ourselves); just as those who have travelled far from their friends at home, when they turn to reach again the place from which they started, first leave that district which they reached at the end of their outward journey. Marriage, then, is the last stage of our separation from the life that was led in Paradise; marriage therefore, as our discourse has been suggesting, is the first thing to be left; it is the first station as it were for our departure to Christ. Next, we must retire from all anxious toil upon the land, such as man was bound to after his sin. Next we must divest ourselves of those coverings of our nakedness, the coats of skins, namely the wisdom of the flesh; we must renounce all shameful things done in secret 2 Corinthians 4:2, and be covered no longer with the fig-leaves of this bitter world; then, when we have torn off the coatings of this life's perishable leaves, we must stand again in the sight of our Creator; and repelling all the illusion of taste and sight, take for our guide God's commandment only, instead of the venom-spitting serpent. That commandment was, to touch nothing but what was Good, and to leave what was evil untasted; because impatience to remain any longer in ignorance of evil would be but the beginning of the long train of actual evil. For this reason it was forbidden to our first parents to grasp the knowledge of the opposite to the good, as well as that of the good itself; they were to keep themselves from *"the knowledge of good and evil* Genesis 2:17,"* and to enjoy the Good in its purity, unmixed with one particle of evil: and to enjoy *that*, is in my judgment nothing else than to be ever with God, and to feel ceaselessly and continually this delight, unalloyed by anything that could tear us away from it. One might even be bold to say that this might be found the way by which a man could be again caught up into Paradise out of this world which lies in the Evil, into that Paradise where Paul was when he saw the unspeakable sights which it is not lawful for a man to talk of 2 Corinthians 12:4 .

Chapter 13

But seeing that Paradise is the home of living spirits, and will not admit those who are dead in sin, and that we on the other hand are fleshly, subject to death, and sold under sin , how is it possible that one who is a subject of death's empire should ever dwell in this land where all is life? What method of release from this jurisdiction can be devised? Here too the Gospel teaching is abundantly sufficient. We hear our Lord saying to Nicodemus, *"That which is born of the flesh is flesh; and that which is born of the Spirit is spirit. "* We know too that the flesh is subject to death because of sin, but the Spirit of God is both incorruptible, and life-giving, and deathless. As at our physical birth there comes into the world with us a potentiality of being again turned to dust, plainly the Spirit also imparts a life-giving potentiality to the children begotten by Himself. What lesson, then, results from these remarks? This: that we should wean ourselves from this life in the flesh, which has an inevitable follower, death; and that we should search for a manner of life which does not bring death in its train. Now the life of Virginity is such a life. We will add a few other things to show how true this is. Every one knows that the propagation of mortal frames is the work which the intercourse of the sexes has to do; whereas for those who are joined to the Spirit, life and immortality instead of children are produced by this latter intercourse; and the words of the Apostle beautifully suit their case, for the joyful mother of such children as these *"shall be saved in child-*

bearing 1 Timothy 2:15;" as the Psalmist in his divine songs thankfully cries, *"He makes the barren woman to keep house, and to be a joyful mother of children."* Truly a joyful mother is the virgin mother who by the operation of the Spirit conceives the deathless children, and who is called by the Prophet barren because of her modesty only. This life, then, which is stronger than the power of death, is, to those who think, the preferable one. The physical bringing of children into the world— I speak without wishing to offend— is as much a starting-point of death as of life; because from the moment of birth the process of dying commences. But those who by virginity have desisted from this process have drawn within themselves the boundary line of death, and by their own deed have checked his advance; they have made themselves, in fact, a frontier between life and death, and a barrier too, which thwarts him. If, then, death cannot pass beyond virginity, but finds his power checked and shattered there, it is demonstrated that virginity is a stronger thing than death; and that body is rightly named undying which does not lend its service to a dying world, nor brook to become the instrument of a succession of dying creatures. In such a body the long unbroken career of decay and death, which has intervened between the first man and the lives of virginity which have been led, is interrupted. It could not be indeed that death should cease working as long as the human race by marriage was working too; he walked the path of life with all preceding generations; he started with every new-born child and accompanied it to the end: but he found in virginity a barrier, to pass which was an impossible feat. Just as, in the age of Mary the mother of God, he who had reigned from Adam to her time found, when he came to her and dashed his forces against the fruit of her virginity as against a rock, that he was shattered to pieces upon her, so in every soul which passes through this life in the flesh under the protection of virginity, the strength of death is in a manner broken and annulled, for he does not find the places upon which he may fix his sting. If you do not throw into the fire wood, or straw, or grass, or something that it can consume, it has not the force to last by itself; so the power of death cannot go on working, if marriage does not supply it with material and prepare victims for this executioner. If you have any doubts left, consider the actual names of those afflictions which death brings upon mankind, and which were detailed in the first part of this discourse. Whence do they get their meaning? *"Widowhood," "orphanhood," "loss of children,"* could they be a subject for grief, if marriage did not precede? Nay, all the dearly-prized blisses, and transports, and comforts of marriage end in these agonies of grief. The hilt of a sword is smooth and handy, and polished and glittering outside; it seems to grow to the outline of the hand ; but the other part is steel and the instrument of death, formidable to look at, more formidable still to come across. Such a thing is marriage. It offers for the grasp of the senses a smooth surface of delights, like a hilt of rare polish and beautiful workmanship; but when a man has taken it up and has got it into his hands, he finds the pain that has been wedded to it is in his hands as well; and it becomes to him the worker of mourning and of loss. It is marriage that has the heartrending spectacles to show of children left desolate in the tenderness of their years, a mere prey to the powerful, yet smiling often at their misfortune from ignorance of coming woes. What is the cause of widowhood but marriage? And retirement from this would bring with it an immunity from the whole burden of these sad taxes on our hearts. Can we expect it otherwise? When the verdict that was pronounced on the delinquents in the beginning is annulled, then too the mothers' *"sorrows* Genesis 3:16 " are no longer *"multiplied,"* nor does *"sorrow"* herald the births of men; then all calamity has been removed from life and *"tears wiped from off all faces* Isaiah 25:8;" conception is no more an iniquity, nor child-bearing a sin; and births shall be no more *"of bloods,"* or *"of the will of man,"* or *"of the will of the flesh "*, but of God alone. This is always happening whenever any one in a lively heart conceives all the integrity of the Spirit, and brings forth wisdom and righteousness, and sanctification and redemption too. It is possible for any one to be the mother of such a son; as our Lord says, *"He that does my will is my brother, my sister, and my mother* Matthew 12:50 ." What room is there for death in such parturitions? Indeed in them death is swallowed up by life. In fact, the Life of Virginity seems to be an actual representation of the blessedness in the world to come, showing as it does in itself so many signs of the presence of those expected blessings which are reserved for us there. That the truth of this statement may be perceived, we will verify it thus. It is so, first, because a man who has thus died once for all to sin lives for the future to God; he brings forth no more fruit unto death; and having so far as in him lies made an end of this life within him according to the flesh, he awaits thenceforth the expected blessing of the manifestation of the great God, refraining from putting any distance between himself and this coming of God by an

Selected Works

intervening posterity: secondly, because he enjoys even in this present life a certain exquisite glory of all the blessed results of our resurrection. For our Lord has announced that the life after our resurrection shall be as that of the angels. Now the peculiarity of the angelic nature is that they are strangers to marriage; therefore the blessing of this promise has been already received by him who has not only mingled his own glory with the halo of the Saints, but also by the stainlessness of his life has so imitated the purity of these incorporeal beings. If virginity then can win us favours such as these, what words are fit to express the admiration of so great a grace? What other gift of the soul can be found so great and precious as not to suffer by comparison with this perfection?

Chapter 14

But if we apprehend at last the perfection of this grace, we must understand as well what necessarily follows from it; namely that it is not a single achievement, ending in the subjugation of the body, but that in intention it reaches to and pervades everything that is, or is considered, a right condition of the soul. That soul indeed which in virginity cleaves to the true Bridegroom will not remove herself merely from all bodily defilement; she will make that abstension only the beginning of her purity, and will carry this security from failure equally into everything else upon her path. Fearing lest, from a too partial heart, she should by contact with evil in any one direction give occasion for the least weakness of unfaithfulness (to suppose such a case: but I will begin again what I was going to say), that soul which cleaves to her Master so as to become with Him one spirit, and by the compact of a wedded life has staked the love of all her heart and all her strength on Him alone— that soul will no more commit any other of the offenses contrary to salvation, than imperil her union with Him by cleaving to fornication; she knows that between all sins there is a single kinship of impurity, and that if she were to defile herself with but one , she could no longer retain her spotlessness. An illustration will show what we mean. Suppose all the water in a pool remaining smooth and motionless, while no disturbance of any kind comes to mar the peacefulness of the spot; and then a stone thrown into the pool; the movement in that one part will extend to the whole, and while the stone's weight is carrying it to the bottom, the waves that are set in motion round it pass in circles into others, and so through all the intervening commotion are pushed on to the very edge of the water, and the whole surface is ruffled with these circles, feeling the movement of the depths. So is the broad serenity and calm of the soul troubled by one invading passion, and affected by the injury of a single part. They tell us too, those who have investigated the subject, that the virtues are not disunited from each other, and that to grasp the principle of any one virtue will be impossible to one who has not seized that which underlies the rest, and that the man who shows one virtue in his character will necessarily show them all. Therefore, by contraries, the depravation of anything in our moral nature will extend to the whole virtuous life; and in very truth, as the Apostle tells us, the whole is affected by the parts, and *"if one member suffer, all the members suffer with it," "if one be honoured, all rejoice."*

Chapter 15

But the ways in our life which turn aside towards sin are innumerable; and their number is told by Scripture in various manners. *"Many are they that trouble me and persecute,"* and *"Many are they that fight against me from on high "*; and many other texts like that. We may affirm, indeed, absolutely, that many are they who plot in the adulterer's fashion to destroy this truly honourable marriage, and to defile this inviolate bed; and if we must name them one by one, we charge with this adulterous spirit anger, avarice, envy, revenge, enmity, malice, hatred, and whatever the Apostle puts in the class of those things which are contrary to sound doctrine. Now let us suppose a lady, prepossessing and lovely above her peers, and on that account wedded to a king, but besieged because of her beauty by profligate lovers. As long as she remains indignant at these would-be seducers and complains of them to her lawful husband, she keeps her chastity and has no one before her eyes but her bridegroom; the profligates find no vantage ground for their attack upon her. But if she were to listen to a single one of them, her chastity with regard to the rest would not exempt her from the retribution; it would be sufficient to condemn her, that she had allowed that one to defile the marriage bed. So the soul whose life is in God will find her pleasure in no single one of those things which make a beauteous show to deceive her. If she were, in some fit of weakness, to admit the defilement to her heart, she would herself have broken the covenant of her spiritual marriage; and, as the Scripture tells us, *"into the malicious soul Wisdom cannot come* Wisdom 1:4 ." It may, in a word, be truly said that the Good Husband cannot come to dwell with the soul that is irascible, or malice-bearing, or harbours any other disposition which jars with that concord. No way has been discovered of harmonizing things whose nature is antagonistic and which have nothing in common. The Apostle tells us there is *"no communion of light with darkness* 2 Corinthians 6:14,*"* or of righteousness with iniquity, or, in a word, of all the qualities which we perceive and name as the essence of God's nature, with all the opposite which are perceived in evil. Seeing, then, the impossibility of any union between mutual repellents, we understand that the vicious soul is estranged from entertaining the company of the Good. What then is the practical lesson from this? The chaste and thoughtful virgin must sever herself from any affection which can in any way impart contagion to her soul; she must keep herself pure for the Husband who has married her, *"not having spot or blemish or any such thing."*

Chapter 16

There is only one right path. It is narrow and contracted. It has no turnings either on the one side or the other. No matter how we leave it, there is the same danger of straying hopelessly away. This being so, the habit which many have got into must be as far as possible corrected; those, I mean, who while they fight strenuously against the baser pleasures, yet still go on hunting for pleasure in the shape of worldly honour and positions which will gratify their love of power. They act like some domestic who longed for liberty, but instead of exerting himself to get away from slavery proceeded only to change his masters, and thought liberty consisted in that change. But all alike are slaves, even though they should not all go on being ruled by the same masters, as long as a dominion of any sort, with power to enforce it, is set over them. There are others again who after a long battle against all the pleasures , yield themselves easily on another field, where feelings of an opposite kind come in; and in the intense exactitude of their lives fall a ready prey to melancholy and irritation, and to brooding over injuries, and to everything that is the direct opposite of pleasurable feelings; from which they are very reluctant to extricate themselves. This is always happening, whenever any emotion, instead of virtuous reason, controls the course of a life. For the commandment of the Lord is exceedingly far-shining, so as to *"enlighten the eyes"* even of *"the simple ,"* declaring that good cleaves only unto God. But God is not pain any more than He is pleasure; He is not cowardice any more than boldness; He is not fear, nor anger, nor any other emotion which sways the untutored soul, but, as the Apostle says, He is Very Wisdom and Sanctification, Truth and Joy and Peace, and everything like that. If He is such, how can any one be said to cleave to Him, who is mastered by the very opposite? Is it not want of reason in any one to suppose that when he has striven successfully to escape the dominion of one particular passion, he will find virtue in its opposite? For instance, to suppose that when he has escaped pleasure, he will find virtue in letting pain have possession of him; or when he has by an effort remained proof against anger, in crouching with fear. It matters not whether we miss virtue, or rather God Himself Who is the Sum of virtue, in this way, or in that. Take the case of great bodily prostration; one would say that the sadness of this failure was just the same, whether the cause has been excessive under-feeding, or immoderate eating; both failures to stop in time end in the same result. He therefore who watches over the life and the sanity of the soul will confine himself to the moderation of the truth; he will continue without touching either of those opposite states which run along-side virtue. This teaching is not mine; it comes from the Divine lips. It is clearly contained in that passage where our Lord says to His disciples, that they are as sheep wandering among wolves, yet are not to be as doves only, but are to have something of the serpent too in their disposition; and that means that they should neither carry to excess the practice of that which seems praiseworthy in simplicity, as such a habit would come very near to downright madness, nor on the other hand should deem the cleverness which most admire to be a virtue, while unsoftened by any mixture with its opposite; they were in fact to form another disposition, by a compound of these two seeming opposites, cutting off its silliness from the one, its evil cunning from the other; so that one single beautiful character should be created from the two, a union of simplicity of purpose with shrewdness. *"Be,"* He says, *"wise as serpents, and harmless as doves."*

Chapter 17

Let that which was then said by our Lord be the general maxim for every life; especially let it be the maxim for those who are coming nearer God through the gateway of virginity, that they should never in watching for a perfection in one direction present an unguarded side in another and contrary one; but should in all directions realize the good, so that they may guarantee in all things their holy life against failure. A soldier does not arm himself only on some points, leaving the rest of his body to take its chance unprotected. If he were to receive his death-wound upon that, what would have been the advantage of this partial armour? Again, who would call that feature faultless, which from some accident had lost one of those requisites which go to make up the sum of beauty? The disfigurement of the mutilated part mars the grace of the part untouched. The Gospel implies that he who undertakes the building of a tower, but spends all his labour upon the foundations without ever reaching the completion, is worthy of ridicule; and what else do we learn from the Parable of the Tower, but to strive to come to the finish of every lofty purpose, accomplishing the work of God in all the multiform structures of His commandments? One stone, indeed, is no more the whole edifice of the Tower, than one commandment kept will raise the soul's perfection to the required height. The foundation must by all means first be laid but over it, as the Apostle says 1 Corinthians 3:12, the edifice of gold and precious gems must be built; for so is the doing of the commandment put by the Prophet who cries, *"I have loved Your commandment above gold and many a precious stone."* Let the virtuous life have for its substructure the love of virginity; but upon this let every result of virtue be reared. If virginity is believed to be a vastly precious thing and to have a divine look (as indeed is the case, as well as men believe of it), yet, if the whole life does not harmonize with this perfect note, and it be marred by the succeeding discord of the soul, this thing becomes but *"the jewel of gold in the swine's snout"* or *"the pearl that is trodden under the swine's feet."* But we have said enough upon this.

Chapter 18

If any one supposes that this want of mutual harmony between his life and a single one of its circumstances is quite unimportant, let him be taught the meaning of our maxim by looking at the management of a house. The master of a private dwelling will not allow any untidiness or unseemliness to be seen in the house, such as a couch upset, or the table littered with rubbish, or vessels of price thrown away into dirty corners, while those which serve ignobler uses are thrust forward for entering guests to see. He has everything arranged neatly and in the proper place, where it stands to most advantage; and then he can welcome his guests, without any misgivings that he need be ashamed of opening the interior of his house to receive them. The same duty, I take it, is incumbent on that master of our *"tabernacle,"* the mind; it has to arrange everything within us, and to put each particular faculty of the soul, which the Creator has fashioned to be our implement or our vessel, to fitting and noble uses. We will now mention in detail the way in which any one might manage his life, with its present advantages, to his improvement, hoping that no one will accuse us of trifling , or over-minuteness. We advise, then, that love's passion be placed in the soul's purest shrine, as a thing chosen to be the first fruits of all our gifts, and devoted entirely to God; and when once this has been done, to keep it untouched and unsullied by any secular defilement. Then indignation, and anger, and hatred must be as watch-dogs to be roused only against attacking sins; they must follow their natural impulse only against the thief and the enemy who is creeping in to plunder the divine treasure-chamber, and who comes only for that, that he may steal, and mangle, and destroy. Courage and confidence are to be weapons in our hands to baffle any sudden surprise and attack of the wicked who advance. Hope and patience are to be the staffs to lean upon, whenever we are weary with the trials of the world. As for sorrow, we must have a stock of it ready to apply, if need should happen to arise for it, in the hour of repentance for our sins; believing at the same time that it is never useful, except to minister to that. Righteousness will be our rule of straightforwardness, guarding us from stumbling either in word or deed, and guiding us in the disposal of the faculties of our soul, as well as in the due consideration for every one we meet. The love of gain, which is a large, incalculably large, element in every soul, when once applied to the desire for God, will bless the man who has it; for he will be violent where it is right to be violent. Wisdom and prudence will be our advisers as to our best interests; they will order our lives so as never to suffer from any thoughtless folly. But suppose a man does not apply the aforesaid faculties of the soul to their proper use, but reverses their intended purpose; suppose he wastes his love upon the basest objects, and stores up his hatred only for his own kinsmen; suppose he welcomes iniquity, plays the man only against his parents, is bold only in absurdities, fixes his hopes on emptiness, chases prudence and wisdom from his company, takes gluttony and folly for his mistresses, and uses all his other opportunities in the same fashion, he would indeed be a strange and unnatural character to a degree beyond any one's power to express. If we could imagine any one putting his armour on all the wrong way, reversing the helmet so as to cover his face while the plume nodded backward, putting his feet into the cuirass, and fitting the greaves on to his breast, changing to the right side all that ought to go on the left and *vice versa*, and how such a hoplite would be likely to fare in battle, then we should have an idea of the fate in life which is sure to await him whose confused judgment makes him reverse the proper uses of his soul's faculties. We must therefore provide this balance in all feeling; the true sobriety of mind is naturally able to supply it; and if one had to find an exact definition of this sobriety, one might declare absolutely, that it amounts to our ordered control, by dint of wisdom and prudence, over every emotion of the soul. Moreover, such a condition in the soul will be no longer in need of any laborious method to attain to the high and heavenly realities; it will accomplish with the greatest ease that which erewhile seemed so unattainable; it will grasp the object of its search as a natural consequence of rejecting the opposite attractions. A man who comes out of darkness is necessarily in the light; a man who is not dead is necessarily alive. Indeed, if a man is not to have received his soul to no purpose , he will certainly be upon the path of truth; the prudence and the science employed to guard against error will be itself a sure guidance along the right road. Slaves who have been freed and cease to serve their former masters, the very moment they become their own masters, direct all their thoughts towards themselves so, I take it, the soul which has been freed from ministering to the body becomes at once cognizant of its own inherent energy. But this liberty consists, as we learn from the Apostle Galatians 5:1, in not again being held in the yoke of slavery, and in not being bound again, like a runaway or a criminal, with the fetters of marriage. But I must return here to what I said at first; that the perfection of this liberty does not consist only in that one point of abstaining from marriage. Let no one suppose that the prize of virginity is so insignificant and so easily won as that; as if one little observance of the flesh could settle so vital a matter. But we have seen that every man who does a sin is the servant of sin John 8:34; so that a declension towards vice in any act, or in any practice whatever, makes a slave, and still more, a branded slave, of the man, covering him through sin's lashes with bruises and seared spots. Therefore it behooves the man who grasps at the transcendent aim of all virginity to be true to himself in every respect, and to manifest his purity equally in every relation of his life. If any of the inspired words are required to aid our pleading, the Truth Itself will be sufficient to corroborate the truth when It inculcates this very kind of teaching in the veiled meaning of a Gospel Parable: the good and eatable fish are separated by the fishers' skill from the bad and poisonous fish, so that the enjoyment of the good should not be spoilt by any of the bad getting into the *"vessels"* with them. The work of true sobriety is the same; from all pursuits and habits to choose that which is pure and improving, rejecting in every case that which does not seem likely to be useful, and letting it go back into the universal and secular life, called *"the sea Matthew 13:47-48,"* in the imagery of the Parable. The Psalmist also, when expounding the doctrine of a full confession, calls this restless suffering tumultuous life, *"waters coming in even unto the soul," "depths of waters,"* and a *"hurricane"*; in which sea indeed every rebellious thought sinks, as the Egyptian did, with a stone's weight into the deeps. Exodus 15:10 But all in us that is dear to God, and has a piercing insight into the truth (called *"Israel"* in the narrative), passes, but that alone, over that sea as if it were dry land, and is never reached by the bitterness and the brine of life's billows. Thus, typically, under the leadership of the Law (for Moses was a type of the Law that was coming) Israel passes unwetted over that sea, while the Egyptian who crosses in her track is overwhelmed. Each fares according to the disposition which he carries with him; one walks lightly enough, the other is dragged into the deep water. For virtue is a light and buoyant thing, and all who live in her way *"fly like clouds,"* as Isaiah says, *"and as doves with their young ones"*; but sin is a heavy affair, *"sitting,"* as another of the prophets says, *"upon a talent of lead."* If, however, this reading of the history appears to any forced and inapplicable, and the miracle at the Red Sea does not present itself to him as written for our profit, let him listen to the Apostle: *"Now all these things happened unto them for types, and they are written for our admonition."*

Chapter 19

But besides other things the action of Miriam the prophetess also gives rise to these surmisings of ours. Directly the sea was crossed she took in her hand a dry and sounding timbrel and conducted the women's dance. Exodus 15:20 By this timbrel the story may mean to imply virginity, as first perfected by Miriam; whom indeed I would believe to be a type of Mary the mother of God. Just as the timbrel emits a loud sound because it is devoid of all moisture and reduced to the highest degree of dryness, so has virginity a clear and ringing report among men because it repels from itself the vital sap of merely physical life. Thus, Miriam's timbrel being a dead thing, and virginity being a deadening of the bodily passions, it is perhaps not very far removed from the bounds of probability that Miriam was a virgin. However, we can but guess and surmise, we cannot clearly prove, that this was so, and that Miriam the prophetess led a dance of virgins, even though many of the learned have affirmed distinctly that she was unmarried, from the fact that the history makes no mention either of her marriage or of her being a mother; and surely she would have been named and known, not as *"the sister of Aaron* Exodus 15:20,*"* but from her husband, if she had had one; since the head of the woman is not the brother but the husband. But if, among a people with whom motherhood was sought after and classed as a blessing and regarded as a public duty, the grace of virginity, nevertheless, came to be regarded as a precious thing, how does it behoove us to feel towards it, who do not *"judge"* of the Divine blessings *"according to the flesh"*? Indeed it has been revealed in the oracles of God, on what occasion to conceive and to bring forth is a good thing, and what species of fecundity was desired by God's saints; for both the Prophet Isaiah and the divine Apostle have made this clear and certain. The one cries, *"From fear of You, O Lord, have I conceived,"* the other boasts that he is the parent of the largest family of any, bringing to the birth whole cities and nations; not the Corinthians and Galatians only whom by his travailings he moulded for the Lord, but all in the wide circuit from Jerusalem to Illyricum; his children filled the world, *"begotten"* by him in Christ through the Gospel. In the same strain the womb of the Holy Virgin, which ministered to an Immaculate Birth, is pronounced blessed in the Gospel ; for that birth did not annul the Virginity, nor did the Virginity impede so great a birth. When the *"spirit of salvation ,"* as Isaiah names it, is being born, the willings of the flesh are useless. There is also a particular teaching of the Apostle, which harmonizes with this; viz. each man of us is a double man 2 Corinthians 4:16; one the outwardly visible, whose natural fate it is to decay; the other perceptible only in the secret of the heart, yet capable of renovation. If this teaching is true—and it must be true because Wisdom is speaking there—then there is no absurdity in supposing a double marriage also which answers in every detail to either man; and, maybe, if one was to assert boldly that the body's virginity was the cooperator and the agent of the inward marriage, this assertion would not be much beside the probable fact.

Chapter 20

Now it is impossible, as far as manual exercise goes, to ply two arts at once; for instance, husbandry and sailing, or tinkering and carpentering. If one is to be honestly taken in hand, the other must be left alone. Just so, there are these two marriages for our choice, the one effected in the flesh, the other in the spirit; and preoccupation in the one must cause of necessity alienation from the other. No more is the eye able to look at two objects at once; but it must concentrate its special attention on one at a time; no more can the tongue effect utterances in two different languages, so as to pronounce, for instance, a Hebrew word and a Greek word in the same moment: no more can the ear take in at one and the same time a narrative of facts, and a hortatory discourse; if each special tone is heard separately, it will impress its ideas upon the hearers' minds; but if they are combined and so poured into the ear, an inextricable confusion of ideas will be the result, one meaning being mutually lost in the other: and no more, by analogy, do our emotional powers possess a nature which can at once pursue the pleasures of sense and court the spiritual union; nor, besides, can both those ends be gained by the same courses of life; continence, mortification of the passions, scorn of fleshly needs, are the agents of the one union; but all that are the reverse of these are the agents of bodily habitation. As, when two masters are before us to choose between, and we cannot be subject to both, for *"no man can serve two masters,"* he who is wise will choose the one most useful to himself, so, when two marriages are before us to choose between, and we cannot contract both, for *"he that is unmarried cares for the things of the Lord, but he that is married cares for the things of the world* 1 Corinthians 7:32,*"* I repeat that it would be the aim of a sound mind not to miss choosing the more profitable one; and not to be ignorant either of the way which will lead it to this, a way which cannot be learned but by some such comparison as the following. In the case of a marriage of this world a man who is anxious to avoid appearing altogether insignificant pays the greatest attention both to physical health, and becoming adornment, and amplitude of means and the security from any disgraceful revelations as to his antecedents or his parentage; for so he thinks things will be most likely to turn out as he wishes. Now just in the same way the man who is courting the spiritual alliance will first of all display himself, by the renewal of his mind , a young man, without a single touch of age upon him; next he will reveal a lineage rich in that in which it is a noble ambition to be rich, not priding himself on worldly wealth, but luxuriating only in the heavenly treasures. As for family distinction, he will not vaunt that which comes by the mere routine of devolution even to numbers of the worthless, but that which is gained by the successful efforts of his own zeal and labours; a distinction which only those can boast of who are *"sons of the light"* and children of God, and are styled *"nobles from the sunrise"* because of their splendid deeds. Strength and health he will not try to gain by bodily training and feeding, but by all that is the contrary of this, perfecting the spirit's strength in the body's weakness. I could tell also of the suitor's gifts to the bride in such a wedding ; they are not procured by the money that perishes, but are contributed out of the wealth peculiar to the soul. Would you know their names? You must hear from Paul, that excellent adorner of the Bride , in what the wealth of those consists who in everything commend themselves. He mentions much else that is priceless in it, and adds, *"in chastity* 2 Corinthians 6:6 "; and besides this all the recognized fruits of the spirit from any quarter whatever are gifts of this marriage. If a man is going to carry out the advice of Solomon and take for helpmate and life-companion that true Wisdom of which he says, *"Love her, and she shall keep you,"* *"honour her, that she may embrace you* Proverbs 4:6,*"* then he will prepare himself in a manner worthy of such a love, so as to feast with all the joyous wedding guests in spotless raiment, and not be cast forth, while claiming to sit at that feast, for not having put on the wedding garment. It is plain moreover that the argument applies equally to men and women, to move them towards such a marriage. *"There is neither male nor female* Galatians 3:28,*"* the Apostle says; *"Christ is all, and in all* Colossians 3:11 "; and so it is equally reasonable that he who is enamoured of wisdom should hold the Object of his passionate desire, Who is the True Wisdom; and that the soul which cleaves to the undying Bridegroom should have the fruition of her love for the true Wisdom, which is God. We have now sufficiently revealed the nature of the spiritual union, and the Object of the pure and heavenly Love.

Chapter 21

It is perfectly clear that no one can come near the purity of the Divine Being who has not first himself become such; he must therefore place between himself and the pleasures of the senses a high strong wall of separation, so that in this his approach to the Deity the purity of his own heart may not become soiled again. Such an impregnable wall will be found in a complete estrangement from everything wherein passion operates.

Now pleasure is one in kind, as we learn from the experts; as water parted into various channels from one single fountain, it spreads itself over the pleasure-lover through the various avenues of the senses; so that it has been on his heart that the man, who through any one particular sensation succumbs to the resulting pleasure, has received a wound from that sensation. This accords with the teaching given from the Divine lips, that *"he who has satisfied the lust of the eyes has received the mischief already in his heart"*; for I take it that our Lord was speaking in that particular example of any of the senses; so that we might well carry on His saying, and add, *"He who has heard, to lust after,"* and what follows, *"He who has touched to lust after,"* *"He who has lowered any faculty within us to the service of pleasure, has sinned in his heart."*

To prevent this, then, we want to apply to our own lives that rule of all temperance, never to let the mind dwell on anything wherein pleasure's bait is hid; but above all to be specially watchful against the pleasure of taste. For that seems in a way the most deeply rooted, and to be the mother as it were of all forbidden enjoyment. The pleasures of eating and drinking, leading to boundless excess, inflict upon the body the doom of the most dreadful sufferings ; for over-indulgence is the parent of most of the painful diseases. To secure for the body a continuous tranquillity, unstirred by the pains of surfeit, we must make up our minds to a more sparing regimen, and constitute the need of it on each occasion not the pleasure of it, as the measure and limit of our indulgence. If the sweetness will nevertheless mingle itself with the satisfaction of the need (for hunger knows how to sweeten everything , and by the vehemence of appetite she gives the zest of pleasure to every discoverable supply of the need), we must not because of the resulting enjoyment reject the satisfaction, nor yet make this latter our leading aim. In everything we must select the expedient quantity, and leave untouched what merely feasts the senses.

Chapter 22

We see how the husbandmen have a method for separating the chaff, which is united with the wheat, with a view to employ each for its proper purpose, the one for the sustenance of man, the other for burning and the feeding of animals. The labourer in the field of temperance will in like manner distinguish the satisfaction from the mere delight, and will fling this latter nature to savages *"whose end is to be burned ,"* as the Apostle says, but will take the other, in proportion to the actual need, with thankfulness. Many, however, slide into the very opposite kind of excess, and unconsciously to themselves, in their over-preciseness, laboriously thwart their own design; they let their soul fall down the other side from the heights of Divine elevation to the level of dull thoughts and occupations, where their minds are so bent upon regulations which merely affect the body, that they can no longer walk in their heavenly freedom and gaze above; their only inclination is to this tormenting and afflicting of the flesh. It would be well, then, to give this also careful thought, so as to be equally on our guard against either over-amount , neither stifling the mind beneath the wound of the flesh, nor, on the other hand, by gratuitously inflicted weakenings sapping and lowering the powers, so that it can have no thought but of the body's pain ; and let every one remember that wise precept, which warns us from turning to the right hand or to the left. I have heard a certain physician of my acquaintance, in the course of explaining the secrets of his art, say that our body consists of four elements, not of the same species, but disposed to be conflicting: yet the hot penetrated the cold, and an equally unexpected union of the wet and the dry took place, the contradictories of each pair being brought into contact by their relationship to the intervening pair. He added an extremely subtle explanation of this account of his studies in nature. Each of these elements was in its essence *diametrically* opposed to its contradictory; but then it had two other qualities lying on each side of it, and by virtue of its kinship with them it came into contact with its contradictory; for example, the cold and the hot each unite with the wet, or the dry; and again, the wet and the dry each unite with the hot, or the cold: and so this sameness of quality, when it manifests itself in contradictories, is itself the agent which affects the union of those contradictories. What business of mine, however, is it to explain exactly the details of this change from this mutual separation and repugnance of nature, to this mutual union through the medium of kindred qualities, except for the purpose for which we mentioned it? And that purpose was to add that the author of this analysis of the body's constitution advised that all possible care be taken to preserve a balance between these properties, for that in fact health consisted in not letting any one of them gain the mastery within us. If his doctrine has truth in it, then, for our health's continuance, we must secure such a habit, and by no irregularity of diet produce either an excess or a defect in any member of these our constituent elements. The chariot-master, if the young horses which he has to drive will not work well together, does not urge a fast one with the whip, and rein in a slow one; nor, again, does he let a horse that shies in the traces or is hard-mouthed gallop his own way to the confusion of orderly driving; but he quickens the pace of the first, checks the second, reaches the third with cuts of his whip, till he has made them all breathe evenly together in a straight career. Now our mind in like manner holds in its grasp the reins of this chariot of the body; and in that capacity it will not devise, in the time of youth, when heat of temperament is abundant, ways of heightening that fever; nor will it multiply the cooling and the thinning things when the body is already chilled by illness or by time; and in the case of all these physical qualities it will be guided by the Scripture, so as actually to realize it: *"He that gathered much had nothing over; and he that had gathered little had no lack."* It will curtail immoderate lengths in either direction, and so will be careful to replenish where there is much lack. The inefficiency of the body from either cause will be that which it guards against; it will train the flesh, neither making it wild and ungovernable by excessive pampering, nor sickly and unstrung and nerveless for the required work by immoderate mortification. That is temperance's highest aim; it looks not to the afflicting of the body, but to the peaceful action of the soul's functions.

Chapter 23

Now the details of the life of him who has chosen to live in such a philosophy as this, the things to be avoided, the exercises to be engaged in, the rules of temperance, the whole method of the training, and all the daily regimen which contributes towards this great end, has been dealt with in certain written manuals of instruction for the benefit of those who love details. Yet there is a plainer guide to be found than verbal instruction; and that is practice:

and there is nothing vexatious in the maxim that when we are undertaking a long journey or voyage we should get an instructor. *"But,"* says the Apostle , *"the word is near you;"* the grace begins at home; there is the manufactory of all the virtues; there this life has become exquisitely refined by a continual progress towards consummate perfection; there, whether men are silent or whether they speak, there is large opportunity for being instructed in this heavenly citizenship through the actual practice of it. Any theory divorced from living examples, however admirably it may be dressed out, is like the unbreathing statue, with its show of a blooming complexion impressed in tints and colours; but the man who acts as well as teaches, as the Gospel tells us, he is the man who is truly living, and has the bloom of beauty, and is efficient and stirring. It is to him that we must go, if we mean, according to the saying of Scripture, to *"retain"* virginity. One who wants to learn a foreign language is not a competent instructor of himself; he gets himself taught by experts, and can then talk with foreigners. So, for this high life, which does not advance in nature's groove, but is estranged from her by the novelty of its course, a man cannot be instructed thoroughly unless he puts himself into the hands of one who has himself led it in perfection; and indeed in all the other professions of life the candidate is more likely to achieve success if he gets from tutors a scientific knowledge of each part of the subject of his choice, than if he undertook to study it by himself; and this particular profession is not one where everything is so clear that judgment as to our best course in it is necessarily left to ourselves; it is one where to hazard a step into the unknown at once brings us into danger. The science of medicine once did not exist; it has come into being by the experiments which men have made, and has gradually been revealed through their various observations; the healing and the harmful drug became known from the attestation of those who had tried them, and this distinction was adopted into the theory of the art, so that the close observation of former practitioners became a precept for those who succeeded; and now any one who studies to attain this art is under no necessity to ascertain at his own peril the power of any drug, whether it be a poison or a medicine; he has only to learn from others the known facts, and may then practise with success. It is so also with that medicine of the soul, philosophy, from which we learn the remedy for every weakness that can touch the soul. We need not hunt after a knowledge of these remedies by dint of guess-work and surmisings; we have abundant means of learning them from him who by a long and rich experience has gained the possession which we seek. In any matter youth is generally a giddy guide; and it would not be easy to find anything of importance succeeding, in which gray hairs have not been called in to share in the deliberations. Even in all other undertakings we must, in proportion to their greater importance, take the more precaution against failure; for in them too the thoughtless designs of youth have brought loss; on property, for instance; or have compelled the surrender of a position in the world, and even of renown. But in this mighty and sublime ambition it is not property, or secular glory lasting for its hour, or any external fortune, that is at stake—of such things , whether they settle themselves well or the reverse, the wise take small account—here rashness can affect the soul itself; and we run the awful hazard, not of losing any of those other things whose recovery even may perhaps be possible, but of ruining our very selves and making the soul a bankrupt. A man who has spent or lost his patrimony does not despair, as long as he is in the land of the living, of perchance coming again through contrivances into his former competence; but the man who has ejected himself from this calling, deprives himself as well of all hope of a return to better things. Therefore, since most embrace virginity while still young and unformed in understanding, this before anything else should be their employment, to search out a fitting guide and master of this way, lest, in their present ignorance, they should wander from the direct route, and strike out new paths of their own in trackless wilds. *"Two are better than one,"* says the Preacher Ecclesiastes 4:9; but a single one is easily vanquished by the foe who infests the path which leads to God; and verily *"woe to him that is alone when he falls, for he has not another to help him up. "* Some ere now in their enthusiasm for the stricter life have shown a dexterous alacrity; but, as if in the very moment of their choice they had already touched perfection, their pride has had a shocking fall , and they have been tripped up from madly deluding themselves into thinking that that to which their own mind inclined them was the true beauty. In this number are those whom Wisdom calls the *"slothful ones* Proverbs 15:19, *"* who bestrew their *"way"* with *"thorns";* who think it a moral loss to be anxious about keeping the commandments; who erase from their own minds the Apostolic teaching, and instead of eating the bread of their own honest earning fix on that of others, and make their idleness itself into an art of living. From this number, too, come the Dreamers, who put more faith in the illusions of their dreams than in the Gospel teaching, and style their own phantasies *"revelations."* Hence, too, those who *"creep into the houses"*; and again others who suppose virtue to consist in savage bearishness, and have never known the fruits of long-suffering and humility of spirit. Who could enumerate all the pitfalls into which any one might slip, from refusing to have recourse to men of godly celebrity? Why, we have known ascetics of this class who have persisted in their fasting even unto death, as if *"with such sacrifices God were well pleased* Hebrews 13:16;" and, again, others who rush off into the extreme diametrically opposite, practising celibacy in name only and leading a life in no way different from the secular; for they not only indulge in the pleasures of the table, but are openly known to have a woman in their houses ; and they call such a friendship a brotherly affection, as if, forsooth, they could veil their own thought, which is inclined to evil, under a sacred term. It is owing to them that this pure and holy profession of virginity is *"blasphemed among the Gentiles."*

Chapter 24

It would therefore be to their profit, for the young to refrain from laying down *for themselves* their future course in this profession; and indeed, examples of holy lives for them to follow are not wanting in the living generation. Now, if ever before, saintliness abounds and penetrates our world; by gradual advances it has reached the highest mark of perfectness; and one who follows such footsteps in his daily rounds may catch this halo; one who tracks the scent of this preceding perfume may be drenched in the sweet odours of Christ Himself. As, when one torch has been fired, flame is transmitted to all the neighbouring candlesticks, without either the first light being lessened or blazing with unequal brilliance on the other points where it has been caught; so the saintliness of a life is transmitted from him who has achieved it, to those who come within his circle; for there is truth in the Prophet's saying , that one who lives with a man who is *"holy"* and *"clean"* and *"elect,"* will become such himself. If you would wish to know the sure signs, which will secure you the real model, it is not hard to take a sketch from life. If you see a man so standing between death and life, as to select from each helps for the contemplative course, never letting death's stupor paralyze his zeal to keep all the commandments, nor yet placing both feet in the world of the living, since he has weaned himself from secular ambitions;— a man who remains more insensate than the dead themselves to everything that is found on examination to be living for the flesh, but instinct with life and energy and strength in the achievements of virtue, which are the sure marks of the spiritual life—then look to that man for the rule of your life; let him be the leading light of your course of devotion, as the constellations that never set are to the pilot; imitate his youth and his gray hairs: or, rather, imitate the old man and the stripling who are joined in him; for even now in his declining years time has not blunted the keen activity of his soul, nor was his youth active in the sphere of youth's well-known employments; in both seasons of life he has shown a wonderful combination of opposites, or rather an exchange of the peculiar qualities of each; for in age he shows, in the direction of the good, a young man's energy, while, in the hours of youth, in the direction of evil, his passions were powerless. If you wish to know what were the passions of that glorious youth of his, you will have for your imitation the intensity and glow of his godlike love of wisdom, which grew with him from his childhood, and has continued with him into his old age. But if you cannot gaze upon him, as the weak-sighted cannot gaze upon the sun, at all events watch that band of holy men who are ranged beneath him, and who by the illumination of their lives are a model for this age. God has placed them as a beacon for us who live around; many among them have been young men there in their prime, and have grown gray in the unbroken practice of continence and temperance; they were old in reasonableness before their time, and in character outstripped their years. The only love they tasted was that of wisdom; not that their natural instincts were different from the rest; for in all alike *"the flesh lusts against the spirit* Galatians 5:17;" but they listened to some purpose to him who said that Temperance *"is a tree of life to them that lay hold upon her ;"* and they sailed across the swelling billows of existence upon this tree of life, as upon a skiff; and anchored in the haven of the will of God; enviable now after so fair a voyage, they rest their souls in that sunny cloudless calm. They now ride safe themselves at the anchor of a good hope, far out of reach of the tumult of the billows; and for others who will follow they radiate the splendour of their lives as beacon-fires on some high watchtower. We have indeed a mark to guide us safely over the ocean of temptations; and why make the too curious inquiry, whether some with such thoughts as these have not fallen nevertheless, and why therefore despair, as if the achievement was beyond your reach? Look on him who has succeeded, and boldly launch upon the voyage with confidence that it will be prosperous, and sail on under the breeze of the Holy Spirit with Christ your pilot and with the oarage of good cheer. For those who *"go down to the sea in ships and occupy their business in great waters"* do not let the shipwreck that has befallen some one else prevent their being of good cheer; they rather shield their hearts in this very confidence, and so sweep on to accomplish their successful feat. Surely it is the most absurd thing in the world to reprobate him who has slipped in a course which requires the greatest nicety, while one considers those who all their lives have been growing old in failures and in errors, to have chosen the better part. If one single approach to sin is such an awful thing that you deem it safer not to take in hand at all this loftier aim, how much more awful a thing it is to make sin the practice of a whole life, and to remain thereby absolutely ignorant of the purer course! How can you in your full life obey the Crucified? How can you, hale in sin, obey Him Who died to sin? How can you, who are not crucified to the world, and will not accept the mortification of the flesh, obey Him Who bids you follow after Him, and Who bore the Cross in His own body, as a trophy from the foe? How can you obey Paul when he exhorts you *"to present your body a living sacrifice, holy, acceptable unto God,"* when you are *"conformed to this world,"* and not transformed by the renewing of your mind, when you are not *"walking"* in this *"newness of life,"* but still pursuing the routine of *"the old man"*? How can you be a priest unto God, anointed though you are for this very office, to offer a gift to God; a gift in no way another's, no counterfeited gift from sources outside yourself, but a gift that is really your own, namely, *"the inner man* Ephesians 3:16,*"* who must be perfect and blameless, as it is required of a lamb to be without spot or blemish? How can you offer this to God, when you do not listen to the law forbidding the unclean to offer sacrifices? If you long for God to manifest Himself to you, why do you not hear Moses, when he commands the people to be pure from the stains of marriage, that they may take in the vision of God. Exodus 19:15 If this all seems little in your eyes, to be crucified with Christ, to present yourself a sacrifice to God, to become a priest unto the most high God, to make yourself worthy of the vision of the Almighty, what higher blessings than these can we imagine for you, if indeed you make light of the consequences of these as well? And the consequence of being crucified with Christ is that we shall live with Him, and be glorified with Him, and reign with Him; and the consequence of presenting ourselves to God is that we shall be changed from the rank of human nature and human dignity to that of Angels; for so speaks Daniel, that *"thousand thousands stood before him* Daniel 7:10 ." He too who has taken his share in the true priesthood and placed himself beside the Great High Priest remains altogether himself a priest for ever, prevented for eternity from remaining any more in death. To say, again, that one makes oneself worthy to see God, produces no less a result than this; that one is made worthy to see God. Indeed, the crown of every hope, and of every desire, of every blessing, and of every promise of God, and of all those unspeakable delights which we believe to exist beyond our perception and our knowledge—the crowning result of them all, I say, is this. Moses longed earnestly to see it, and many prophets and kings have desired to see the same: but the only class deemed worthy of it are the pure in heart, those who are, and are named *"blessed,"* for this very reason, that *"they shall see God. "* Wherefore we would that you too should become crucified with Christ, a holy priest standing before God, a pure offering in all chastity, preparing yourself by your own holiness for God's coming; that you also may have a pure heart in which to see God, according to the promise of God, and of our Saviour Jesus Christ, to Whom be glory for ever and ever. Amen.

On the Making of Man
Introduction

Gregory, Bishop of Nyssa, to his brother Peter, the servant of God.

If we had to honour with rewards of money those who excel in virtue, the whole world of money, as Solomon says , would seem but small to be made equal to your virtue in the balance. Since, however, the debt of gratitude due to your Reverence is greater than can be valued in money, and the holy Eastertide demands the accustomed gift of love, we offer to your greatness of mind, O man of God, a gift too small indeed to be worthy of presentation to you, yet not falling short of the extent of our power. The gift is a discourse, like a mean garment, woven not without toil from our poor wit, and the subject of the discourse, while it will perhaps be generally thought audacious, yet seemed not unfitting. For he alone has worthily considered the creation of God who truly was created after God, and whose soul was fashioned in the image of Him Who created him—Basil, our common father and teacher—who by his own speculation made the sublime ordering of the universe generally intelligible, making the world as established by God in the true Wisdom known to those who by means of his understanding are led to such contemplation: but we, who fall short even of worthily admiring him, yet intend to add to the great writer's speculations that which is lacking in them, not so as to interpolate his work by insertion (for it is not to be thought of that that lofty mouth should suffer the insult of being given as authority for our discourses), but so that the glory of the teacher may not seem to be failing among his disciples.

For if, the consideration of man being lacking in his Hexaëmeron, none of those who had been his disciples contributed any earnest effort to supply the defect, the scoffer would perhaps have had a handle against his great fame, on the ground that he had not cared to produce in his hearers any habit of intelligence. But now that we venture according to our powers upon the exposition of what was lacking, if anything should be found in our work such as to be not unworthy of his teaching, it will surely be referred to our teacher: while if our discourse does not reach the height of his sublime speculation, he will be free from this charge and escape the blame of seeming not to wish that his disciples should have any skill at all, though we perhaps may be answerable to our censurers as being unable to contain in the littleness of our heart the wisdom of our instructor.

The scope of our proposed enquiry is not small: it is second to none of the wonders of the world—perhaps even greater than any of those known to us, because no other existing thing, save the human creation, has been made like to God: thus we shall readily find that allowance will be made for what we say by kindly readers, even if our discourse is far behind the merits of the subject. For it is our business, I suppose, to leave nothing unexamined of all that concerns man—of what we believe to have taken place previously, of what we now see, and of the results which are expected afterwards to appear (for surely our effort would be convicted of failing of its promise, if, when man is proposed for contemplation, any of the questions which bear upon the subject were to be omitted); and, moreover, we must fit together, according to the explanation of Scripture and to that derived from reasoning, those statements concerning him which seem, by a kind of necessary sequence, to be opposed, so that our whole subject may be consistent in train of thought and in order, as the statements that seem to be contrary are brought (if the Divine power so discovers a hope for what is beyond hope, and a way for what is inextricable) to one and the same end: and for clearness' sake I think it well to set forth to you the discourse by chapters, that you may be able briefly to know the force of the several arguments of the whole work.

I. *Wherein is a partial inquiry into the nature of the world, and a more minute exposition of the things which preceded the genesis of man*

1. *"This is the book of the generation of heaven and earth ,"* says the Scripture, when all that is seen was finished, and each of the things that are betook itself to its own separate place, when the body of heaven compassed all things round, and those bodies which are heavy and of downward tendency, the earth and the water, holding each other in, took the middle place of the universe; while, as a sort of bond and stability for the things that were made, the Divine power and skill was implanted in the growth of things, guiding all things with the reins of a double operation (for it was by rest and motion that it devised the genesis of the things that were not, and the continuance of the things that are), driving around, about the heavy and changeless element contributed by the creation that does not move, as about some fixed path, the exceedingly rapid motion of the

sphere, like a wheel, and preserving the indissolubility of both by their mutual action, as the circling substance by its rapid motion compresses the compact body of the earth round about, while that which is firm and unyielding, by reason of its unchanging fixedness, continually augments the whirling motion of those things which revolve round it, and intensity is produced in equal measure in each of the natures which thus differ in their operation, in the stationary nature, I mean, and in the mobile revolution; for neither is the earth shifted from its own base, nor does the heaven ever relax in its vehemence, or slacken its motion.

2. These, moreover, were first framed before other things, according to the Divine wisdom, to be as it were a beginning of the whole machine, the great Moses indicating, I suppose, where he says that the heaven and the earth were made by God *"in the beginning* Genesis 1:1 " that all things that are seen in the creation are the offspring of rest and motion, brought into being by the Divine will. Now the heaven and the earth being diametrically opposed to each other in their operations, the creation which lies between the opposites, and has in part a share in what is adjacent to it, itself acts as a mean between the extremes, so that there is manifestly a mutual contact of the opposites through the mean; for all in a manner imitates the perpetual motion and subtlety of the fiery substance, both in the lightness of its nature, and in its suitableness for motion; yet it is not such as to be alienated from the solid substance, for it is no more in a state of continual flux and dispersion than in a permanent state of immobility, but becomes, in its affinity to each, a kind of borderland of the opposition between operations, at once uniting in itself and dividing things which are naturally distinct.

3. In the same way, liquid substance also is attached by double qualities to each of the opposites; for in so far as it is heavy and of downward tendency it is closely akin to the earthy; but in so far as it partakes of a certain fluid and mobile energy it is not altogether alien from the nature which is in motion; and by means of this also there is effected a kind of mixture and concurrence of the opposites, weight being transferred to motion, and motion finding no hindrance in weight, so that things most extremely opposite in nature combine with one another, and are mutually joined by those which act as means between them.

4. But to speak strictly, one should rather say that the very nature of the contraries themselves is not entirely without mixture of properties, each with the other, so that, as I think, all that we see in the world mutually agree, and the creation, though discovered in properties of contrary natures, is yet at union with itself. For as motion is not conceived merely as local shifting, but is also contemplated in change and alteration, and on the other hand the immovable nature does not admit motion by way of alteration, the wisdom of God has transposed these properties, and wrought unchangeableness in that which is ever moving, and change in that which is immovable; doing this, it may be, by a providential dispensation, so that that property of nature which constitutes its immutability and immobility might not, when viewed in any created object, cause the creature to be accounted as God; for that which may happen to move or change would cease to admit of the conception of Godhead. Hence the earth is stable without being immutable, while the heaven, on the contrary, as it has no mutability, so has not stability either, that the Divine power, by interweaving change in the stable nature and motion with that which is not subject to change, might, by the interchange of attributes, at once join them both closely to each other, and make them alien from the conception of Deity; for as has been said, neither of these (neither that which is unstable, nor that which is mutable) can be considered to belong to the more Divine nature.

5. Now all things were already arrived at their own end: *"the heaven and the earth* Genesis 2:1*,"* as Moses says, *"were finished,"* and all things that lie between them, and the particular things were adorned with their appropriate beauty; the heaven with the rays of the stars, the sea and air with the living creatures that swim and fly, and the earth with all varieties of plants and animals, to all which, empowered by the Divine will, it gave birth together; the earth was full, too, of her produce, bringing forth fruits at the same time with flowers; the meadows were full of all that grows therein, and all the mountain ridges, and summits, and every hillside, and slope, and hollow, were crowned with young grass, and with the varied produce of the trees, just risen from the ground, yet shot up at once into their perfect beauty; and all the beasts that had come into life at God's command were rejoicing, we may suppose, and skipping about, running to and fro in the thickets in herds according to their kind, while every

sheltered and shady spot was ringing with the chants of the songbirds. And at sea, we may suppose, the sight to be seen was of the like kind, as it had just settled to quiet and calm in the gathering together of its depths, where havens and harbours spontaneously hollowed out on the coasts made the sea reconciled with the land; and the gentle motion of the waves vied in beauty with the meadows, rippling delicately with light and harmless breezes that skimmed the surface; and all the wealth of creation by land and sea was ready, and none was there to share it.

II. *Why man appeared last, after the creation*

1. For not as yet had that great and precious thing, man, come into the world of being; it was not to be looked for that the ruler should appear before the subjects of his rule; but when his dominion was prepared, the next step was that the king should be manifested. When, then, the Maker of all had prepared beforehand, as it were, a royal lodging for the future king (and this was the land, and islands, and sea, and the heaven arching like a roof over them), and when all kinds of wealth had been stored in this palace (and by wealth I mean the whole creation, all that is in plants and trees, and all that has sense, and breath, and life; and— if we are to account materials also as wealth— all that for their beauty are reckoned precious in the eyes of men, as gold and silver, and the substances of your jewels which men delight in— having concealed, I say, abundance of all these also in the bosom of the earth as in a royal treasure-house), he thus manifests man in the world, to be the beholder of some of the wonders therein, and the lord of others; that by his enjoyment he might have knowledge of the Giver, and by the beauty and majesty of the things he saw might trace out that power of the Maker which is beyond speech and language.

2. For this reason man was brought into the world last after the creation, not being rejected to the last as worthless, but as one whom it behooved to be king over his subjects at his very birth. And as a good host does not bring his guest to his house before the preparation of his feast, but, when he has made all due preparation, and decked with their proper adornments his house, his couches, his table, brings his guest home when things suitable for his refreshment are in readiness—in the same manner the rich and munificent Entertainer of our nature, when He had decked the habitation with beauties of every kind, and prepared this great and varied banquet, then

introduced man, assigning to him as his task not the acquiring of what was not there, but the enjoyment of the things which were there; and for this reason He gives him as foundations the instincts of a twofold organization, blending the Divine with the earthy, that by means of both he may be naturally and properly disposed to each enjoyment, enjoying God by means of his more divine nature, and the good things of earth by the sense that is akin to them.

III. *That the nature of man is more precious than all the visible creation*

1. But it is right that we should not leave this point without consideration, that while the world, great as it is, and its parts, are laid as an elemental foundation for the formation of the universe, the creation is, so to say, made offhand by the Divine power, existing at once on His command, while counsel precedes the making of man; and that which is to be is foreshown by the Maker in verbal description, and of what kind it is fitting that it should be, and to what archetype it is fitting that it should bear a likeness, and for what it shall be made, and what its operation shall be when it is made, and of what it shall be the ruler—all these things the saying examines beforehand, so that he has a rank assigned him before his genesis, and possesses rule over the things that are before his coming into being; for it says, *"God said, Let us make man in our image, after our likeness, and let them have dominion over the fish of the sea, and the beasts of the earth, and the fowls of the heaven, and the cattle, and all the earth."*

2. O marvellous! A sun is made, and no counsel precedes; a heaven likewise; and to these no single thing in creation is equal. So great a wonder is formed by a word alone, and the saying indicates neither when, nor how, nor any such detail. So too in all particular cases, the æther, the stars, the intermediate air, the sea, the earth, the animals, the plants—all are brought into being with a word, while only to the making of man does the Maker of all draw near with circumspection, so as to prepare beforehand for him material for his formation, and to liken his form to an archetypal beauty, and, setting before him a mark for which he is to come into being, to make for him a nature appropriate and allied to the operations, and suitable for the object in hand.

IV. *That the construction of man throughout signifies his ruling power.*

1. For as in our own life artificers fashion a tool in the way suitable to its use, so the best Artificer made our nature as it were a formation fit for the exercise of royalty, preparing it at once by superior advantages of soul, and by the very form of the body, to be such as to be adapted for royalty: for the soul immediately shows its royal and exalted character, far removed as it is from the lowliness of private station, in that it owns no lord, and is self-governed, swayed autocratically by its own will; for to whom else does this belong than to a king? And further, besides these facts, the fact that it is the image of that Nature which rules over all means nothing else than this, that our nature was created to be royal from the first. For as, in men's ordinary use, those who make images of princes both mould the figure of their form, and represent along with this the royal rank by the vesture of purple, and even the likeness is commonly spoken of as *"a king,"* so the human nature also, as it was made to rule the rest, was, by its likeness to the King of all, made as it were a living image, partaking with the archetype both in rank and in name, not vested in purple, nor giving indication of its rank by sceptre and diadem (for the archetype itself is not arrayed with these), but instead of the purple robe, clothed in virtue, which is in truth the most royal of all raiment, and in place of the sceptre, leaning on the bliss of immortality, and instead of the royal diadem, decked with the crown of righteousness; so that it is shown to be perfectly like to the beauty of its archetype in all that belongs to the dignity of royalty.

V. *That man is a likeness of the Divine sovereignty.*

1. It is true, indeed, that the Divine beauty is not adorned with any shape or endowment of form, by any beauty of colour, but is contemplated as excellence in unspeakable bliss. As then painters transfer human forms to their pictures by the means of certain colours, laying on their copy the proper and corresponding tints, so that the beauty of the original may be accurately transferred to the likeness, so I would have you understand that our Maker also, painting the portrait to resemble His own beauty, by the addition of virtues, as it were with colours, shows in us His own sovereignty: and manifold and varied are the tints, so to say, by which His true form is portrayed: not red, or white , or the blending of these, whatever it may be called, nor a touch of black that paints the eyebrow and the eye, and shades, by some combination, the depressions in the figure, and all such arts which the hands of painters contrive, but instead of

these, purity, freedom from passion, blessedness, alienation from all evil, and all those attributes of the like kind which help to form in men the likeness of God: with such hues as these did the Maker of His own image mark our nature.

2. And if you were to examine the other points also by which the Divine beauty is expressed, you will find that to them too the likeness in the image which we present is perfectly preserved. The Godhead is mind and word: for *"in the beginning was the Word"* and the followers of Paul *"have the mind of Christ"* which *"speaks"* in them : humanity too is not far removed from these: you see in yourself word and understanding, an imitation of the very Mind and Word. Again, God is love, and the fount of love: for this the great John declares, that *"love is of God,"* and *"God is love"* 1 John 4:7-8: the Fashioner of our nature has made this to be our feature too: for *"hereby,"* He says, *"shall all men know that you are my disciples, if you love one another"*: — thus, if this be absent, the whole stamp of the likeness is transformed. The Deity beholds and hears all things, and searches all things out: you too have the power of apprehension of things by means of sight and hearing, and the understanding that inquires into things and searches them out.

VI. *An examination of the kindred of mind to nature: wherein, by way of digression, is refuted the doctrine of the Anomœans.*

1. And let no one suppose me to say that the Deity is in touch with existing things in a manner resembling human operation, by means of different faculties. For it is impossible to conceive in the simplicity of the Godhead the varied and diverse nature of the apprehensive operation: not even in our own case are the faculties which apprehend things numerous, although we are in touch with those things which affect our life in many ways by means of our senses; for there is one faculty, the implanted mind itself, which passes through each of the organs of sense and grasps the things beyond: this it is that, by means of the eyes, beholds what is seen; this it is that, by means of hearing, understands what is said; that is content with what is to our taste, and turns from what is unpleasant; that uses the hand for whatever it wills, taking hold or rejecting by its means, using the help of the organ for this purpose precisely as it thinks expedient.

2. If in men, then, even though the organs formed by nature for purposes of perception may be different, that which operates and

moves by means of all, and uses each appropriately for the object before it, is one and the same, not changing its nature by the differences of operations, how could any one suspect multiplicity of essence in God on the ground of His varied powers? For *"He that made the eye,"* as the prophet says, and *"that planted the ear,"* stamped on human nature these operations to be as it were significant characters, with reference to their models in Himself: for He says, *"Let us make man in our image* Genesis 1:26."

3. But what, I would ask, becomes of the heresy of the Anomœans? What will they say to this utterance? How will they defend the vanity of their dogma in view of the words cited? Will they say that it is possible that one image should be made like to different forms? If the Son is in nature unlike the Father, how comes it that the likeness He forms of the different natures is one? For He Who said, *"Let us make after our image,"* and by the plural signification revealed the Holy Trinity, would not, if the archetypes were unlike one another, have mentioned the image in the singular: for it would be impossible that there should be one likeness displayed of things which do not agree with one another: if the natures were different he would assuredly have begun their images also differently, making the appropriate image for each: but since the image is one, while the archetype is not one, who is so far beyond the range of understanding as not to know that the things which are like the same thing, surely resemble one another? Therefore He says (the word, it may be, cutting short this wickedness at the very formation of human life), *"Let us make man in our image, after our likeness."*

VII. *Why man is destitute of natural weapons and covering*

1. But what means the uprightness of his figure? And why is it that those powers which aid life do not naturally belong to his body? But man is brought into life bare of natural covering, an unarmed and poor being, destitute of all things useful, worthy, according to appearances, of pity rather than of admiration, not armed with prominent horns or sharp claws, nor with hoofs nor with teeth, nor possessing by nature any deadly venom in a sting—things such as most animals have in their own power for defence against those who do them harm: his body is not protected with a covering of hair: and yet possibly it was to be expected that he who was promoted to rule over the rest of the creatures should be defended by nature with arms of his own so that he might not need assistance from others for his

own security. Now, however, the lion, the boar, the tiger, the leopard, and all the like have natural power sufficient for their safety: and the bull has his horn, the hare his speed, the deer his leap and the certainty of his sight, and another beast has bulk, others a proboscis, the birds have their wings, and the bee her sting, and generally in all there is some protective power implanted by nature: but man alone of all is slower than the beasts that are swift of foot, smaller than those that are of great bulk, more defenceless than those that are protected by natural arms; and how, one will say, has such a being obtained the sovereignty over all things?

2. Well, I think it would not be at all hard to show that what seems to be a deficiency of our nature is a means for our obtaining dominion over the subject creatures. For if man had had such power as to be able to outrun the horse in swiftness, and to have a foot that, from its solidity, could not be worn out, but was strengthened by hoofs or claws of some kind, and to carry upon him horns and stings and claws, he would be, to begin with, a wild-looking and formidable creature, if such things grew with his body: and moreover he would have neglected his rule over the other creatures if he had no need of the co-operation of his subjects; whereas now, the needful services of our life are divided among the individual animals that are under our sway, for this reason— to make our dominion over them necessary.

3. It was the slowness and difficult motion of our body that brought the horse to supply our need, and tamed him: it was the nakedness of our body that made necessary our management of sheep, which supplies the deficiency of our nature by its yearly produce of wool: it was the fact that we import from others the supplies for our living which subjected beasts of burden to such service: furthermore, it was the fact that we cannot eat grass like cattle which brought the ox to render service to our life, who makes our living easy for us by his own labour; and because we needed teeth and biting power to subdue some of the other animals by grip of teeth, the dog gave, together with his swiftness, his own jaw to supply our need, becoming like a live sword for man; and there has been discovered by men iron, stronger and more penetrating than prominent horns or sharp claws, not, as those things do with the beasts, always growing naturally with us, but entering into alliance with us for the time, and for the rest abiding by itself: and to compensate for the crocodile's scaly hide, one may make that very hide serve as armour, by putting it on his skin

upon occasion: or, failing that, art fashions iron for this purpose too, which, when it has served him for a time for war, leaves the man-at-arms once more free from the burden in time of peace: and the wing of the birds, too, ministers to our life, so that by aid of contrivance we are not left behind even by the speed of wings: for some of them become tame and are of service to those who catch birds, and by their means others are by contrivance subdued to serve our needs: moreover art contrives to make our arrows feathered, and by means of the bow gives us for our needs the speed of wings: while the fact that our feet are easily hurt and worn in travelling makes necessary the aid which is given by the subject animals: for hence it comes that we fit shoes to our feet.

VIII. *Why man's form is upright; and that hands were given him because of reason; wherein also is a speculation on the difference of souls.*

1. But man's form is upright, and extends aloft towards heaven, and looks upwards: and these are marks of sovereignty which show his royal dignity. For the fact that man alone among existing things is such as this, while all others bow their bodies downwards, clearly points to the difference of dignity between those which stoop beneath his sway and that power which rises above them: for all the rest have the foremost limbs of their bodies in the form of feet, because that which stoops needs something to support it: but in the formation of man these limbs were made hands, for the upright body found one base, supporting its position securely on two feet, sufficient for its needs.

2. Especially do these ministering hands adapt themselves to the requirements of the reason: indeed if one were to say that the ministration of hands is a special property of the rational nature, he would not be entirely wrong; and that not only because his thought turns to the common and obvious fact that we signify our reasoning by means of the natural employment of our hands in written characters. It is true that this fact, that we speak by writing, and, in a certain way, converse by the aid of our hands, preserving sounds by the forms of the alphabet, is not unconnected with the endowment of reason; but I am referring to something else when I say that the hands co-operate with the bidding of reason.

3. Let us, however, before discussing this point, consider the matter we passed over (for the subject of the order of created things almost escaped our notice), why the growth of things that spring from the earth takes precedence, and the irrational animals come next, and then, after the making of these, comes man: for it may be that we learn from these facts not only the obvious thought, that grass appeared to the Creator useful for the sake of the animals, while the animals were made because of man, and that for this reason, before the animals there was made their food, and before man that which was to minister to human life.

4. But it seems to me that by these facts Moses reveals a hidden doctrine, and secretly delivers that wisdom concerning the soul, of which the learning that is without had indeed some imagination, but no clear comprehension. His discourse then hereby teaches us that the power of life and soul may be considered in three divisions. For one is only a power of growth and nutrition supplying what is suitable for the support of the bodies that are nourished, which is called the vegetative soul, and is to be seen in plants; for we may perceive in growing plants a certain vital power destitute of sense; and there is another form of life besides this, which, while it includes the form above mentioned, is also possessed in addition of the power of management according to sense; and this is to be found in the nature of the irrational animals: for they are not only the subjects of nourishment and growth, but also have the activity of sense and perception. But perfect bodily life is seen in the rational (I mean the human) nature, which both is nourished and endowed with sense, and also partakes of reason and is ordered by mind.

5. We might make a division of our subject in some such way as this. Of things existing, part are intellectual, part corporeal. Let us leave alone for the present the division of the intellectual according to its properties, for our argument is not concerned with these. Of the corporeal, part is entirely devoid of life, and part shares in vital energy. Of a living body, again, part has sense conjoined with life, and part is without sense: lastly, that which has sense is again divided into rational and irrational. For this reason the lawgiver says that after inanimate matter (as a sort of foundation for the form of animate things), this vegetative life was made, and had earlier existence in the growth of plants: then he proceeds to introduce the genesis of those creatures which are regulated by sense: and since, following the same

order, of those things which have obtained life in the flesh, those which have sense can exist by themselves even apart from the intellectual nature, while the rational principle could not be embodied save as blended with the sensitive—for this reason man was made last after the animals, as nature advanced in an orderly course to perfection. For this rational animal, man, is blended of every form of soul; he is nourished by the vegetative kind of soul, and to the faculty of growth was added that of sense, which stands midway, if we regard its peculiar nature, between the intellectual and the more material essence being as much coarser than the one as it is more refined than the other: then takes place a certain alliance and commixture of the intellectual essence with the subtle and enlightened element of the sensitive nature: so that man consists of these three: as we are taught the like thing by the apostle in what he says to the Ephesians , praying for them that the complete grace of their *"body and soul and spirit"* may be preserved at the coming of the Lord; using, the word *"body"* for the nutritive part, and denoting the sensitive by the word *"soul,"* and the intellectual by *"spirit."* Likewise too the Lord instructs the scribe in the Gospel that he should set before every commandment that love to God which is exercised with all the heart and soul and mind : for here also it seems to me that the phrase indicates the same difference, naming the more corporeal existence *"heart,"* the intermediate *"soul,"* and the higher nature, the intellectual and mental faculty, *"mind."*

6. Hence also the apostle recognizes three divisions of dispositions, calling one *"carnal,"* which is busied with the belly and the pleasures connected with it, another *"natural ,"* which holds a middle position with regard to virtue and vice, rising above the one, but without pure participation in the other; and another *"spiritual,"* which perceives the perfection of godly life: wherefore he says to the Corinthians, reproaching their indulgence in pleasure and passion, *"You are carnal* 1 Corinthians 3:3*,"* and incapable of receiving the more perfect doctrine; while elsewhere, making a comparison of the middle kind with the perfect, he says, *"but the natural man receives not the things of the Spirit: for they are foolishness unto him: but he that is spiritual judges all things, yet he himself is judged of no man* 1 Corinthians 2:14-15 *."* As, then, the natural man is higher than the carnal, by the same measure also the spiritual man rises above the natural.

7. If, therefore, Scripture tells us that man was made last, after every animate thing, the lawgiver is doing nothing else than declaring to us the doctrine of the soul, considering that what is perfect comes last, according to a certain necessary sequence in the order of things: for in the rational are included the others also, while in the sensitive there also surely exists the vegetative form, and that again is conceived only in connection with what is material: thus we may suppose that nature makes an ascent as it were by steps— I mean the various properties of life— from the lower to the perfect form.

8. Now since man is a rational animal, the instrument of his body must be made suitable for the use of reason ; as you may see musicians producing their music according to the form of their instruments, and not piping with harps nor harping upon flutes, so it must needs be that the organization of these instruments of ours should be adapted for reason, that when struck by the vocal organs it might be able to sound properly for the use of words. For this reason the hands were attached to the body; for though we can count up very many uses in daily life for which these skilfully contrived and helpful instruments, our hands, that easily follow every art and every operation, alike in war and peace , are serviceable, yet nature added them to our body pre-eminently for the sake of reason. For if man were destitute of hands, the various parts of his face would certainly have been arranged like those of the quadrupeds, to suit the purpose of his feeding: so that its form would have been lengthened out and pointed towards the nostrils, and his lips would have projected from his mouth, lumpy, and stiff, and thick, fitted for taking up the grass, and his tongue would either have lain between his teeth, of a kind to match his lips, fleshy, and hard, and rough, assisting his teeth to deal with what came under his grinder, or it would have been moist and hanging out at the side like that of dogs and other carnivorous beasts, projecting through the gaps in his jagged row of teeth. If, then, our body had no hands, how could articulate sound have been implanted in it, seeing that the form of the parts of the mouth would not have had the configuration proper for the use of speech, so that man must of necessity have either bleated, or *"baaed,"* or barked, or neighed, or bellowed like oxen or asses, or uttered some bestial sound? But now, as the hand is made part of the body, the mouth is at leisure for the service of the reason. Thus the hands are shown to be the property of

the rational nature, the Creator having thus devised by their means a special advantage for reason.

IX. *That the form of man was framed to serve as an instrument for the use of reason.*

1. Now since our Maker has bestowed upon our formation a certain Godlike grace, by implanting in His image the likeness of His own excellences, for this reason He gave, of His bounty, His other good gifts to human nature; but mind and reason we cannot strictly say that He *gave*, but that He *imparted* them, adding to the image the proper adornment of His own nature. Now since the mind is a thing intelligible and incorporeal, its grace would have been incommunicable and isolated, if its motion were not manifested by some contrivance. For this cause there was still need of this instrumental organization, that it might, like a plectrum, touch the vocal organs and indicate by the quality of the notes struck, the motion within.

2. And as some skilled musician, who may have been deprived by some affection of his own voice, and yet wish to make his skill known, might make melody with voices of others, and publish his art by the aid of flutes or of the lyre, so also the human mind being a discoverer of all sorts of conceptions, seeing that it is unable, by the mere soul, to reveal to those who hear by bodily senses the motions of its understanding, touches, like some skilful composer, these animated instruments, and makes known its hidden thoughts by means of the sound produced upon them.

3. Now the music of the human instrument is a sort of compound of flute and lyre, sounding together in combination as in a concerted piece of music. For the breath, as it is forced up from the air-receiving vessels through the windpipe, when the speaker's impulse to utterance attunes the harmony to sound, and as it strikes against the internal protuberances which divide this flute-like passage in a circular arrangement, imitates in a way the sound uttered through a flute, being driven round and round by the membranous projections. But the palate receives the sound from below in its own concavity, and dividing the sound by the two passages that extend to the nostrils, and by the cartilages about the perforated bone, as it were by some scaly protuberance, makes its resonance louder; while the cheek, the tongue, the mechanism of the pharynx by which the chin is

relaxed when drawn in, and tightened when extended to a point— all these in many different ways answer to the motion of the plectrum upon the strings, varying very quickly, as occasion requires, the arrangement of the tones; and the opening and closing of the lips has the same effect as players produce when they check the breath of the flute with their fingers according to the measure of the tune.

X. *That the mind works by means of the senses.*

1. As the mind then produces the music of reason by means of our instrumental construction, we are born rational, while, as I think, we should not have had the gift of reason if we had had to employ our lips to supply the need of the body— the heavy and toilsome part of the task of providing food. As things are, however, our hands appropriate this ministration to themselves, and leave the mouth available for the service of reason.

2. The operation of the instrument, however, is twofold; one for the production of sound, the other for the reception of concepts from without; and the one faculty does not blend with the other, but abides in the operation for which it was appointed by nature, not interfering with its neighbour either by the sense of hearing undertaking to speak, or by the speech undertaking to hear; for the latter is always uttering something, while the ear, as Solomon somewhere says, is not filled with continual hearing.

3. That point as to our internal faculties which seems to me to be even in a special degree matter for wonder, is this:— what is the extent of that inner receptacle into which flows everything that is poured in by our hearing? Who are the recorders of the sayings that are brought in by it? What sort of storehouses are there for the concepts that are being put in by our hearing? And how is it, that when many of them, of varied kinds, are pressing one upon another, there arises no confusion and error in the relative position of the things that are laid up there? And one may have the like feeling of wonder also with regard to the operation of sight; for by it also in like manner the mind apprehends those things which are external to the body, and draws to itself the images of phenomena, marking in itself the impressions of the things which are seen.

4. And just as if there were some extensive city receiving all comers by different entrances, all will not congregate at any particular place, but some will go to the market, some to the houses, others to the

churches, or the streets, or lanes, or the theatres, each according to his own inclination—some such city of our mind I seem to discern established in us, which the different entrances through the senses keep filling, while the mind, distinguishing and examining each of the things that enters, ranks them in their proper departments of knowledge.

5. And as, to follow the illustration of the city, it may often be that those who are of the same family and kindred do not enter by the same gate, coming in by different entrances, as it may happen, but are none the less, when they come within the circuit of the wall, brought together again, being on close terms with each other (and one may find the contrary happen; for those who are strangers and mutually unknown often take one entrance to the city, yet their community of entrance does not bind them together; for even when they are within they can be separated to join their own kindred); something of the same kind I seem to discern in the spacious territory of our mind; for often the knowledge which we gather from the different organs of sense is one, as the same object is divided into several parts in relation to the senses; and again, on the contrary, we may learn from some one sense many and varied things which have no affinity one with another.

6. For instance— for it is better to make our argument clear by illustration— let us suppose that we are making some inquiry into the property of tastes— what is sweet to the sense, and what is to be avoided by tasters. We find, then, by experience, both the bitterness of gall and the pleasant character of the quality of honey; but when these facts are known, the knowledge is one which is given to us (the same thing being introduced to our understanding in several ways) by taste, smell, hearing, and often by touch and sight. For when one sees honey, and hears its name, and receives it by taste, and recognizes its odour by smell, and tests it by touch, he recognizes the same thing by means of each of his senses.

7. On the other hand we get varied and multiform information by some one sense, for as hearing receives all sorts of sounds, and our visual perception exercises its operation by beholding things of different kinds— for it lights alike on black and white, and all things that are distinguished by contrariety of colour—so with taste, with smell, with perception by touch; each implants in us by means of its own perceptive power the knowledge of things of every kind.

XI. *That the nature of mind is invisible.*

1. What then is, in its own nature, this mind that distributes itself into faculties of sensation, and duly receives, by means of each, the knowledge of things? That it is something else besides the senses, I suppose no reasonable man doubts; for if it were identical with sense, it would reduce the proper character of the operations carried on by sense to one, on the ground that it is itself simple, and that in what is simple no diversity is to be found. Now however, as all agree that touch is one thing and smell another, and as the rest of the senses are in like manner so situated with regard to each other as to exclude intercommunion or mixture, we must surely suppose, since the mind is duly present in each case, that it is something else besides the sensitive nature, so that no variation may attach to a thing intelligible.

2. *"Who has known the mind of the Lord* Romans 11:34*?"* the apostle asks; and I ask further, who has understood his own mind? Let those tell us who consider the nature of God to be within their comprehension, whether they understand themselves— if they know the nature of their own mind. *"It is manifold and much compounded."* How then can that which is intelligible be composite? Or what is the mode of mixture of things that differ in kind? Or, *"It is simple, and incomposite."* How then is it dispersed into the manifold divisions of the senses? How is there diversity in unity? How is unity maintained in diversity?

3. But I find the solution of these difficulties by recourse to the very utterance of God; for He says, *"Let us make man in our image, after our likeness* Genesis 1:26 *."* The image is properly an image so long as it fails in none of those attributes which we perceive in the archetype; but where it falls from its resemblance to the prototype it ceases in that respect to be an image; therefore, since one of the attributes we contemplate in the Divine nature is incomprehensibility of essence, it is clearly necessary that in this point the image should be able to show its imitation of the archetype.

4. For if, while the archetype transcends comprehension, the nature of the image were comprehended, the contrary character of the attributes we behold in them would prove the defect of the image; but since the nature of our mind, which is the likeness of the Creator evades our knowledge, it has an accurate resemblance to the superior

nature, figuring by its own unknowableness the incomprehensible Nature.

XII. *An examination of the question where the ruling principle is to be considered to reside; wherein also is a discussion of tears and laughter, and a physiological speculation as to the inter-relation of matter, nature, and mind.*

1. Let there be an end, then, of all the vain and conjectural discussion of those who confine the intelligible energy to certain bodily organs; of whom some lay it down that the ruling principle is in the heart, while others say that the mind resides in the brain, strengthening such opinions by some plausible superficialities. For he who ascribes the principal authority to the heart makes its local position evidence of his argument (because it seems that it somehow occupies the middle position in the body), on the ground that the motion of the will is easily distributed from the centre to the whole body, and so proceeds to operation; and he makes the troublesome and passionate disposition of man a testimony for his argument, because such affections seem to move this part sympathetically. Those, on the other hand, who consecrate the brain to reasoning, say that the head has been built by nature as a kind of citadel of the whole body, and that in it the mind dwells like a king, with a bodyguard of senses surrounding it like messengers and shield-bearers. And these find a sign of their opinion in the fact that the reasoning of those who have suffered some injury to the membrane of the brain is abnormally distorted, and that those whose heads are heavy with intoxication ignore what is seemly.

2. Each of those who uphold these views puts forward some reasons of a more physical character on behalf of his opinion concerning the ruling principle. One declares that the motion which proceeds from the understanding is in some way akin to the nature of fire, because fire and the understanding are alike in perpetual motion; and since heat is allowed to have its source in the region of the heart, he says on this ground that the motion of mind is compounded with the mobility of heat, and asserts that the heart, in which heat is enclosed, is the receptacle of the intelligent nature. The other declares that the cerebral membrane (for so they call the tissue that surrounds the brain) is as it were a foundation or root of all the senses, and hereby makes good his own argument, on the ground that the intellectual energy cannot have its seat save in that part where the ear, connected

with it, comes into concussion with the sounds that fall upon it, and the sight (which naturally belongs to the hollow of the place where the eyes are situated) makes its internal representation by means of the images that fall upon the pupils, while the qualities of scents are discerned in it by being drawn in through the nose, and the sense of taste is tried by the test of the cerebral membrane, which sends down from itself, by the veterbræ of the neck, sensitive nerve-processes to the isthmoidal passage, and unites them with the muscles there.

3. I admit it to be true that the intellectual part of the soul is often disturbed by prevalence of passions; and that the reason is blunted by some bodily accident so as to hinder its natural operation; and that the heart is a sort of source of the fiery element in the body, and is moved in correspondence with the impulses of passion; and moreover, in addition to this, I do not reject (as I hear very much the same account from those who spend their time on anatomical researches) the statement that the cerebral membrane (according to the theory of those who take such a physiological view), enfolding in itself the brain, and steeped in the vapours that issue from it, forms a foundation for the senses; yet I do not hold this for a proof that the incorporeal nature is bounded by any limits of place.

4. Certainly we are aware that mental aberrations do not arise from heaviness of head alone, but skilled physicians declare that our intellect is also weakened by the membranes that underlie the sides being affected by disease, when they call the disease frenzy, since the name given to those membranes is φρένες . And the sensation resulting from sorrow is mistakenly supposed to arise at the heart; for while it is not the heart, but the entrance of the belly that is pained, people ignorantly refer the affection to the heart. Those, however, who have carefully studied the affections in question give some such account as follows:— by a compression and closing of the pores, which naturally takes place over the whole body in a condition of grief, everything that meets a hindrance in its passage is driven to the cavities in the interior of the body, and hence also (as the respiratory organs too are pressed by what surrounds them), the drawing of breath often becomes more violent under the influence of nature endeavouring to widen what has been contracted, so as to open out the compressed passages; and such breathing we consider a symptom of grief and call it a groan or a shriek. That, moreover, which appears to oppress the region of the heart is a painful affection, not of the

heart, but of the entrance of the stomach, and occurs from the same cause (I mean, that of the compression of the pores), as the vessel that contains the bile, contracting, pours that bitter and pungent juice upon the entrance of the stomach; and a proof of this is that the complexion of those in grief becomes sallow and jaundiced, as the bile pours its own juice into the veins by reason of excessive pressure.

5. Furthermore, the opposite affection, that, I mean, of mirth and laughter, contributes to establish the argument; for the pores of the body, in the case of those who are dissolved in mirth by hearing something pleasant, are also somehow dissolved and relaxed. Just as in the former case the slight and insensible exhalations of the pores are checked by grief, and, as they compress the internal arrangement of the higher viscera, drive up towards the head and the cerebral membrane the humid vapour which, being retained in excess by the cavities of the brain, is driven out by the pores at its base , while the closing of the eyelids expels the moisture in the form of drops (and the drop is called a tear), so I would have you think that when the pores, as a result of the contrary condition, are unusually widened, some air is drawn in through them into the interior, and thence again expelled by nature through the passage of the mouth, while all the viscera (and especially, as they say, the liver) join in expelling this air by a certain agitation and throbbing motion; whence it comes that nature, contriving to give facility for the exit of the air, widens the passage of the mouth, extending the cheeks on either side round about the breath; and the result is called laughter.

6. We must not, then, on this account ascribe the ruling principle any more to the liver than we must think, because of the heated state of the blood about the heart in wrathful dispositions, that the seat of the mind is in the heart; but we must refer these matters to the character of our bodily organization, and consider that the mind is equally in contact with each of the parts according to a kind of combination which is indescribable.

7. Even if any should allege to us on this point the Scripture which claims the ruling principle for the heart, we shall not receive the statement without examination; for he who makes mention of the heart speaks also of the reins, when he says, *"God tries the hearts and reins"* ; so that they must either confine the intellectual principle to the two combined or to neither.

8. And although I am aware that the intellectual energies are blunted, or even made altogether ineffective in a certain condition of the body, I do not hold this a sufficient evidence for limiting the faculty of the mind by any particular place, so that it should be forced out of its proper amount of free space by any inflammations that may arise in the neighbouring parts of the body (for such an opinion is a corporeal one, that when the receptacle is already occupied by something placed in it, nothing else can find place there); for the intelligible nature neither dwells in the empty spaces of bodies, nor is extruded by encroachments of the flesh; but since the whole body is made like some musical instrument, just as it often happens in the case of those who know how to play, but are unable, because the unfitness of the instrument does not admit of their art, to show their skill (for that which is destroyed by time, or broken by a fall, or rendered useless by rust or decay, is mute and inefficient, even if it be breathed upon by one who may be an excellent artist in flute-playing); so too the mind, passing over the whole instrument, and touching each of the parts in a mode corresponding to its intellectual activities, according to its nature, produces its proper effect on those parts which are in a natural condition, but remains inoperative and ineffective upon those which are unable to admit the movement of its art; for the mind is somehow naturally adapted to be in close relation with that which is in a natural condition, but to be alien from that which is removed from nature.

9. And here, I think there is a view of the matter more close to nature, by which we may learn something of the more refined doctrines. For since the most beautiful and supreme good of all is the Divinity Itself, to which incline all things that have a tendency towards what is beautiful and good , we therefore say that the mind, as being in the image of the most beautiful, itself also remains in beauty and goodness so long as it partakes as far as is possible in its likeness to the archetype; but if it were at all to depart from this it is deprived of that beauty in which it was. And as we said that the mind was adorned by the likeness of the archetypal beauty, being formed as though it were a mirror to receive the figure of that which it expresses, we consider that the nature which is governed by it is attached to the mind in the same relation, and that it too is adorned by the beauty that the mind gives, being, so to say, a mirror of the

mirror; and that by it is swayed and sustained the material element of that existence in which the nature is contemplated.

10. Thus so long as one keeps in touch with the other, the communication of the true beauty extends proportionally through the whole series, beautifying by the superior nature that which comes next to it; but when there is any interruption of this beneficent connection, or when, on the contrary, the superior comes to follow the inferior, then is displayed the misshapen character of matter, when it is isolated from nature (for in itself matter is a thing without form or structure), and by its shapelessness is also destroyed that beauty of nature with which it is adorned through the mind; and so the transmission of the ugliness of matter reaches through the nature to the mind itself, so that the image of God is no longer seen in the figure expressed by that which was moulded according to it; for the mind, setting the idea of good like a mirror behind the back, turns off the incident rays of the effulgence of the good, and it receives into itself the impress of the shapelessness of matter.

11. And in this way is brought about the genesis of evil, arising through the withdrawal of that which is beautiful and good. Now all is beautiful and good that is closely related to the First Good; but that which departs from its relation and likeness to this is certainly devoid of beauty and goodness. If, then, according to the statement we have been considering, that which is truly good is one, and the mind itself also has its power of being beautiful and good, in so far as it is in the image of the good and beautiful, and the nature, which is sustained by the mind, has the like power, in so far as it is an image of the image, it is hereby shown that our material part holds together, and is upheld when it is controlled by nature; and on the other hand is dissolved and disorganized when it is separated from that which upholds and sustains it, and is dissevered from its conjunction with beauty and goodness.

12. Now such a condition as this does not arise except when there takes place an overturning of nature to the opposite state, in which the desire has no inclination for beauty and goodness, but for that which is in need of the adorning element; for it must needs be that that which is made like to matter, destitute as matter is of form of its own, should be assimilated to it in respect of the absence alike of form and of beauty.

13. We have, however, discussed these points in passing, as following on our argument, since they were introduced by our speculation on the point before us; for the subject of enquiry was, whether the intellectual faculty has its seat in any of the parts of us, or extends equally over them all; for as for those who shut up the mind locally in parts of the body, and who advance for the establishment of this opinion of theirs the fact that the reason has not free course in the case of those whose cerebral membranes are in an unnatural condition, our argument showed that in respect of every part of the compound nature of man, whereby every man has some natural operation, the power of the soul remains equally ineffective if the part does not continue in its natural condition. And thus there came into our argument, following out this line of thought, the view we have just stated, by which we learn that in the compound nature of man the mind is governed by God, and that by it is governed our material life, provided the latter remains in its natural state, but if it is perverted from nature it is alienated also from that operation which is carried on by the mind.

14. Let us return however once more to the point from which we started— that in those who are not perverted from their natural condition by some affection, the mind exercises its own power, and is established firmly in those who are in sound health, but on the contrary is powerless in those who do not admit its operation; for we may confirm our opinion on these matters by yet other arguments: and if it is not tedious for those to hear who are already wearied with our discourse, we shall discuss these matters also, so far as we are able, in a few words.

XIII. *A Rationale of sleep, of yawning, and of dreams.*

1. This life of our bodies, material and subject to flux, always advancing by way of motion, finds the power of its being in this, that it never rests from its motion: and as some river, flowing on by its own impulse, keeps the channel in which it runs well filled, yet is not seen in the same water always at the same place, but part of it glides away while part comes flowing on, so, too, the material element of our life here suffers change in the continuity of its succession of opposites by way of motion and flux, so that it never can desist from change, but in its inability to rest keeps up unceasingly its motion alternating by like ways : and if it should ever cease moving it will assuredly have cessation also of its being.

2. For instance, emptying succeeds fullness, and on the other hand after emptiness comes in turn a process of filling: sleep relaxes the strain of waking, and, again, awakening braces up what had become slack: and neither of these abides continually, but both give way, each at the other's coming; nature thus by their interchange so renewing herself as, while partaking of each in turn, to pass from the one to the other without break. For that the living creature should always be exerting itself in its operations produces a certain rupture and severance of the overstrained part; and continual quiescence of the body brings about a certain dissolution and laxity in its frame: but to be in touch with each of these at the proper times in a moderate degree is a staying-power of nature, which, by continual transference to the opposed states, gives herself in each of them rest from the other. Thus she finds the body on the strain through wakefulness, and devises relaxation for the strain by means of sleep, giving the perceptive faculties rest for the time from their operations, loosing them like horses from the chariots after the race.

3. Further, rest at proper times is necessary for the framework of the body, that the nutriment may be diffused over the whole body through the passages which it contains, without any strain to hinder its progress. For just as certain misty vapours are drawn up from the recesses of the earth when it is soaked with rain, whenever the sun heats it with rays of any considerable warmth, so a similar result happens in the earth that is in us, when the nutriment within is heated up by natural warmth; and the vapours, being naturally of upward tendency and airy nature, and aspiring to that which is above them, come to be in the region of the head like smoke penetrating the joints of a wall: then they are dispersed thence by exhalation to the passages of the organs of sense, and by them the senses are of course rendered inactive, giving way to the transit of these vapours. For the eyes are pressed upon by the eyelids when some leaden instrument , as it were (I mean such a weight as that I have spoken of), lets down the eyelid upon the eyes; and the hearing, being dulled by these same vapours, as though a door were placed upon the acoustic organs, rests from its natural operation: and such a condition is sleep, when the sense is at rest in the body, and altogether ceases from the operation of its natural motion, so that the digestive processes of nutriment may have free course for transmission by the vapours through each of the passages.

4. And for this reason, if the apparatus of the organs of sense should be closed and sleep hindered by some occupation, the nervous system, becoming filled with the vapours, is naturally and spontaneously extended so that the part which has had its density increased by the vapours is rarefied by the process of extension, just as those do who squeeze the water out of clothes by vehement wringing: and, seeing that the parts about the pharynx are somewhat circular, and nervous tissue abounds there, whenever there is need for the expulsion from that part of the density of the vapours— since it is impossible that the part which is circular in shape should be separated directly, but only by being distended in the outline of its circumference— for this reason, by checking the breath in a yawn the chin is moved downwards so as to leave a hollow to the uvula, and all the interior parts being arranged in the figure of a circle, that smoky denseness which had been detained in the neighbouring parts is emitted together with the exit of the breath. And often the like may happen even after sleep when any portion of those vapours remains in the region spoken of undigested and unexhaled.

5. Hence the mind of man clearly proves its claim to connection with his nature, itself also co-operating and moving with the nature in its sound and waking state, but remaining unmoved when it is abandoned to sleep, unless any one supposes that the imagery of dreams is a motion of the mind exercised in sleep. We for our part say that it is only the conscious and sound action of the intellect which we ought to refer to mind; and as to the fantastic nonsense which occurs to us in sleep, we suppose that some appearances of the operations of the mind are accidentally moulded in the less rational part of the soul; for the soul, being by sleep dissociated from the senses, is also of necessity outside the range of the operations of the mind; for it is through the senses that the union of mind with man takes place; therefore when the senses are at rest, the intellect also must needs be inactive; and an evidence of this is the fact that the dreamer often seems to be in absurd and impossible situations, which would not happen if the soul were then guided by reason and intellect.

6. It seems to me, however, that when the soul is at rest so far as concerns its more excellent faculties (so far, I mean, as concerns the operations of mind and sense), the nutritive part of it alone is operative during sleep, and that some shadows and echoes of those

things which happen in our waking moments— of the operations both of sense and of intellect— which are impressed upon it by that part of the soul which is capable of memory, that these, I say, are pictured as chance will have it, some echo of memory still lingering in this division of the soul.

7. With these, then, the man is beguiled, not led to acquaintance with the things that present themselves by any train of thought, but wandering among confused and inconsequent delusions. But just as in his bodily operations, while each of the parts individually acts in some way according to the power which naturally resides in it, there arises also in the limb that is at rest a state sympathetic with that which is in motion, similarly in the case of the soul, even if one part is at rest and another in motion, the whole is affected in sympathy with the part; for it is not possible that the natural unity should be in any way severed, though one of the faculties included in it is in turn supreme in virtue of its active operation. But as, when men are awake and busy, the mind is supreme, and sense ministers to it, yet the faculty which regulates the body is not dissociated from them (for the mind furnishes the food for its wants, the sense receives what is furnished, and the nutritive faculty of the body appropriates to itself that which is given to it), so in sleep the supremacy of these faculties is in some way reversed in us, and while the less rational becomes supreme, the operation of the other ceases indeed, yet is not absolutely extinguished; but while the nutritive faculty is then busied with digestion during sleep, and keeps all our nature occupied with itself, the faculty of sense is neither entirely severed from it (for that cannot be separated which has once been naturally joined), nor yet can its activity revive, as it is hindered by the inaction during sleep of the organs of sense; and by the same reasoning (the mind also being united to the sensitive part of the soul) it would follow that we should say that the mind moves with the latter when it is in motion, and rests with it when it is quiescent.

8. As naturally happens with fire when it is heaped over with chaff, and no breath fans the flame— it neither consumes what lies beside it, nor is entirely quenched, but instead of flame it rises to the air through the chaff in the form of smoke; yet if it should obtain any breath of air, it turns the smoke to flame— in the same way the mind when hidden by the inaction of the senses in sleep is neither able to shine out through them, nor yet is quite extinguished, but has, so to

say, a smouldering activity, operating to a certain extent, but unable to operate farther.

9. Again, as a musician, when he touches with the plectrum the slackened strings of a lyre, brings out no orderly melody (for that which is not stretched will not sound), but his hand frequently moves skilfully, bringing the plectrum to the position of the notes so far as place is concerned, yet there is no sound, except that he produces by the vibration of the strings a sort of uncertain and indistinct hum; so in sleep the mechanism of the senses being relaxed, the artist is either quite inactive, if the instrument is completely relaxed by satiety or heaviness; or will act slackly and faintly, if the instrument of the senses does not fully admit of the exercise of its art.

10. For this cause memory is confused, and foreknowledge, though rendered doubtful by uncertain veils, is imaged in shadows of our waking pursuits, and often indicates to us something of what is going to happen: for by its subtlety of nature the mind has some advantage, in ability to behold things, over mere corporeal grossness; yet it cannot make its meaning clear by direct methods, so that the information of the matter in hand should be plain and evident, but its declaration of the future is ambiguous and doubtful,— what those who interpret such things call an *"enigma."*

11. So the butler presses the cluster for Pharaoh's cup: so the baker seemed to carry his baskets; each supposing himself in sleep to be engaged in those services with which he was busied when awake: for the images of their customary occupations imprinted on the prescient element of their soul, gave them for a time the power of foretelling, by this sort of prophecy on the part of the mind, what should come to pass.

12. But if Daniel and Joseph and others like them were instructed by Divine power, without any confusion of perception, in the knowledge of things to come, this is nothing to the present statement; for no one would ascribe this to the power of dreams, since he will be constrained as a consequence to suppose that those Divine appearances also which took place in wakefulness were not a miraculous vision but a result of nature brought about spontaneously. As then, while all men are guided by their own minds, there are some few who are deemed worthy of evident Divine communication; so, while the imagination of sleep naturally occurs in a like and

equivalent manner for all, some, not all, share by means of their dreams in some more Divine manifestation: but to all the rest even if a foreknowledge of anything does occur as a result of dreams, it occurs in the way we have spoken of.

13. And again, if the Egyptian and the Assyrian king were guided by God to the knowledge of the future, the dispensation wrought by their means is a different thing: for it was necessary that the hidden wisdom of the holy men should be made known, that each of them might not pass his life without profit to the state. For how could Daniel have been known for what he was, if the soothsayers and magicians had not been unequal to the task of discovering the dream? And how could Egypt have been preserved while Joseph was shut up in prison, if his interpretation of the dream had not brought him to notice? Thus we must reckon these cases as exceptional, and not class them with common dreams.

14. But this ordinary seeing of dreams is common to all men, and arises in our fancies in different modes and forms: for either there remain, as we have said, in the reminiscent part of the soul, the echoes of daily occupations; or, as often happens, the constitution of dreams is framed with regard to such and such a condition of the body: for thus the thirsty man seems to be among springs, the man who is in need of food to be at a feast, and the young man in the heat of youthful vigour is beset by fancies corresponding to his passion.

15. I also knew another cause of the fancies of sleep, when attending one of my relations attacked by frenzy; who being annoyed by food being given him in too great quantity for his strength, kept crying out and finding fault with those who were about him for filling intestines with dung and putting them upon him: and when his body was rapidly tending to perspire he blamed those who were with him for having water ready to wet him with as he lay: and he did not cease calling out till the result showed the meaning of these complaints: for all at once a copious sweat broke out over his body, and a relaxation of the bowels explained the weight in the intestines. The same condition then which, while his sober judgment was dulled by disease, his nature underwent, being sympathetically affected by the condition of the body— not being without perception of what was amiss, but being unable clearly to express its pain, by reason of the distraction resulting from the disease— this, probably, if the intelligent principle of the soul were lulled to rest, not from infirmity

but by natural sleep, might appear as a dream to one similarly situated, the breaking out of perspiration being expressed by water, and the pain occasioned by the food, by the weight of intestines.

16. This view also is taken by those skilled in medicine, that according to the differences of complaints the visions of dreams appear differently to the patients: that the visions of those of weak stomach are of one kind, those of persons suffering from injury to the cerebral membrane of another, those of persons in fevers of yet another; that those of patients suffering from bilious and from phlegmatic affections are diverse, and those again of plethoric patients, and of patients in wasting disease, are different; whence we may see that the nutritive and vegetative faculty of the soul has in it by commixture some seed of the intelligent element, which is in some sense brought into likeness to the particular state of the body, being adapted in its fancies according to the complaint which has seized upon it.

17. Moreover, most men's dreams are conformed to the state of their character: the brave man's fancies are of one kind, the coward's of another; the wanton man's dreams of one kind, the continent man's of another; the liberal man and the avaricious man are subject to different fancies; while these fancies are nowhere framed by the intellect, but by the less rational disposition of the soul, which forms even in dreams the semblances of those things to which each is accustomed by the practice of his waking hours.

XIV. *That the mind is not in a part of the body; wherein also is a distinction of the movements of the body and of the soul.*

1. But we have wandered far from our subject, for the purpose of our argument was to show that the mind is not restricted to any part of the body, but is equally in touch with the whole, producing its motion according to the nature of the part which is under its influence. There are cases, however, in which the mind even follows the bodily impulses, and becomes, as it were, their servant; for often the bodily nature takes the lead by introducing either the sense of that which gives pain or the desire for that which gives pleasure, so that it may be said to furnish the first beginnings, by producing in us the desire for food, or, generally, the impulse towards some pleasant thing; while the mind, receiving such an impulse, furnishes the body by its own intelligence with the proper means towards the desired

object. Such a condition, indeed, does not occur in all, save in those of a somewhat slavish disposition, who bring the reason into bondage to the impulses of their nature and pay servile homage to the pleasures of sense by allowing them the alliance of their mind; but in the case of more perfect men this does not happen; for the mind takes the lead, and chooses the expedient course by reason and not by passion, while their nature follows in the tracks of its leader.

2. But since our argument discovered in our vital faculty three different varieties— one which receives nourishment without perception, another which at once receives nourishment and is capable of perception, but is without the reasoning activity, and a third rational, perfect, and co-extensive with the whole faculty— so that among these varieties the advantage belongs to the intellectual,— let no one suppose on this account that in the compound nature of man there are three souls welded together, contemplated each in its own limits, so that one should think man's nature to be a sort of conglomeration of several souls. The true and perfect soul is naturally one, the intellectual and immaterial, which mingles with our material nature by the agency of the senses; but all that is of material nature, being subject to mutation and alteration, will, if it should partake of the animating power, move by way of growth: if, on the contrary, it should fall away from the vital energy, it will reduce its motion to destruction.

3. Thus, neither is there perception without material substance, nor does the act of perception take place without the intellectual faculty.

XV. *That the soul proper, in fact and name, is the rational soul, while the others are called so equivocally; wherein also is this statement, that the power of the mind extends throughout the whole body in fitting contact with every part.*

1. Now, if some things in creation possess the nutritive faculty, and others again are regulated by the perceptive faculty, while the former have no share of perception nor the latter of the intellectual nature, and if for this reason any one is inclined to the opinion of a plurality of souls, such a man will be positing a variety of souls in a way not in accordance with their distinguishing definition. For everything which we conceive among existing things, if it be perfectly that which it is, is also properly called by the name it bears: but of that which is not every respect what it is called, the appellation also is vain. For

instance:— if one were to show us true bread, we say that he properly applies the name to the subject: but if one were to show us instead that which had been made of stone to resemble the natural bread, which had the same shape, and equal size, and similarity of colour, so as in most points to be the same with its prototype, but which yet lacks the power of being food, on this account we say that the stone receives the name of *"bread,"* not properly, but by a misnomer, and all things which fall under the same description, which are not absolutely what they are called, have their name from a misuse of terms.

2. Thus, as the soul finds its perfection in that which is intellectual and rational, everything that is not so may indeed share the name of *"soul,"* but is not really soul, but a certain vital energy associated with the appellation of *"soul."* And for this reason also He Who gave laws on every matter, gave the animal nature likewise, as not far removed from this vegetative life , for the use of man, to be for those who partake of it instead of herbs:— for He says, *"You shall eat all kinds of flesh even as the green herb ;"* for the perceptive energy seems to have but a slight advantage over that which is nourished and grows without it. Let this teach carnal men not to bind their intellect closely to the phenomena of sense, but rather to busy themselves with their spiritual advantages, as the true soul is found in these, while sense has equal power also among the brute creation.

3. The course of our argument, however, has diverged to another point: for the subject of our speculation was not the fact that the energy of mind is of more dignity among the attributes we conceive in man than the material element of his being, but the fact that the mind is not confined to any one part of us, but is equally in all and through all, neither surrounding anything without, nor being enclosed within anything: for these phrases are properly applied to casks or other bodies that are placed one inside the other; but the union of the mental with the bodily presents a connection unspeakable and inconceivable—not being *within* it (for the incorporeal is not enclosed in a body), nor yet surrounding it without (for that which is incorporeal does not include anything), but the mind approaching our nature in some inexplicable and incomprehensible way, and coming into contact with it, is to be regarded as both in it and around it, neither implanted in it nor enfolded with it, but in a way which we cannot speak or think, except

so far as this, that while the nature prospers according to its own order, the mind is also operative; but if any misfortune befalls the former, the movement of the intellect halts correspondingly.

XVI. *A contemplation of the Divine utterance which said— "Let us make man after our image and likeness"; wherein is examined what is the definition of the image, and how the passible and mortal is like to the Blessed and Impassible, and how in the image there are male and female, seeing these are not in the prototype.*

1. Let us now resume our consideration of the Divine word, *"Let us make man in our image, after our likeness* Genesis 1:26 *."* How mean and how unworthy of the majesty of man are the fancies of some heathen writers, who magnify humanity, as they supposed, by their comparison of it to this world! For they say that man is a little world, composed of the same elements with the universe. Those who bestow on human nature such praise as this by a high-sounding name, forget that they are dignifying man with the attributes of the gnat and the mouse: for they too are composed of these four elements—because assuredly about the animated nature of every existing thing we behold a part, greater or less, of those elements without which it is not natural that any sensitive being should exist. What great thing is there, then, in man's being accounted a representation and likeness of the world—of the heaven that passes away, of the earth that changes, of all things that they contain, which pass away with the departure of that which compasses them round?

2. In what then does the greatness of man consist, according to the doctrine of the Church? Not in his likeness to the created world, but in his being in the image of the nature of the Creator.

3. What therefore, you will perhaps say, is the definition of the image? How is the incorporeal likened to body? How is the temporal like the eternal? That which is mutable by change like to the immutable? That which is subject to passion and corruption to the impassible and incorruptible? That which constantly dwells with evil, and grows up with it, to that which is absolutely free from evil? There is a great difference between that which is conceived in the archetype, and a thing which has been made in its image: for the image is properly so called if it keeps its resemblance to the prototype; but if the imitation be perverted from its subject, the thing is something else, and no longer an image of the subject.

4. How then is man, this mortal, passible, shortlived being, the image of that nature which is immortal, pure, and everlasting? The true answer to this question, indeed, perhaps only the very Truth knows: but this is what we, tracing out the truth so far as we are capable by conjectures and inferences, apprehend concerning the matter. Neither does the word of God lie when it says that man was made in the image of God, nor is the pitiable suffering of man's nature like to the blessedness of the impassible Life: for if any one were to compare our nature with God, one of two things must needs be allowed in order that the definition of the likeness may be apprehended in both cases in the same terms—either that the Deity is passible, or that humanity is impassible: but if neither the Deity is passible nor our nature free from passion, what other account remains whereby we may say that the word of God speaks truly, which says that man was made in the image of God?

5. We must, then, take up once more the Holy Scripture itself, if we may perhaps find some guidance in the question by means of what is written. After saying, *"Let us make man in our image,"* and for what purposes it was said *"Let us make him,"* it adds this saying:— *"and God created man; in the image of God created He him; male and female created He them* Genesis 1:27 ." We have already said in what precedes, that this saying was uttered for the destruction of heretical impiety, in order that being instructed that the Only-begotten God made man in the image of God, we should in no wise distinguish the Godhead of the Father and the Son, since Holy Scripture gives to each equally the name of God—to Him Who made man, and to Him in Whose image he was made.

6. However, let us pass by our argument upon this point: let us turn our inquiry to the question before us—how it is that while the Deity is in bliss, and humanity is in misery, the latter is yet in Scripture called *"like"* the former?

7. We must, then, examine the words carefully: for we find, if we do so, that that which was made *"in the image"* is one thing, and that which is now manifested in wretchedness is another. *"God created man,"* it says; *"in the image of God created He him* Genesis 1:27 ." There is an end of the creation of that which was made *"in the image"*: then it makes a resumption of the account of creation, and says, *"male and female created He them."* I presume that every one knows that this is a departure from the Prototype: for *"in Christ*

Jesus," as the apostle says, *"there is neither male nor female."* Yet the phrase declares that man is thus divided.

8. Thus the creation of our nature is in a sense twofold: one made like to God, one divided according to this distinction: for something like this the passage darkly conveys by its arrangement, where it first says, *"God created man, in the image of God created He him* Genesis 1:27," and then, adding to what has been said, *"male and female created He them* Genesis 1:27,"— a thing which is alien from our conceptions of God.

9. I think that by these words Holy Scripture conveys to us a great and lofty doctrine; and the doctrine is this. While two natures— the Divine and incorporeal nature, and the irrational life of brutes— are separated from each other as extremes, human nature is the mean between them: for in the compound nature of man we may behold a part of each of the natures I have mentioned—of the Divine, the rational and intelligent element, which does not admit the distinction of male and female; of the irrational, our bodily form and structure, divided into male and female: for each of these elements is certainly to be found in all that partakes of human life. That the intellectual element, however, precedes the other, we learn as from one who gives in order an account of the making of man; and we learn also that his community and kindred with the irrational is for man a provision for reproduction. For he says first that *"God created man in the image of God"* (showing by these words, as the Apostle says, that in such a being there is no male or female): then he adds the peculiar attributes of human nature, *"male and female created He them* Genesis 1:27."

10. What, then, do we learn from this? Let no one, I pray, be indignant if I bring from far an argument to bear upon the present subject. God is in His own nature all that which our mind can conceive of good—rather, transcending all good that we can conceive or comprehend. He creates man for no other reason than that He is good; and being such, and having this as His reason for entering upon the creation of our nature, He would not exhibit the power of His goodness in an imperfect form, giving our nature some one of the things at His disposal, and grudging it a share in another: but the perfect form of goodness is here to be seen by His both bringing man into being from nothing, and fully supplying him with all good gifts: but since the list of individual good gifts is a long one, it is out of the question to apprehend it numerically. The language of Scripture

therefore expresses it concisely by a comprehensive phrase, in saying that man was made *"in the image of God"*: for this is the same as to say that He made human nature participant in all good; for if the Deity is the fullness of good, and this is His image, then the image finds its resemblance to the Archetype in being filled with all good.

11. Thus there is in us the principle of all excellence, all virtue and wisdom, and every higher thing that we conceive: but pre-eminent among all is the fact that we are free from necessity, and not in bondage to any natural power, but have decision in our own power as we please; for virtue is a voluntary thing, subject to no dominion: that which is the result of compulsion and force cannot be virtue.

12. Now as the image bears in all points the semblance of the archetypal excellence, if it had not a difference in some respect, being absolutely without divergence it would no longer be a likeness, but will in that case manifestly be absolutely identical with the Prototype. What difference then do we discern between the Divine and that which has been made like to the Divine? We find it in the fact that the former is uncreate, while the latter has its being from creation: and this distinction of property brings with it a train of other properties; for it is very certainly acknowledged that the uncreated nature is also immutable, and always remains the same, while the created nature cannot exist without change; for its very passage from nonexistence to existence is a certain motion and change of the nonexistent transmuted by the Divine purpose into being.

13. As the Gospel calls the stamp upon the coin *"the image of Cæsar Matthew 22:20-21,"* whereby we learn that in that which was fashioned to resemble Cæsar there was resemblance as to outward look, but difference as to material, so also in the present saying, when we consider the attributes contemplated both in the Divine and human nature, in which the likeness consists, to be in the place of the features, we find in what underlies them the difference which we behold in the uncreated and in the created nature.

14. Now as the former always remains the same, while that which came into being by creation had the beginning of its existence from change, and has a kindred connection with the like mutation, for this reason He Who, as the prophetical writing says, *"knows all things before they be ,"* following out, or rather perceiving beforehand by His power of foreknowledge what, in a state of independence and

freedom, is the tendency of the motion of man's will,— as He saw, I say, what would be, He devised for His image the distinction of male and female, which has no reference to the Divine Archetype, but, as we have said, is an approximation to the less rational nature.

15. The cause, indeed, of this device, only those can know who were eye-witnesses of the truth and ministers of the Word; but we, imagining the truth, as far as we can, by means of conjectures and similitudes, do not set forth that which occurs to our mind authoritatively, but will place it in the form of a theoretical speculation before our kindly hearers.

16. What is it then which we understand concerning these matters? In saying that *"God created man"* the text indicates, by the indefinite character of the term, all mankind; for was not Adam here named together with the creation, as the history tells us in what follows? Yet the name given to the man created is not the particular, but the general name: thus we are led by the employment of the general name of our nature to some such view as this— that in the Divine foreknowledge and power all humanity is included in the first creation; for it is fitting for God not to regard any of the things made by Him as indeterminate, but that each existing thing should have some limit and measure prescribed by the wisdom of its Maker.

17. Now just as any particular man is limited by his bodily dimensions, and the peculiar size which is conjoined with the superficies of his body is the measure of his separate existence, so I think that the entire plenitude of humanity was included by the God of all, by His power of foreknowledge, as it were in one body, and that this is what the text teaches us which says, *"God created man, in the image of God created He him."* For the image is not in part of our nature, nor is the grace in any one of the things found in that nature, but this power extends equally to all the race: and a sign of this is that mind is implanted alike in all: for all have the power of understanding and deliberating, and of all else whereby the Divine nature finds its image in that which was made according to it: the man that was manifested at the first creation of the world, and he that shall be after the consummation of all, are alike: they equally bear in themselves the Divine image.

18. For this reason the whole race was spoken of as one man, namely, that to God's power nothing is either past or future, but even that

which we expect is comprehended, equally with what is at present existing, by the all-sustaining energy. Our whole nature, then, extending from the first to the last, is, so to say, one image of Him Who is; but the distinction of kind in male and female was added to His work last, as I suppose, for the reason which follows.

XVII. What we must answer to those who raise the question—"If procreation is after sin, how would souls have come into being if the first of mankind had remained sinless?"

1. It is better for us however, perhaps, rather to inquire, before investigating this point, the solution of the question put forward by our adversaries; for they say that before the sin there is no account of birth, or of travail, or of the desire that tends to procreation, but when they were banished from Paradise after their sin, and the woman was condemned by the sentence of travail, Adam thus entered with his consort upon the intercourse of married life, and then took place the beginning of procreation. If, then, marriage did not exist in Paradise, nor travail, nor birth, they say that it follows as a necessary conclusion that human souls would not have existed in plurality had not the grace of immortality fallen away to mortality, and marriage preserved our race by means of descendants, introducing the offspring of the departing to take their place, so that in a certain way the sin that entered into the world was profitable for the life of man: for the human race would have remained in the pair of the first-formed, had not the fear of death impelled their nature to provide succession.

2. Now here again the true answer, whatever it may be, can be clear to those only who, like Paul, have been instructed in the mysteries of Paradise; but our answer is as follows. When the Sadducees once argued against the doctrine of the resurrection, and brought forward, to establish their own opinion, that woman of many marriages, who had been wife to seven brethren, and thereupon inquired whose wife she will be after the resurrection, our Lord answered their argument so as not only to instruct the Sadducees, but also to reveal to all that come after them the mystery of the resurrection-life: *"for in the resurrection,"* He says, *"they neither marry, nor are given in marriage; neither can they die any more, for they are equal to the angels, and are the children of God, being the children of the resurrection* Luke 20:35-36 *."* Now the resurrection promises us nothing else than the restoration of the fallen to their ancient state; for the grace we look for is a certain return to the first life, bringing back again to

Paradise him who was cast out from it. If then the life of those restored is closely related to that of the angels, it is clear that the life before the transgression was a kind of angelic life, and hence also our return to the ancient condition of our life is compared to the angels. Yet while, as has been said, there is no marriage among them, the armies of the angels are in countless myriads; for so Daniel declared in his visions: so, in the same way, if there had not come upon us as the result of sin a change for the worse, and removal from equality with the angels, neither should we have needed marriage that we might multiply; but whatever the mode of increase in the angelic nature is (unspeakable and inconceivable by human conjectures, except that it assuredly exists), it would have operated also in the case of men, who were *"made a little lower than the angels,"* to increase mankind to the measure determined by its Maker.

3. But if any one finds a difficulty in an inquiry as to the manner of the generation of souls, had man not needed the assistance of marriage, we shall ask him in turn, what is the mode of the angelic existence, how they exist in countless myriads, being one essence, and at the same time numerically many; for we shall be giving a fit answer to one who raises the question how man would have been without marriage, if we say, *"as the angels are without marriage;"* for the fact that man was in a like condition with them before the transgression is shown by the restoration to that state.

4. Now that we have thus cleared up these matters, let us return to our former point—how it was that after the making of His image God contrived for His work the distinction of male and female. I say that the preliminary speculation we have completed is of service for determining this question; for He Who brought all things into being and fashioned Man as a whole by His own will to the Divine image, did not wait to see the number of souls made up to its proper fullness by the gradual additions of those coming after; but while looking upon the nature of man in its entirety and fullness by the exercise of His foreknowledge, and bestowing upon it a lot exalted and equal to the angels, since He saw beforehand by His all-seeing power the failure of their will to keep a direct course to what is good, and its consequent declension from the angelic life, in order that the multitude of human souls might not be cut short by its fall from that mode by which the angels were increased and multiplied—for this reason, I say, He formed for our nature that contrivance for increase

which befits those who had fallen into sin, implanting in mankind, instead of the angelic majesty of nature, that animal and irrational mode by which they now succeed one another.

5. Hence also, it seems to me, the great David pitying the misery of man mourns over his nature with such words as these, that, *"man being in honour knew it not"* (meaning by *"honour"* the equality with the angels), therefore, he says, *"he is compared to the beasts that have no understanding, and made like them. "* For he truly was made like the beasts, who received in his nature the present mode of transient generation, on account of his inclination to material things.

XVIII. *That our irrational passions have their rise from kindred with irrational nature.*

1. For I think that from this beginning all our passions issue as from a spring, and pour their flood over man's life; and an evidence of my words is the kinship of passions which appears alike in ourselves and in the brutes; for it is not allowable to ascribe the first beginnings of our constitutional liability to passion to that human nature which was fashioned in the Divine likeness; but as brute life first entered into the world, and man, for the reason already mentioned, took something of their nature (I mean the mode of generation), he accordingly took at the same time a share of the other attributes contemplated in that nature; for the likeness of man to God is not found in anger, nor is pleasure a mark of the superior nature; cowardice also, and boldness, and the desire of gain, and the dislike of loss, and all the like, are far removed from that stamp which indicates Divinity.

2. These attributes, then, human nature took to itself from the side of the brutes; for those qualities with which brute life was armed for self-preservation, when transferred to human life, became passions; for the carnivorous animals are preserved by their anger, and those which breed largely by their love of pleasure; cowardice preserves the weak, fear that which is easily taken by more powerful animals, and greediness those of great bulk; and to miss anything that tends to pleasure is for the brutes a matter of pain. All these and the like affections entered man's composition by reason of the animal mode of generation.

3. I may be allowed to describe the human image by comparison with some wonderful piece of modelling. For, as one may see in models those carved shapes which the artificers of such things contrive for the

wonder of beholders, tracing out upon a single head two forms of faces; so man seems to me to bear a double likeness to opposite things — being moulded in the Divine element of his mind to the Divine beauty, but bearing, in the passionate impulses that arise in him, a likeness to the brute nature; while often even his reason is rendered brutish, and obscures the better element by the worse through its inclination and disposition towards what is irrational; for whenever a man drags down his mental energy to these affections, and forces his reason to become the servant of his passions, there takes place a sort of conversion of the good stamp in him into the irrational image, his whole nature being traced anew after that design, as his reason, so to say, cultivates the beginnings of his passions, and gradually multiplies them; for once it lends its co-operation to passion, it produces a plenteous and abundant crop of evils.

4. Thus our love of pleasure took its beginning from our being made like to the irrational creation, and was increased by the transgressions of men, becoming the parent of so many varieties of sins arising from pleasure as we cannot find among the irrational animals. Thus the rising of anger in us is indeed akin to the impulse of the brutes; but it grows by the alliance of thought: for thence come malignity, envy, deceit, conspiracy, hypocrisy; all these are the result of the evil husbandry of the mind; for if the passion were divested of the aid it receives from thought, the anger that is left behind is short-lived and not sustained, like a bubble, perishing straightway as soon as it comes into being. Thus the greediness of swine introduces covetousness, and the high spirit of the horse becomes the origin of pride; and all the particular forms that proceed from the want of reason in brute nature become vice by the evil use of the mind.

5. So, likewise, on the contrary, if reason instead assumes sway over such emotions, each of them is transmuted to a form of virtue; for anger produces courage, terror caution, fear obedience, hatred aversion from vice, the power of love the desire for what is truly beautiful; high spirit in our character raises our thought above the passions, and keeps it from bondage to what is base; yea, the great Apostle, even, praises such a form of mental elevation when he bids us constantly to *"think those things that are above* Colossians 3:2;*"* and so we find that every such motion, when elevated by loftiness of mind, is conformed to the beauty of the Divine image.

Selected Works

6. But the other impulse is greater, as the tendency of sin is heavy and downward; for the ruling element of our soul is more inclined to be dragged downwards by the weight of the irrational nature than is the heavy and earthy element to be exalted by the loftiness of the intellect; hence the misery that encompasses us often causes the Divine gift to be forgotten, and spreads the passions of the flesh, like some ugly mask, over the beauty of the image.

7. Those, therefore, are in some sense excusable, who do not admit, when they look upon such cases, that the Divine form is there; yet we may behold the Divine image in men by the medium of those who have ordered their lives aright. For if the man who is subject to passion, and carnal, makes it incredible that man was adorned, as it were, with Divine beauty, surely the man of lofty virtue and pure from pollution will confirm you in the better conception of human nature.

8. For instance (for it is better to make our argument clear by an illustration), one of those noted for wickedness— some Jechoniah, say, or some other of evil memory— has obliterated the beauty of his nature by the pollution of wickedness; yet in Moses and in men like him the form of the image was kept pure. Now where the beauty of the form has not been obscured, there is made plain the faithfulness of the saying that man is an image of God.

9. It may be, however, that some one feels shame at the fact that our life, like that of the brutes, is sustained by food, and for this reason deems man unworthy of being supposed to have been framed in the image of God; but he may expect that freedom from this function will one day be bestowed upon our nature in the life we look for; for, as the Apostle says, *"the Kingdom of God is not meat and drink* Romans 14:17;" and the Lord declared that *"man shall not live by bread alone, but by every word that proceeds out of the mouth of God."* Further, as the resurrection holds forth to us a life equal with the angels, and with the angels there is no food, there is sufficient ground for believing that man, who will live in like fashion with the angels, will be released from such a function.

XIX. *To those who say that the enjoyment of the good things we look for will again consist in meat and drink, because it is written that by these means man at first lived in Paradise.*

1. But some one perhaps will say that man will not be returning to the same form of life, if as it seems, we formerly existed by eating, and shall hereafter be free from that function. I, however, when I hear the Holy Scripture, do not understand only bodily meat, or the pleasure of the flesh; but I recognize another kind of food also, having a certain analogy to that of the body, the enjoyment of which extends to the soul alone: *"Eat of my bread* Proverbs 9:5,*"* is the bidding of Wisdom to the hungry; and the Lord declares those blessed who hunger for such food as this, and says, *"If any man thirst, let him come unto Me, and drink"*: and *"drink ye joy,"* is the great Isaiah's charge to those who are able to hear his sublimity. There is a prophetic threatening also against those worthy of vengeance, that they shall be punished with famine; but the *"famine"* is not a lack of bread and water, but a failure of the word:— *"not a famine of bread, nor a thirst for water, but a famine of hearing the word of the Lord* Amos 8:11 *."*

2. We ought, then, to conceive that the fruit in Eden was something worthy of God's planting (and Eden is interpreted to mean *"delight"*), and not to doubt that man was hereby nourished: nor should we at all conceive, concerning the mode of life in Paradise, this transitory and perishable nutriment: *"of every tree of the garden,"* He says, *"you may freely eat* Genesis 2.16 *."*

3. Who will give to him that has a healthful hunger that tree that is in Paradise, which includes all good, which is named *"every tree,"* in which this passage bestows on man the right to share? For in the universal and transcendent saying every form of good is in harmony with itself, and the whole is one. And who will keep me back from that tasting of the tree which is of mixed and doubtful kind? For surely it is clear to all who are at all keen-sighted what that *"every"* tree is whose fruit is life, and what again that mixed tree is whose end is death: for He Who presents ungrudgingly the enjoyment of *"every"* tree, surely by some reason and forethought keeps man from participation in those which are of doubtful kind.

4. It seems to me that I may take the great David and the wise Solomon as my instructors in the interpretation of this text: for both understand the grace of the permitted delight to be one—that very actual Good, which in truth is *"every"* good—David, when he says, *"Delight thou in the Lord,"* and Solomon, when he names Wisdom herself (which is the Lord) *"a tree of life* Proverbs 3:18 *."*

5. Thus the *"every"* tree of which the passage gives food to him who was made in the likeness of God, is the same with the tree of life; and there is opposed to this tree another tree, the food given by which is the knowledge of good and evil:— not that it bears in turn as fruit each of these things of opposite significance, but that it produces a fruit blended and mixed with opposite qualities, the eating of which the Prince of Life forbids, and the serpent counsels, that he may prepare an entrance for death: and he obtained credence for his counsel, covering over the fruit with a fair appearance and the show of pleasure, that it might be pleasant to the eyes and stimulate the desire to taste.

XX. What was the life in Paradise, and what was the forbidden tree?

1. What then is that which includes the knowledge of good and evil blended together, and is decked with the pleasures of sense? I think I am not aiming wide of the mark in employing, as a starting-point for my speculation, the sense of *"knowable."* It is not, I think, *"science"* which the Scripture here means by *"knowledge"*; but I find a certain distinction, according to Scriptural use, between *"knowledge"* and *"discernment"*: for to *"discern"* skilfully the good from the evil, the Apostle says is a mark of a more perfect condition and of *"exercised senses,"* for which reason also he bids us *"prove all things* 1 Thessalonians 5:21," and says that *"discernment"* belongs to the spiritual man 1 Corinthians 2:15: but *"knowledge"* is not always to be understood of skill and acquaintance with anything, but of the disposition towards what is agreeable—as *"the Lord knows them that are His* 2 Timothy 2:19"; and He says to Moses, *"I knew you above all"*; while of those condemned in their wickedness He Who knows all things says, *"I never knew you* Matthew 7:23."

2. The tree, then, from which comes this fruit of mixed knowledge, is among those things which are forbidden; and that fruit is combined of opposite qualities, which has the serpent to commend it, it may be for this reason, that the evil is not exposed in its nakedness, itself appearing in its own proper nature— for wickedness would surely fail of its effect were it not decked with some fair colour to entice to the desire of it him whom it deceives— but now the nature of evil is in a manner mixed, keeping destruction like some snare concealed in its depths, and displaying some phantom of good in the deceitfulness of its exterior. The beauty of the substance seems good to those who

love money: yet *"the love of money is a root of all evil* 1 Timothy 6:10*"*: and who would plunge into the unsavoury mud of wantonness, were it not that he whom this bait hurries into passion thinks pleasure a thing fair and acceptable? So, too, the other sins keep their destruction hidden, and seem at first sight acceptable, and some deceit makes them earnestly sought after by unwary men instead of what is good.

3. Now since the majority of men judge the good to lie in that which gratifies the senses, and there is a certain identity of name between that which is, and that which appears to be *"good,"*— for this reason that desire which arises towards what is evil, as though towards good, is called by Scripture *"the knowledge of good and evil;" "knowledge,"* as we have said, expressing a certain mixed disposition. It speaks of the fruit of the forbidden tree not as a thing absolutely evil (because it is decked with good), nor as a thing purely good (because evil is latent in it), but as compounded of both, and declares that the tasting of it brings to death those who touch it; almost proclaiming aloud the doctrine that the very actual good is in its nature simple and uniform, alien from all duplicity or conjunction with its opposite, while evil is many-coloured and fairly adorned, being esteemed to be one thing and revealed by experience as another, the knowledge of which (that is, its reception by experience) is the beginning and antecedent of death and destruction.

4. It was because he saw this that the serpent points out the evil fruit of sin, not showing the evil manifestly in its own nature (for man would not have been deceived by manifest evil), but giving to what the woman beheld the glamour of a certain beauty, and conjuring into its taste the spell of a sensual pleasure, he appeared to her to speak convincingly: *"and the woman saw,"* it says, *"that the tree was good for food, and that it was pleasant to the eyes to behold, and fair to see; and she took of the fruit thereof and did eat ,"* and that eating became the mother of death to men. This, then, is that fruit-bearing of mixed character, where the passage clearly expresses the sense in which the tree was called *"capable of the knowledge of good and evil,"* because, like the evil nature of poisons that are prepared with honey, it appears to be good in so far as it affects the senses with sweetness: but in so far as it destroys him who touches it, it is the worst of all evil. Thus when the evil poison worked its effect against man's life,

then man, that noble thing and name, the image of God's nature, was made, as the prophet says, *"like vanity."*

5. The image, therefore, properly belongs to the better part of our attributes; but all in our life that is painful and miserable is far removed from the likeness to the Divine.

XXI. *That the resurrection is looked for as a consequence, not so much from the declaration of Scripture as from the very necessity of things.*

1. Wickedness, however, is not so strong as to prevail over the power of good; nor is the folly of our nature more powerful and more abiding than the wisdom of God: for it is impossible that that which is always mutable and variable should be more firm and more abiding than that which always remains the same and is firmly fixed in goodness: but it is absolutely certain that the Divine counsel possesses immutability, while the changeableness of our nature does not remain settled even in evil.

2. Now that which is always in motion, if its progress be to good, will never cease moving onwards to what lies before it, by reason of the infinity of the course to be traversed:— for it will not find any limit of its object such that when it has apprehended it, it will at last cease its motion: but if its bias be in the opposite direction, when it has finished the course of wickedness and reached the extreme limit of evil, then that which is ever moving, finding no halting point for its impulse natural to itself when it has run through the lengths that can be run in wickedness, of necessity turns its motion towards good: for as evil does not extend to infinity, but is comprehended by necessary limits, it would appear that good once more follows in succession upon the limit of evil; and thus, as we have said, the ever-moving character of our nature comes to run its course at the last once more back towards good, being taught the lesson of prudence by the memory of its former misfortunes, to the end that it may never again be in like case.

3. Our course, then, will once more lie in what is good, by reason of the fact that the nature of evil is bounded by necessary limits. For just as those skilled in astronomy tell us that the whole universe is full of light, and that darkness is made to cast its shadow by the interposition of the body formed by the earth; and that this darkness is shut off from the rays of the sun, in the shape of a cone, according

to the figure of the sphere-shaped body, and behind it; while the sun, exceeding the earth by a size many times as great as its own, enfolding it round about on all sides with its rays, unites at the limit of the cone the concurrent streams of light; so that if (to suppose the case) any one had the power of passing beyond the measure to which the shadow extends, he would certainly find himself in light unbroken by darkness—even so I think that we ought to understand about ourselves, that on passing the limit of wickedness we shall again have our conversation in light, as the nature of good, when compared with the measure of wickedness, is incalculably superabundant.

4. Paradise therefore will be restored, that tree will be restored which is in truth the tree of life—there will be restored the grace of the image, and the dignity of rule. It does not seem to me that our hope is one for those things which are now subjected by God to man for the necessary uses of life, but one for another kingdom, of a description that belongs to unspeakable mysteries.

XXII. *To those who say, "If the resurrection is a thing excellent and good, how is it that it has not happened already, but is hoped for in some periods of time?"*

1. Let us give our attention, however, to the next point of our discussion. It may be that some one, giving his thought wings to soar towards the sweetness of our hope, deems it a burden and a loss that we are not more speedily placed in that good state which is above man's sense and knowledge, and is dissatisfied with the extension of the time that intervenes between him and the object of his desire. Let him cease to vex himself like a child that is discontented at the brief delay of something that gives him pleasure; for since all things are governed by reason and wisdom, we must by no means suppose that anything that happens is done without reason itself and the wisdom that is therein.

2. You will say then, What is this reason, in accordance with which the change of our painful life to that which we desire does not take place at once, but this heavy and corporeal existence of ours waits, extended to some determinate time, for the term of the consummation of all things, that then man's life may be set free as it were from the reins, and revert once more, released and free, to the life of blessedness and impassibility?

3. Well, whether our answer is near the truth of the matter, the Truth Itself may clearly know; but at all events what occurs to our intelligence is as follows. I take up then once more in my argument our first text:— God says, *"Let us make man in our image, after our likeness, and God created man, in the image of God created He him* Genesis 1:26-27 ."* Accordingly, the Image of God, which we behold in universal humanity, had its consummation then ; but Adam as yet was not; for the thing formed from the earth is called Adam, by etymological nomenclature, as those tell us who are acquainted with the Hebrew tongue— wherefore also the apostle, who was specially learned in his native tongue, the tongue of the Israelites, calls the man *"of the earth* 1 Corinthians 15:47 *"* χοϊκός, as though translating the name Adam into the Greek word.

4. Man, then, was made in the image of God; that is, the universal nature, the thing like God; not part of the whole, but all the fullness of the nature together was so made by omnipotent wisdom. He saw, Who holds all limits in His grasp, as the Scripture tells us which says, *"in His hand are all the corners of the earth ,"* He saw, *"Who knows all things"* even *"before they be ,"* comprehending them in His knowledge, how great in number humanity will be in the sum of its individuals. But as He perceived in our created nature the bias towards evil, and the fact that after its voluntary fall from equality with the angels it would acquire a fellowship with the lower nature, He mingled, for this reason, with His own image, an element of the irrational (for the distinction of male and female does not exist in the Divine and blessed nature);— transferring, I say, to man the special attribute of the irrational formation, He bestowed increase upon our race not according to the lofty character of our creation; for it was not when He made that which was in His own image that He bestowed on man the power of increasing and multiplying; but when He divided it by sexual distinctions, then He said, *"Increase and multiply, and replenish the earth* Genesis 1:28 ."* For this belongs not to the Divine, but to the irrational element, as the history indicates when it narrates that these words were first spoken by God in the case of the irrational creatures; since we may be sure that, if He had bestowed on man, before imprinting on our nature the distinction of male and female, the power for increase conveyed by this utterance, we should not have needed this form of generation by which the brutes are generated.

5. Now seeing that the full number of men pre-conceived by the operation of foreknowledge will come into life by means of this animal generation, God, Who governs all things in a certain order and sequence—since the inclination of our nature to what was beneath it (which He Who beholds the future equally with the present saw before it existed) made some such form of generation absolutely necessary for mankind—therefore also foreknew the time coextensive with the creation of men, so that the extent of time should be adapted for the entrances of the pre-determined souls, and that the flux and motion of time should halt at the moment when humanity is no longer produced by means of it; and that when the generation of men is completed, time should cease together with its completion, and then should take place the restitution of all things, and with the World-Reformation humanity also should be changed from the corruptible and earthly to the impassible and eternal.

6. And this it seems to me the Divine apostle considered when he declared in his epistle to the Corinthians the sudden stoppage of time, and the change of the things that are now moving on back to the opposite end where he says, *"Behold, I show you a mystery; we shall not all sleep, but we shall all be changed, in a moment, in the twinkling of an eye, at the last trump* 1 Corinthians 15:51-52 *."* For when, as I suppose, the full complement of human nature has reached the limit of the pre-determined measure, because there is no longer anything to be made up in the way of increase to the number of souls, he teaches us that the change in existing things will take place in an instant of time, giving to that limit of time which has no parts or extension the names of *"a moment,"* and *"the twinkling of an eye"*; so that it will no more be possible for one who reaches the verge of time (which is the last and extreme point, from the fact that nothing is lacking to the attainment of its extremity) to obtain by death this change which takes place at a fixed period, but only when the trumpet of the resurrection sounds, which awakens the dead, and transforms those who are left in life, after the likeness of those who have undergone the resurrection change, at once to incorruptibility; so that the weight of the flesh is no longer heavy, nor does its burden hold them down to earth, but they rise aloft through the air— for, *"we shall be caught up,"* he tells us, *"in the clouds to meet the Lord in the air; and so shall we ever be with the Lord* 1 Thessalonians 4:17 *."*

7. Let him therefore wait for that time which is necessarily made co-extensive with the development of humanity. For even Abraham and the patriarchs, while they had the desire to see the promised good things, and ceased not to seek the heavenly country, as the apostle says, are yet even now in the condition of hoping for that grace, *"God having provided some better thing for us,"* according to the words of Paul, *"that they without us should not be made perfect* Hebrews 11:40 *."* If they, then, bear the delay who by faith only and by hope saw the good things *"afar off"* and *"embraced them* Hebrews 11:13,*"* as the apostle bears witness, placing their certainty of the enjoyment of the things for which they hoped in the fact that they *"judged Him faithful Who has promised* Hebrews 11:11,*"* what ought most of us to do, who have not, it may be, a hold upon the better hope from the character of our lives? Even the prophet's soul fainted with desire, and in his psalm he confesses this passionate love, saying that his *"soul has a desire and longing to be in the courts of the Lord ,"* even if he must needs be rejected to a place among the lowest, as it is a greater and more desirable thing to be last there than to be first among the ungodly tents of this life; nevertheless he was patient of the delay, deeming, indeed, the life there blessed, and accounting a brief participation in it more desirable than *"thousands"* of time— for he says, *"one day in Your courts is better than thousands "*— yet he did not repine at the necessary dispensation concerning existing things, and thought it sufficient bliss for man to have those good things even by way of hope; wherefore he says at the end of the Psalm, *"O Lord of hosts, blessed is the man that hopes in You. "*

8. Neither, then, should we be troubled at the brief delay of what we hope for, but give diligence that we may not be cast out from the object of our hopes; for just as though, if one were to tell some inexperienced person beforehand, *"the gathering of the crops will take place in the season of summer, and the stores will be filled, and the table abundantly supplied with food at the time of plenty,"* it would be a foolish man who should seek to hurry on the coming of the fruit-time, when he ought to be sowing seeds and preparing the crops for himself by diligent care; for the fruit-time will surely come, whether he wishes or not, at the appointed time; and it will be looked on differently by him who has secured for himself beforehand abundance of crops, and by him who is found by the fruit-time destitute of all preparation. Even so I think it is one's duty, as the proclamation is

clearly made to all that the time of change will come, not to trouble himself about times (for He said that *"it is not for us to know the times and the seasons* Acts 1:7 "), nor to pursue calculations by which he will be sure to sap the hope of the resurrection in the soul; but to make his confidence in the things expected as a prop to lean on, and to purchase for himself, by good conversation, the grace that is to come.

XXIII. *That he who confesses the beginning of the world's existence must necessarily also agree as to its end.*

But if some one, beholding the present course of the world, by which intervals of time are marked, going on in a certain order, should say that it is not possible that the predicted stoppage of these moving things should take place, such a man clearly also does not believe that in the beginning the heaven and the earth were made by God; for he who admits a beginning of motion surely does not doubt as to its also having an end; and he who does not allow its end, does not admit its beginning either; but as it is by believing that *"we understand that the worlds were framed by the word of God,"* as the apostle says, *"so that things which are seen were not made of things which do appear,"* we must use the same faith as to the word of God when He foretells the necessary stoppage of existing things.

2. The question of the *"how"* must, however, be put beyond the reach of our meddling; for even in the case mentioned it was *"by faith"* that we admitted that the thing seen was framed from things not yet apparent, omitting the search into things beyond our reach. And yet our reason suggests difficulties on many points, offering no small occasions for doubt as to the things which we believe.

3. For in that case too, argumentative men might by plausible reasoning upset our faith, so that we should not think that statement true which Holy Scripture delivers concerning the material creation, when it asserts that all existing things have their beginning of being from God. For those who abide by the contrary view maintain that matter is co-eternal with God, and employ in support of their own doctrine some such arguments as these. If God is in His nature simple and immaterial, without quantity, or size, or combination, and removed from the idea of circumscription by way of figure, while all matter is apprehended in extension measured by intervals, and does not escape the apprehension of our senses, but becomes known to us in colour, and figure, and bulk, and size, and resistance, and the

other attributes belonging to it, none of which it is possible to conceive in the Divine nature,— what method is there for the production of matter from the immaterial, or of the nature that has dimensions from that which is unextended? For if these things are believed to have their existence from that source, they clearly come into existence after being in Him in some mysterious way; but if material existence was in Him, how can He be immaterial while including matter in Himself? And similarly with all the other marks by which the material nature is differentiated; if quantity exists in God, how is God without quantity? If the compound nature exists in Him, how is He simple, without parts and without combination? So that the argument forces us to think either that He is material, because matter has its existence from Him as a source; or, if one avoids this, it is necessary to suppose that matter was imported by Him *ab extra* for the making of the universe.

4. If, then, it was external to God, something else surely existed besides God, conceived, in respect of eternity, together with Him Who exists ungenerately; so that the argument supposes two eternal and unbegotten existences, having their being concurrently with each other— that of Him Who operates as an artificer, and that of the thing which admits this skilled operation; and if any one under pressure of this argument should assume a material substratum for the Creator of all things, what a support will the Manichæan find for his special doctrine, who opposes by virtue of ungenerateness a material existence to a Good Being. Yet we do believe that all things are of God, as we hear the Scripture say so; and as to the question how they were in God, a question beyond our reason, we do not seek to pry into it, believing that all things are within the capacity of God's power— both to give existence to what is not, and to implant qualities at His pleasure in what is.

5. Consequently, as we suppose the power of the Divine will to be a sufficient cause to the things that are, for their coming into existence out of nothing, so too we shall not repose our belief on anything beyond probability in referring the World-Reformation to the same power. Moreover, it might perhaps be possible, by some skill in the use of words, to persuade those who raise frivolous objections on the subject of matter not to think that they can make an unanswerable attack on our statement.

XXIV. *An argument against those who say that matter is co-eternal with God.*

1. For after all that opinion on the subject of matter does not turn out to be beyond what appears consistent, which declares that it has its existence from Him Who is intelligible and immaterial. For we shall find all matter to be composed of certain qualities, of which if it is divested it can, in itself, be by no means grasped by idea. Moreover in idea each kind of quality is separated from the substratum; but idea is an intellectual and not a corporeal method of examination. If, for instance, some animal or tree is presented to our notice, or any other of the things that have material existence, we perceive in our mental discussion of it many things concerning the substratum, the idea of each of which is clearly distinguished from the object we contemplate: for the idea of colour is one, of weight another; so again that of quantity and of such and such a peculiar quality of touch: for *"softness,"* and *"two cubits long,"* and the rest of the attributes we spoke of, are not connected in idea either with one another or with the body: each of them has conceived concerning it its own explanatory definition according to its being, having nothing in common with any other of the qualities that are contemplated in the substratum.

2. If, then, colour is a thing intelligible, and resistance also is intelligible, and so with quantity and the rest of the like properties, while if each of these should be withdrawn from the substratum, the whole idea of the body is dissolved; it would seem to follow that we may suppose the concurrence of those things, the absence of which we found to be a cause of the dissolution of the body, to produce the material nature: for as that is not a body which has not colour, and figure, and resistance, and extension, and weight, and the other properties, while each of these in its proper existence is found to be not the body but something else besides the body, so, conversely, whenever the specified attributes concur they produce bodily existence. Yet if the perception of these properties is a matter of intellect, and the Divinity is also intellectual in nature, there is no incongruity in supposing that these intellectual occasions for the genesis of bodies have their existence from the incorporeal nature, the intellectual nature on the one hand giving being to the intellectual potentialities, and the mutual concurrence of these bringing to its genesis the material nature.

3. Let this discussion, however, be by way of digression: we must direct our discourse once more to the faith by which we accept the statement that the universe took being from nothing, and do not doubt, when we are taught by Scripture, that it will again be transformed into some other state.

XXV. *How one even of those who are without may be brought to believethe Scripture when teaching of the resurrection.*

1. Some one, perhaps, having regard to the dissolution of bodies, and judging the Deity by the measure of his own power, asserts that the idea of the resurrection is impossible, saying that it cannot be that both those things which are now in motion should become stationary, and those things which are now without motion should rise again.

2. Let such an one, however, take as the first and greatest evidence of the truth touching the resurrection the credibility of the herald who proclaims it. Now the faith of what is said derives its certainty from the result of the other predictions: for as the Divine Scripture delivers statements many and various, it is possible by examining how the rest of the utterances stand in the matter of falsehood and truth to survey also, in the light of them, the doctrine concerning the resurrection. For if in the other matters the statements are found to be false and to have failed of true fulfilment, neither is this out of the region of falsehood; but if all the others have experience to vouch for their truth, it would seem logical to esteem as true, on their account, the prediction concerning the resurrection also. Let us therefore recall one or two of the predictions that have been made, and compare the result with what was foretold, so that we may know by means of them whether the idea has a truthful aspect.

3. Who knows not how the people of Israel flourished of old, raised up against all the powers of the world; what were the palaces in the city of Jerusalem, what the walls, the towers, the majestic structure of the Temple? Things that seemed worthy of admiration even to the disciples of the Lord, so that they asked the Lord to take notice of them, in their disposition to marvel, as the Gospel history shows us, saying, *"What works, and what buildings!"* But He indicates to those who wondered at its present state the future desolation of the place and the disappearance of that beauty, saying that after a little while nothing of what they saw should be left. And, again, at the time of

His Passion, the women followed, bewailing the unjust sentence against Him—for they could not yet see into the dispensation of what was being done:— but He bids them be silent as to what is befalling Him, for it does not demand their tears, but to reserve their wailing and lamentation for the true time for tears, when the city should be compassed by besiegers, and their sufferings reach so great a strait that they should deem him happy who had not been born: and herein He foretold also the horrid deed of her who devoured her child, when He said that in those days the womb should be accounted blest that never bare. Luke 23:27-29 Where then are those palaces? Where is the Temple? Where are the walls? Where are the defences of the towers? Where is the power of the Israelites? Were not they scattered in different quarters over almost the whole world? And in their overthrow the palaces also were brought to ruin.

4. Now it seems to me that the Lord foretold these things and others like them not for the sake of the matters themselves— for what great advantage to the hearers, at any rate, was the prediction of what was about to happen? They would have known by experience, even if they had not previously learned what would come—but in order that by these means faith on their part might follow concerning more important matters: for the testimony of facts in the former cases is also a proof of truth in the latter.

5. For just as though, if a husbandman were explaining the virtue of seeds, it were to happen that some person inexperienced in husbandry should disbelieve him, it would be sufficient as proof of his statement for the agriculturist to show him the virtue existing in one seed of those in the bushel and make it a pledge of the rest— for he who should see the single grain of wheat or barley, or whatever might chance to be the contents of the bushel, grow into an ear after being cast into the ground, would by the means of the one cease also to disbelieve concerning the others— so the truthfulness which confessedly belongs to the other statements seems to me to be sufficient also for evidence of the mystery of the resurrection.

6. Still more, however, is this the case with the experience of actual resurrection which we have learned not so much by words as by actual facts: for as the marvel of resurrection was great and passing belief, He begins gradually by inferior instances of His miraculous power, and accustoms our faith, as it were, for the reception of the greater.

7. For as a mother who nurses her babe with due care for a time supplies milk by her breast to its mouth while still tender and soft; and when it begins to grow and to have teeth she gives it bread, not hard or such as it cannot chew, so that the tender and unpractised gums may not be chafed by rough food; but softening it with her own teeth, she makes it suitable and convenient for the powers of the eater; and then as its power increases by growth she gradually leads on the babe, accustomed to tender food, to more solid nourishment; so the Lord, nourishing and fostering with miracles the weakness of the human mind, like some babe not fully grown, makes first of all a prelude of the power of the resurrection in the case of a desperate disease, which prelude, though it was great in its achievement, yet was not such a thing that the statement of it would be disbelieved: for by *"rebuking the fever"* which was fiercely consuming Simon's wife's mother, He produced so great a removal of the evil as to enable her who was already expected to be near death, to *"minister"* to those present.

8. Next He makes a slight addition to the power, and when the nobleman's son lies in acknowledged danger of death (for so the history tells us, that he was about to die, as his father cried, *"come down, ere my child die"*), He again brings about the resurrection of one who was believed about to die; accomplishing the miracle with a greater act of power in that He did not even approach the place, but sent life from afar off by the force of His command.

9. Once more in what follows He ascends to higher wonders. For having set out on His way to the ruler of the synagogue's daughter, he voluntarily made a halt in His way, while making public the secret cure of the woman with an issue of blood, that in this time death might overcome the sick. When, then, the soul had just been parted from the body, and those who were wailing over the sorrow were making a tumult with their mournful cries, He raises the damsel to life again, as if from sleep, by His word of command, leading on human weakness, by a sort of path and sequence, to greater things.

10. Still in addition to these acts He exceeds them in wonder, and by a more exalted act of power prepares for men the way of faith in the resurrection. The Scripture tells us of a city called Nain in Judæa: a widow there had an only child, no longer a child in the sense of being among boys, but already passing from childhood to man's estate: the narrative calls him *"a young man."* The story conveys much in few

words: the very recital is a real lamentation: the dead man's mother, it says, *"was a widow."* See you the weight of her misfortune, how the text briefly sets out the tragedy of her suffering? For what does the phrase mean? That she had no more hope of bearing sons, to cure the loss she had just sustained in him who had departed; for the woman was a widow: she had not in her power to look to another instead of to him who had gone; for he was her only child; and how great a grief is here expressed any one may easily see who is not an utter stranger to natural feeling. Him alone she had known in travail, him alone she had nursed at her breast; he alone made her table cheerful, he alone was the cause of brightness in her home, in play, in work, in learning, in gaiety, at processions, at sports, at gatherings of youth; he alone was all that is sweet and precious in a mother's eyes. Now at the age of marriage, he was the stock of her race, the shoot of its succession, the staff of her old age. Moreover, even the additional detail of his time of life is another lament: for he who speaks of him as *"a young man"* tells of the flower of his faded beauty, speaks of him as just covering his face with down, not yet with a full thick beard, but still bright with the beauty of his cheeks. What then, think you, were his mother's sorrows for him? How would her heart be consumed as it were with a flame; how bitterly would she prolong her lament over him, embracing the corpse as it lay before her, lengthening out her mourning for him as far as possible, so as not to hasten the funeral of the dead, but to have her fill of sorrow! Nor does the narrative pass this by: for Jesus *"when He saw her,"* it says, *"had compassion"*; *"and He came and touched the bier; and they that bare him stood still;"* and He said to the dead, *"Young man, I say unto you, arise* Luke 7:13-15,*" "and He delivered him to his mother"* alive. Observe that no short time had intervened since the dead man had entered upon that state, he was all but laid in the tomb; the miracle wrought by the Lord is greater, though the command is the same.

11. His miraculous power proceeds to a still more exalted act, that its display may more closely approach that miracle of the resurrection which men doubt. One of the Lord's companions and friends is ill (Lazarus is the sick man's name); and the Lord deprecates any visiting of His friend, though far away from the sick man, that in the absence of the Life, death might find room and power to do his own work by the agency of disease. The Lord informs His disciples in Galilee of what has befallen Lazarus, and also of his own setting out to him to

raise him up when laid low. They, however, were exceedingly afraid on account of the fury of the Jews, thinking it a difficult and dangerous matter to turn again towards Judæa, in the midst of those who sought to slay Him: and thus, lingering and delaying, they return slowly from Galilee: but they do return, for His command prevailed, and the disciples were led by the Lord to be initiated at Bethany in the preliminary mysteries of the general resurrection. Four days had already passed since the event; all due rites had been performed for the departed; the body was hidden in the tomb: it was probably already swollen and beginning to dissolve into corruption, as the body mouldered in the dank earth and necessarily decayed: the thing was one to turn from, as the dissolved body under the constraint of nature changed to offensiveness. At this point the doubted fact of the general resurrection is brought to proof by a more manifest miracle; for one is not raised from severe sickness, nor brought back to life when at the last breath— nor is a child just dead brought to life, nor a young man about to be conveyed to the tomb released from his bier; but a man past the prime of life, a corpse, decaying, swollen, yea already in a state of dissolution, so that even his own kinsfolk could not suffer that the Lord should draw near the tomb by reason of the offensiveness of the decayed body there enclosed, brought into life by a single call, confirms the proclamation of the resurrection, that is to say, that expectation of it as universal, which we learn by a particular experience to entertain. For as in the regeneration of the universe the Apostle tells us that *"the Lord Himself will descend with a shout, with the voice of the archangel 1 Thessalonians 4:16,"* and by a trumpet sound raise up the dead to incorruption— so now too he who is in the tomb, at the voice of command, shakes off death as if it were a sleep, and ridding himself from the corruption that had come upon his condition of a corpse, leaps forth from the tomb whole and sound, not even hindered in his egress by the bonds of the grave-cloths round his feet and hands.

12. Are these things too small to produce faith in the resurrection of the dead? Or do you seek that your judgment on this point should be confirmed by yet other proofs? In truth the Lord seems to me not to have spoken in vain to them of Capernaum, when He said to Himself, as in the person of men, *"You will surely say unto me this proverb, 'Physician, heal yourself.'"* For it behooved Him, when He had accustomed men to the miracle of the resurrection in other

bodies, to confirm His word in His own humanity. You saw the thing proclaimed working in others— those who were about to die, the child which had just ceased to live, the young man at the edge of the grave, the putrefying corpse, all alike restored by one command to life. Do you seek for those who have come to death by wounds and bloodshed? Does any feebleness of life-giving power hinder the grace in them? Behold Him Whose hands were pierced with nails: behold Him Whose side was transfixed with a spear; pass your fingers through the print of the nails; thrust your hand into the spear-wound ; you can surely guess how far within it is likely the point would reach, if you reckon the passage inwards by the breadth of the external scar; for the wound that gives admission to a man's hand, shows to what depth within the iron entered. If He then has been raised, well may we utter the Apostle's exclamation, *"How say some that there is no resurrection of the dead* 1 Corinthians 15:12?"

13. Since, then, every prediction of the Lord is shown to be true by the testimony of events, while we not only have learned this by His words, but also received the proof of the promise in deed, from those very persons who returned to life by resurrection, what occasion is left to those who disbelieve? Shall we not bid farewell to those who pervert our simple faith by *"philosophy and vain deceit* Colossians 2:8,"and hold fast to our confession in its purity, learning briefly through the prophet the mode of the grace, by his words, *"You shall take away their breath and they shall fail, and turn to their dust. You shall send forth Your Spirit and they shall be created, and You shall renew the face of the earth ;"* at which time also he says that the Lord rejoices in His works, sinners having perished from the earth: for how shall any one be called by the name of sin, when sin itself exists no longer?

XXVI. *That the resurrection is not beyond probability.*

1. There are, however, some who, owing to the feebleness of human reasoning, judging the Divine power by the compass of our own, maintain that what is beyond our capacity is not possible even to God. They point to the disappearance of the dead of old time, and to the remains of those who have been reduced to ashes by fire; and further, besides these, they bring forward in idea the carnivorous beasts, and the fish that receives in its own body the flesh of the shipwrecked sailor, while this again in turn becomes food for men, and passes by digestion into the bulk of him who eats it: and they

rehearse many such trivialities, unworthy of God's great power and authority, for the overthrow of the doctrine, arguing as though God were not able to restore to man his own, by return through the same ways.

2. But we briefly cut short their long circuits of logical folly by acknowledging that dissolution of the body into its component parts does take place, and not only does earth, according to the Divine word, return to earth, but air and moisture also revert to the kindred element, and there takes place a return of each of our components to that nature to which it is allied; and although the human body be dispersed among carnivorous birds, or among the most savage beasts by becoming their food, and although it pass beneath the teeth of fish, and although it be changed by fire into vapour and dust, wheresoever one may in argument suppose the man to be removed, he surely remains in the world; and the world, the voice of inspiration tells us, is held by the hand of God. If you, then, are not ignorant of any of the things in your hand, do you deem the knowledge of God to be feebler than your own power, that it should fail to discover the most minute of the things that are within the compass of the Divine span?

XXVII. *That it is possible, when the human body is dissolved into the elements of the universe, that each should have his own body restored from the common source.*

1. Yet it may be you think, having regard to the elements of the universe, that it is a hard thing when the air in us has been resolved into its kindred element, and the warmth, and moisture, and the earthy nature have likewise been mingled with their own kind, that from the common source there should return to the individual what belongs to itself.

2. Do you not then judge by human examples that even this does not surpass the limits of the Divine power? You have seen surely somewhere among the habitations of men a common herd of some kind of animals collected from every quarter: yet when it is again divided among its owners, acquaintance with their homes and the marks put upon the cattle serve to restore to each his own. If you conceive of yourself also something like to this, you will not be far from the right way: for as the soul is disposed to cling to and long for the body that has been wedded to it, there also attaches to it in secret

a certain close relationship and power of recognition, in virtue of their commixture, as though some marks had been imprinted by nature, by the aid of which the community remains unconfused, separated by the distinctive signs. Now as the soul attracts again to itself that which is its own and properly belongs to it, what labour, I pray you, that is involved for the Divine power, could be a hindrance to concourse of kindred things when they are urged to their own place by the unspeakable attraction of nature, whatever it may be? For that some signs of our compound nature remain in the soul even after dissolution is shown by the dialogue in Hades Luke 16:24-31, where the bodies had been conveyed to the tomb, but some bodily token still remained in the souls by which both Lazarus was recognized and the rich man was not unknown.

3. There is therefore nothing beyond probability in believing that in the bodies that rise again there will be a return from the common stock to the individual, especially for any one who examines our nature with careful attention. For neither does our being consist altogether in flux and change— for surely that which had by nature no stability would be absolutely incomprehensible— but according to the more accurate statement some one of our constituent parts is stationary while the rest goes through a process of alteration: for the body is on the one hand altered by way of growth and diminution, changing, like garments, the vesture of its successive statures, while the form, on the other hand, remains in itself unaltered through every change, not varying from the marks once imposed upon it by nature, but appearing with its own tokens of identity in all the changes which the body undergoes.

4. We must except, however, from this statement the change which happens to the form as the result of disease: for the deformity of sickness takes possession of the form like some strange mask, and when this is removed by the word , as in the case of Naaman the Syrian, or of those whose story is recorded in the Gospel, the form that had been hidden by disease is once more by means of health restored to sight again with its own marks of identity.

5. Now to the element of our soul which is in the likeness of God it is not that which is subject to flux and change by way of alteration, but this stable and unalterable element in our composition that is allied: and since various differences of combination produce varieties of forms (and combination is nothing else than the mixture of the

elements— by elements we mean those which furnish the substratum for the making of the universe, of which the human body also is composed), while the form necessarily remains in the soul as in the impression of a seal, those things which have received from the seal the impression of its stamp do not fail to be recognized by the soul, but at the time of the World-Reformation, it receives back to itself all those things which correspond to the stamp of the form: and surely all those things would so correspond which in the beginning were stamped by the form; thus it is not beyond probability that what properly belongs to the individual should once more return to it from the common source.

6. It is said also that quicksilver, if poured out from the vessel that contains it down a dusty slope, forms small globules and scatters itself over the ground, mingling with none of those bodies with which it meets: but if one should collect at one place the substance dispersed in many directions, it flows back to its kindred substance, if not hindered by anything intervening from mixing with its own kind. Something of the same sort, I think, we ought to understand also of the composite nature of man, that if only the power were given it of God, the proper parts would spontaneously unite with those belonging to them, without any obstruction on their account arising to Him Who reforms their nature.

7. Furthermore, in the case of plants that grow from the ground, we do not observe any labour on the part of nature spent on the wheat or millet or any other seed of grain or pulse, in changing it into stalk or spike or ears; for the proper nourishment passes spontaneously, without trouble, from the common source to the individuality of each of the seeds. If, then, while the moisture supplied to all the plants is common, each of those plants which is nourished by it draws the due supply for its own growth, what new thing is it if in the doctrine of the resurrection also, as in the case of the seeds, it happens that there is an attraction on the part of each of those who rise, of what belongs to himself?

8. So that we may learn on all hands, that the preaching of the resurrection contains nothing beyond those facts which are known to us experimentally.

9. And yet we have said nothing of the most notable point concerning ourselves; I mean the first beginning of our existence.

Who knows not the miracle of nature, what the maternal womb receives— what it produces? You see how that which is implanted in the womb to be the beginning of the formation of the body is in a manner simple and homogeneous: but what language can express the variety of the composite body that is framed? And who, if he did not learn such a thing in nature generally, would think that to be possible which does take place— that that small thing of no account is the beginning of a thing so great? Great, I say, not only with regard to the bodily formation, but to what is more marvellous than this, I mean the soul itself, and the attributes we behold in it.

XXVIII. *To those who say that souls existed before bodies, or that bodies were formed before souls; wherein there is also a refutation of the fables concerning transmigration of souls.*

1. For it is perhaps not beyond our present subject to discuss the question which has been raised in the churches touching soul and body. Some of those before our time who have dealt with the question of *"principles"* think it right to say that souls have a previous existence as a people in a society of their own, and that among them also there are standards of vice and of virtue, and that the soul there, which abides in goodness, remains without experience of conjunction with the body; but if it does depart from its communion with good, it falls down to this lower life, and so comes to be in a body. Others, on the contrary, marking the order of the making of man as stated by Moses, say, that the soul is second to the body in order of time, since God first took dust from the earth and formed man, and then animated the being thus formed by His breath : and by this argument they prove that the flesh is more noble than the soul; that which was previously formed than that which was afterwards infused into it: for they say that the soul was made for the body, that the thing formed might not be without breath and motion; and that everything that is made for something else is surely less precious than that for which it is made, as the Gospel tells us that *"the soul is more than meat and the body than raiment ,"* because the latter things exist for the sake of the former— for the soul was not made for meat nor our bodies for raiment, but when the former things were already in being the latter were provided for their needs.

2. Since then the doctrine involved in both these theories is open to criticism— the doctrine alike of those who ascribe to souls a fabulous pre-existence in a special state, and of those who think they were

created at a later time than the bodies, it is perhaps necessary to leave none of the statements contained in the doctrines without examination: yet to engage and wrestle with the doctrines on each side completely, and to reveal all the absurdities involved in the theories, would need a large expenditure both of argument and of time; we shall, however, briefly survey as best we can each of the views mentioned, and then resume our subject.

3. Those who stand by the former doctrine, and assert that the state of souls is prior to their life in the flesh, do not seem to me to be clear from the fabulous doctrines of the heathen which they hold on the subject of successive incorporation: for if one should search carefully, he will find that their doctrine is of necessity brought down to this. They tell us that one of their sages said that he, being one and the same person, was born a man, and afterwards assumed the form of a woman, and flew about with the birds, and grew as a bush, and obtained the life of an aquatic creature—and he who said these things of himself did not, so far as I can judge, go far from the truth: for such doctrines as this of saying that one soul passed through so many changes are really fitting for the chatter of frogs or jackdaws, or the stupidity of fishes, or the insensibility of trees.

4. And of such absurdity the cause is this— the supposition of the pre-existence of souls for the first principle of such doctrine leads on the argument by consequence to the next and adjacent stage, until it astonishes us by reaching this point. For if the soul, being severed from the more exalted state by some wickedness after having once, as they say, tasted corporeal life, again becomes a man, and if the life in the flesh is, as may be presumed, acknowledged to be, in comparison with the eternal and incorporeal life, more subject to passion, it naturally follows that that which comes to be in a life such as to contain more occasions of sin, is both placed in a region of greater wickedness and rendered more subject to passion than before (now passion in the human soul is a conformity to the likeness of the irrational); and that being brought into close connection with this, it descends to the brute nature: and that when it has once set out on its way through wickedness, it does not cease its advance towards evil even when found in an irrational condition: for a halt in evil is the beginning of the impulse towards virtue, and in irrational creatures virtue does not exist. Thus it will of necessity be continually changed for the worse, always proceeding to what is more degraded and always

finding out what is worse than the nature in which it is: and just as the sensible nature is lower than the rational, so too there is a descent from this to the insensible.

5. Now so far in its course their doctrine, even if it does overstep the bounds of truth, at all events derives one absurdity from another by a kind of logical sequence: but from this point onwards their teaching takes the form of incoherent fable. Strict inference points to the complete destruction of the soul; for that which has once fallen from the exalted state will be unable to halt at any measure of wickedness, but will pass by means of its relation with the passions from rational to irrational, and from the latter state will be transferred to the insensibility of plants; and on the insensible there borders, so to say, the inanimate; and on this again follows the non-existent, so that absolutely by this train of reasoning they will have the soul to pass into nothing: thus a return once more to the better state is impossible for it: and yet they make the soul return from a bush to the man: they therefore prove that the life in a bush is more precious than an incorporeal state.

6. It has been shown that the process of deterioration which takes place in the soul will probably be extended downwards; and lower than the insensible we find the inanimate, to which, by consequence, the principle of their doctrine brings the soul: but as they will not have this, they either exclude the soul from insensibility, or, if they are to bring it back to human life, they must, as has been said, declare the life of a tree to be preferable to the original state— if, that is, the fall towards vice took place from the one, and the return towards virtue takes place from the other.

7. Thus this doctrine of theirs, which maintains that souls have a life by themselves before their life in the flesh, and that they are by reason of wickedness bound to their bodies, is shown to have neither beginning nor conclusion: and as for those who assert that the soul is of later creation than the body, their absurdity was already demonstrated above.

8. The doctrine of both, then, is equally to be rejected; but I think that we ought to direct our own doctrine in the way of truth between these theories: and this doctrine is that we are not to suppose, according to the error of the heathen that the souls that revolve with the motion of the universe weighed down by some wickedness, fall to

earth by inability to keep up with the swiftness of the motion of the spheres.

XXIX. *An establishment of the doctrine that the cause of the existence of soul and body is one and the same.*

1. Nor again are we in our doctrine to begin by making up man like a clay figure, and to say that the soul came into being for the sake of this; for surely in that case the intellectual nature would be shown to be less precious than the clay figure. But as man is one, the being consisting of soul and body, we are to suppose that the beginning of his existence is one, common to both parts, so that he should not be found to be antecedent and posterior to himself, if the bodily element were first in point of time, and the other were a later addition; but we are to say that in the power of God's foreknowledge (according to the doctrine laid down a little earlier in our discourse), all the fullness of human nature had pre-existence (and to this the prophetic writing bears witness, which says that God *"knows all things before they be "*), and in the creation of individuals not to place the one element before the other, neither the soul before the body, nor the contrary, that man may not be at strife against himself, by being divided by the difference in point of time.

2. For as our nature is conceived as twofold, according to the apostolic teaching, made up of the visible man and the hidden man, if the one came first and the other supervened, the power of Him that made us will be shown to be in some way imperfect, as not being completely sufficient for the whole task at once, but dividing the work, and busying itself with each of the halves in turn.

3. But just as we say that in wheat, or in any other grain, the whole form of the plant is potentially included— the leaves, the stalk, the joints, the grain, the beard— and do not say in our account of its nature that any of these things has pre-existence, or comes into being before the others, but that the power abiding in the seed is manifested in a certain natural order, not by any means that another nature is infused into it— in the same way we suppose the human germ to possess the potentiality of its nature, sown with it at the first start of its existence, and that it is unfolded and manifested by a natural sequence as it proceeds to its perfect state, not employing anything external to itself as a stepping-stone to perfection, but itself advancing its own self in due course to the perfect state; so that it is not true to

say either that the soul exists before the body, or that the body exists without the soul, but that there is one beginning of both, which according to the heavenly view was laid as their foundation in the original will of God; according to the other, came into existence on the occasion of generation.

4. For as we cannot discern the articulation of the limbs in that which is implanted for the conception of the body before it begins to take form, so neither is it possible to perceive in the same the properties of the soul before they advance to operation; and just as no one would doubt that the thing so implanted is fashioned into the different varieties of limbs and interior organs, not by the importation of any other power from without, but by the power which resides in it transforming it to this manifestation of energy—so also we may by like reasoning equally suppose in the case of the soul that even if it is not visibly recognized by any manifestations of activity it none the less is there; for even the form of the future man is there potentially, but is concealed because it is not possible that it should be made visible before the necessary sequence of events allows it; so also the soul is there, even though it is not visible, and will be manifested by means of its own proper and natural operation, as it advances concurrently with the bodily growth.

5. For since it is not from a dead body that the potentiality for conception is secreted, but from one which is animate and alive, we hence affirm that it is reasonable that we should not suppose that what is sent forth from a living body to be the occasion of life is itself dead and inanimate; for in the flesh that which is inanimate is surely dead; and the condition of death arises by the withdrawal of the soul. Would not one therefore in this case be asserting that withdrawal is antecedent to possession— if, that is, he should maintain that the inanimate state which is the condition of death is antecedent to the soul ? And if any one should seek for a still clearer evidence of the life of that particle which becomes the beginning of the living creature in its formation, it is possible to obtain an idea on this point from other signs also, by which what is animate is distinguished from what is dead. For in the case of men we consider it an evidence of life that one is warm and operative and in motion, but the chill and motionless state in the case of bodies is nothing else than deadness.

6. Since then we see that of which we are speaking to be warm and operative, we thereby draw the further inference that it is not

inanimate; but as, in respect of its corporeal part, we do not say that it is flesh, and bones, and hair, and all that we observe in the human being, but that potentially it is each of these things, yet does not visibly appear to be so; so also of the part which belongs to the soul, the elements of rationality, and desire, and anger, and all the powers of the soul are not yet visible; yet we assert that they have their place in it, and that the energies of the soul also grow with the subject in a manner similar to the formation and perfection of the body.

7. For just as a man when perfectly developed has a specially marked activity of the soul, so at the beginning of his existence he shows in himself that co-operation of the soul which is suitable and conformable to his existing need, in its preparing for itself its proper dwelling-place by means of the implanted matter; for we do not suppose it possible that the soul is adapted to a strange building, just as it is not possible that the seal impressed on wax should be fitted to an engraving that does not agree with it.

8. For as the body proceeds from a very small original to the perfect state, so also the operation of the soul, growing in correspondence with the subject, gains and increases with it. For at its first formation there comes first of all its power of growth and nutriment alone, as though it were some root buried in the ground; for the limited nature of the recipient does not admit of more; then, as the plant comes forth to the light and shows its shoot to the sun, the gift of sensibility blossoms in addition, but when at last it is ripened and has grown up to its proper height, the power of reason begins to shine forth like a fruit, not appearing in its whole vigour all at once, but by care increasing with the perfection of the instrument, bearing always as much fruit as the powers of the subject allow.

9. If, however, you seek to trace the operation of the soul in the formation of the body, *"take heed to yourself* Deuteronomy 4:23,*"* as Moses says, and you will read, as in a book, the history of the works of the soul; for nature itself expounds to you, more clearly than any discourse, the varied occupations of the soul in the body, alike in general and in particular acts of construction.

10. But I deem it superfluous to declare at length in words what is to be found in ourselves, as though we were expounding some wonder that lay beyond our boundaries:— who that looks on himself needs words to teach him his own nature? For it is possible for one who

considers the mode of his own life, and learns how closely concerned the body is in every vital operation, to know in what the vegetative principle of the soul was occupied on the occasion of the first formation of that which was beginning its existence; so that hereby also it is clear to those who have given any attention to the matter, that the thing which was implanted by separation from the living body for the production of the living being was not a thing dead or inanimate in the laboratory of nature.

11. Moreover we plant in the ground the kernels of fruits, and portions torn from roots, not deprived by death of the vital power which naturally resides in them, but preserving in themselves, hidden indeed, yet surely living, the property of their prototype; the earth that surrounds them does not implant such a power from without, infusing it from itself (for surely then even dead wood would proceed to growth), but it makes that manifest which resides in them, nourishing it by its own moisture, perfecting the plant into root, and bark, and pith, and shoots of branches, which could not happen were not a natural power implanted with it, which drawing to itself from its surroundings its kindred and proper nourishment, becomes a bush, or a tree, or an ear of grain, or some plant of the class of shrubs.

XXX. *A brief examination of the construction of our bodies from a medical point of view.*

1. Now the exact structure of our body each man teaches himself by his experiences of sight and light and perception, having his own nature to instruct him; any one too may learn everything accurately who takes up the researches which those skilled in such matters have worked out in books. And of these writers some learned by dissection the position of our individual organs; others also considered and expounded the reason for the existence of all the parts of the body; so that the knowledge of the human frame which hence results is sufficient for students. But if any one further seeks that the Church should be his teacher on all these points, so that he may not need for anything the voice of those without (for this is the wont of the spiritual sheep, as the Lord says, that they hear not a strange voice), we shall briefly take in hand the account of these matters also.

2. We note concerning our bodily nature three things, for the sake of which our particular parts were formed. Life is the cause of some, good life of others, others again are adapted with a view to the

succession of descendants. All things in us which are of such a kind that without them it is not possible that human life should exist, we consider as being in three parts; in the brain, the heart, and the liver. Again, all that are a sort of additional blessings, nature's liberality, whereby she bestows on man the gift of living well, are the organs of sense; for such things do not constitute our life, since even where some of them are wanting man is often none the less in a condition of life; but without these forms of activity it is impossible to enjoy participation in the pleasures of life. The third aim regards the future, and the succession of life. There are also certain other organs besides these, which help, in common with all the others, to subserve the continuance of life, importing by their own means the proper supplies, as the stomach and the lungs, the latter fanning by respiration the fire at the heart, the former introducing the nourishment for the internal organs.

3. Our structure, then, being thus divided, we have carefully to mark that our faculty for life is not supported in any one way by some single organ, but nature, while distributing the means for our existence among several parts, makes the contribution of each individual necessary for the whole; just as the things which nature contrives for the security and beauty of life are also numerous, and differ much among themselves.

4. We ought, however, I think, first to discuss briefly the first beginnings of the things which contribute to the constitution of our life. As for the material of the whole body which serves as a common substratum for the particular members, it may for the present be left without remark; for a discussion as to natural substance in general will not be of any assistance to our purpose with regard to the consideration of the parts.

5. As it is then acknowledged by all that there is in us a share of all that we behold as elements in the universe— of heat and cold, and of the other pair of qualities of moisture and dryness— we must discuss them severally.

6. We see then that the powers which control life are three, of which the first by its heat produces general warmth, the second by its moisture keeps damp that which is warmed, so that the living being is kept in an intermediate condition by the equal balance of the forces exerted by the quality of each of the opposing natures (the moist

element not being dried up by excess of heat, nor the hot element quenched by the prevalence of moisture); and the third power by its own agency holds together the separate members in a certain agreement and harmony, connecting them by the ties which it itself furnishes, and sending into them all that self-moving and determining force, on the failure of which the member becomes relaxed and deadened, being left destitute of the determining spirit.

7. Or rather, before dealing with these, it is right that we should mark the skilled workmanship of nature in the actual construction of the body. For as that which is hard and resistent does not admit the action of the senses (as we may see in the instance of our own bones, and in that of plants in the ground, where we remark indeed a certain form of life in that they grow and receive nourishment, yet the resistent character of their substance does not allow them sensation), for this reason it was necessary that some wax-like formation, so to say, should be supplied for the action of the senses, with the faculty of being impressed with the stamp of things capable of striking them, neither becoming confused by excess of moisture (for the impress would not remain in moist substance), nor resisting by extraordinary solidity (for that which is unyielding would not receive any mark from the impressions), but being in a state between softness and hardness, in order that the living being might not be destitute of the fairest of all the operations of nature— I mean the motion of sense.

8. Now as a soft and yielding substance, if it had no assistance from the hard parts, would certainly have, like molluscs, neither motion nor articulation, nature accordingly mingles in the body the hardness of the bones, and uniting these by close connection one to another, and knitting their joints together by means of the sinews, thus plants around them the flesh which receives sensations, furnished with a somewhat harder and more highly-strung surface than it would otherwise have had.

9. While resting, then, the whole weight of the body on this substance of the bones, as on some columns that carry a mass of building, she did not implant the bone undivided through the whole structure: for in that case man would have remained without motion or activity, if he had been so constructed, just like a tree that stands on one spot without either the alternate motion of legs to advance its motion or the service of hands to minister to the conveniences of life: but now we see that she contrived that the instrument should be

rendered capable of walking and working by this device, after she had implanted in the body, by the determining spirit which extends through the nerves, the impulse and power for motion. And hence is produced the service of the hands, so varied and multiform, and answering to every thought. Hence are produced, as though by some mechanical contrivance, the turnings of the neck, and the bending and raising of the head, and the action of the chin, and the separation of the eyelids, that takes place with a thought, and the movements of the other joints, by the tightening or relaxation of certain nerves. And the power that extends through these exhibits a sort of independent impulse, working with the spirit of its will by a sort of natural management, in each particular part; but the root of all, and the principle of the motions of the nerves, is found in the nervous tissue that surrounds the brain.

10. We consider, then, that we need not spend more time in inquiring in which of the vital members such a thing resides, when the energy of motion is shown to be here. But that the brain contributes to life in a special degree is shown clearly by the result of the opposite conditions: for if the tissue surrounding it receives any wound or lesion, death immediately follows the injury, nature being unable to endure the hurt even for a moment; just as, when a foundation is withdrawn, the whole building collapses with the part; and that member, from an injury to which the destruction of the whole living being clearly follows, may properly be acknowledged to contain the cause of life.

11. But as furthermore in those who have ceased to live, when the heat that is implanted in our nature is quenched, that which has become dead grows cold, we hence recognize the vital cause also in heat: for we must of necessity acknowledge that the living being subsists by the presence of that, which failing, the condition of death supervenes. And of such a force we understand the heart to be as it were the fountain-head and principle, as from it pipe-like passages, growing one from another in many ramifications, diffuse in the whole body the warm and fiery spirit.

12. And since some nourishment must needs also be provided by nature for the element of heat— for it is not possible that the fire should last by itself, without being nourished by its proper food— therefore the channels of the blood, issuing from the liver as from a fountainhead, accompany the warm spirit everywhere in its way

throughout the body, that the one may not by isolation from the other become a disease and destroy the constitution. Let this instruct those who go beyond the bounds of fairness, as they learn from nature that covetousness is a disease that breeds destruction.

13. But since the Divinity alone is free from needs, while human poverty requires external aid for its own subsistence, nature therefore, in addition to those three powers by which we said that the whole body is regulated, brings in imported matter from without, introducing by different entrances that which is suitable to those powers.

14. For to the fount of the blood, which is the liver, she furnishes its supply by food: for that which from time to time is imported in this way prepares the springs of blood to issue from the liver, as the snow on the mountain by its own moisture increases the springs in the low ground, forcing its own fluid deep down to the veins below.

15. The breath in the heart is supplied by means of the neighbouring organ, which is called the lungs, and is a receptacle for air, drawing the breath from without through the windpipe inserted in it, which extends to the mouth. The heart being placed in the midst of this organ (and itself also moving incessantly in imitation of the action of the ever-moving fire), draws to itself, somewhat as the bellows do in the forges, a supply from the adjacent air, filling its recesses by dilatation, and while it fans its own fiery element, breathes upon the adjoining tubes; and this it does not cease to do, drawing the external air into its own recesses by dilatation, and by compression infusing the air from itself into the tubes.

16. And this seems to me to be the cause of this spontaneous respiration of ours; for often the mind is occupied in discourse with others, or is entirely quiescent when the body is relaxed in sleep, but the respiration of air does not cease, though the will gives no co-operation to this end. Now I suppose, since the heart is surrounded by the lungs, and in the back part of its own structure is attached to them, moving that organ by its own dilatations and compressions, that the inhaling and exhaling of the air is brought about by the lungs: for as they are a lightly built and porous body, and have all their recesses opening at the base of the windpipe, when they contract and are compressed they necessarily force out by pressure the air that

is left in their cavities; and, when they expand and open, draw the air, by their distention, into the void by suction.

17. This then is the cause of this involuntary respiration— the impossibility that the fiery element should remain at rest: for as the operation of motion is proper to heat, and we understand that the principle of heat is to be found in the heart, the continual motion going on in this organ produces the incessant inspiration and exhalation of the air through the lungs: wherefore also when the fiery element is unnaturally augmented, the breathing of those fevered subjects becomes more rapid, as though the heart were endeavouring to quench the flame implanted in it by more violent breathing.

18. But since our nature is poor and in need of supplies for its own maintenance from all quarters, it not only lacks air of its own, and the breath which excites heat, which it imports from without for the preservation of the living being, but the nourishment it finds to fill out the proportions of the body is an importation. Accordingly, it supplies the deficiency by food and drink, implanting in the body a certain faculty for appropriating that which it requires, and rejecting that which is superfluous, and for this purpose too the fire of the heart gives nature no small assistance.

19. For since, according to the account we have given, the heart which kindles by its warm breath the individual parts, is the most important of the vital organs, our Maker caused it to be operative with its efficacious power at all points, that no part of it might be left ineffectual or unprofitable for the regulation of the whole organism. Behind, therefore, it enters the lungs, and, by its continuous motion, drawing that organ to itself, it expands the passages to inhale the air, and compressing them again it brings about the exspiration of the imprisoned air; while in front, attached to the space at the upper extremity of the stomach, it warms it and makes it respond by motion to its own activity, rousing it, not to inhale air, but to receive its appropriate food: for the entrances for breath and food are near one another, extending lengthwise one alongside the other, and are terminated in their upper extremity by the same boundary, so that their mouths are contiguous and the passages come to an end together in one mouth, from which the entrance of food is effected through the one, and that of the breath through the other.

20. Internally, however, the closeness of the connection of the passages is not maintained throughout; for the heart intervening between the base of the two, infuses in the one the powers for respiration, and in the other for nutriment. Now the fiery element is naturally inclined to seek for the material which serves as fuel, and this necessarily happens with regard to the receptacle of nourishment; for the more it becomes penetrated by fire through the neighbouring warmth, the more it draws to itself what nourishes the heat. And this sort of impulse we call appetite.

21. But if the organ which contains the food should obtain sufficient material, not even so does the activity of the fire become quiescent: but it produces a sort of melting of the material just as in a foundry, and, dissolving the solids, pours them out and transfers them, as it were from a funnel, to the neighbouring passages: then separating the coarser from the pure substance, it passes the fine part through certain channels to the entrance of the liver, and expels the sedimentary matter of the food to the wider passages of the bowels, and by turning it over in their manifold windings retains the food for a time in the intestines, lest if it were easily got rid of by a straight passage it might at once excite the animal again to appetite, and man, like the race of irrational animals, might never cease from this sort of occupation.

22. As we saw, however, that the liver has special need of the co-operation of heat for the conversion of the fluids into blood, while this organ is in position distant from the heart (for it would, I imagine, have been impossible that, being one principle or root of the vital power, it should not be hampered by vicinity with another such principle), in order that the system may suffer no injury by the distance at which the heat-giving substance is placed, a muscular passage (and this, by those skilled in such matters, is called the artery) receives the heated air from the heart and conveys it to the liver, making its opening there somewhere beside the point at which the fluids enter, and, as it warms the moist substance by its heat, blends with the liquid something akin to fire, and makes the blood appear red with the fiery tint it produces.

23. Issuing thence again, certain twin channels, each enclosing its own current like a pipe, disperse air and blood (that the liquid substance may have free course when accompanied and lightened by the motion of the heated substance) in various directions over the

whole body, breaking at every part into countless branching channels; while as the two principles of the vital powers mingle together (that alike which disperses heat, and that which supplies moisture to all parts of the body), they make, as it were, a sort of compulsory contribution from the substance with which they deal to the supreme force in the vital economy.

24. Now this force is that which is considered as residing in the cerebral membranes and the brain, from which it comes that every movement of a joint, every contraction of the muscles, every spontaneous influence that is exerted upon the individual members, renders our earthen statue active and mobile as though by some mechanism. For the most pure form of heat and the most subtle form of liquid, being united by their respective forces through a process of mixture and combination, nourish and sustain by their moisture the brain, and hence in turn, being rarefied to the most pure condition, the exhalation that proceeds from that organ anoints the membrane which encloses the brain, which, reaching from above downwards like a pipe, extending through the successive vertebræ;, is (itself and the marrow which is contained in it) conterminous with the base of the spine, itself giving like a charioteer the impulse and power to all the meeting-points of bones and joints, and to the branches of the muscles, for the motion or rest of the particular parts.

25. For this cause too it seems to me that it has been granted a more secure defence, being distinguished, in the head, by a double shelter of bones round about, and in the vertebræ; of the neck by the bulwarks formed by the projections of the spine as well as by the diversified interlacings of the very form of those vertebræ;, by which it is kept in freedom from all harm, enjoying safety by the defence that surrounds it.

26. So too one might suppose of the heart, that it is itself like some safe house fitted with the most solid defences, fortified by the enclosing walls of the bones round about; for in rear there is the spine, strengthened on either side by the shoulder-blades, and on each flank the enfolding position of the ribs makes that which is in the midst between them difficult to injure; while in front the breast-bone and the juncture of the collar-bone serve as a defence, that its safety may be guarded at all points from external causes of danger.

27. As we see in husbandry, when the rain fall from the clouds or the overflow from the river channels causes the land beneath it to be saturated with moisture (let us suppose for our argument a garden, nourishing within its own compass countless varieties of trees, and all the forms of plants that grow from the ground, and whereof we contemplate the figure, quality, and individuality in great variety of detail); then, as these are nourished by the liquid element while they are in one spot, the power which supplies moisture to each individual among them is one in nature; but the individuality of the plants so nourished changes the liquid element into different qualities; for the same substance becomes bitter in wormwood, and is changed into a deadly juice in hemlock, and becomes different in different other plants, in saffron, in balsam, in the poppy: for in one it becomes hot, in another cold, in another it obtains the middle quality: and in laurel and mastick it is scented, and in the fig and the pear it is sweetened, and by passing through the vine it is turned into the grape and into wine; while the juice of the apple, the redness of the rose, the radiance of the lily, the blue of the violet, the purple of the hyacinthine dye, and all that we behold in the earth, arise from one and the same moisture, and are separated into so many varieties in respect of figure and aspect and quality; the same sort of wonder is wrought in the animated soil of our being by Nature, or rather by Nature's Lord. Bones, cartilages, veins, arteries, nerves, ligatures, flesh, skin, fat, hair, glands, nails, eyes, nostrils, ears—all such things as these, and countless others in addition, while separated from one another by various peculiarities, are nourished by the one form of nourishment in ways proper to their own nature, in the sense that the nourishment, when it is brought into close relation with any of the subjects, is also changed according to that to which it approaches, and becomes adapted and allied to the special nature of the part. For if it should be in the neighbourhood of the eye, it blends with the visual part and is appropriately distributed by the difference of the coats round the eye, among the single parts; or, if it flow to the auditory parts, it is mingled with the auscultatory nature, or if it is in the lip, it becomes lip; and it grows solid in bone, and grows soft in marrow, and is made tense with the sinew, and extended with the surface, and passes into the nails, and is fined down for the growth of the hair, by correspondent exhalations, producing hair that is somewhat curly or wavy if it makes its way through winding passages, while, if the

course of the exhalations that go to form the hair lies straight, it renders the hair stiff and straight.

28. Our argument, however, has wandered far from its purpose, going deep into the works of nature, and endeavouring to describe how and from what materials our particular organs are formed, those, I mean, intended for life and for good life, and any other class which we included with these in our first division.

29. For our purpose was to show that the seminal cause of our constitution is neither a soul without body, nor a body without soul, but that, from animated and living bodies, it is generated at the first as a living and animate being, and that our humanity takes it and cherishes it like a nursling with the resources she herself possesses, and it thus grows on both sides and makes its growth manifest correspondingly in either part:— for it at once displays, by this artificial and scientific process of formation, the power of soul that is interwoven in it, appearing at first somewhat obscurely, but afterwards increasing in radiance concurrently with the perfecting of the work.

30. And as we may see with stone-carvers— for the artist's purpose is to produce in stone the figure of some animal; and with this in his mind, he first severs the stone from its kindred matter, and then, by chipping away the superfluous parts of it, advances somehow by the intermediate step of his first outline to the imitation which he has in his purpose, so that even an unskilled observer may, by what he sees, conjecture the aim of his art; again, by working at it, he brings it more nearly to the semblance of the object he has in view; lastly, producing in the material the perfect and finished figure, he brings his art to its conclusion, and that which a little before was a shapeless stone is a lion, or a man, or whatsoever it may be that the artist has made, not by the change of the material into the figure, but by the figure being wrought upon the material. If one supposes the like in the case of the soul he is not far from probability; for we say that Nature, the all-contriving, takes from its kindred matter the part that comes from the man, and moulds her statue within herself. And as the form follows upon the gradual working of the stone, at first somewhat indistinct, but more perfect after the completion of the work, so too in the moulding of its instrument the form of the soul is expressed in the substratum, incompletely in that which is still incomplete, perfect in that which is perfect; indeed it would have

been perfect from the beginning had our nature not been maimed by evil. Thus our community in that generation which is subject to passion and of animal nature, brings it about that the Divine image does not at once shine forth at our formation, but brings man to perfection by a certain method and sequence, through those attributes of the soul which are material, and belong rather to the animal creation.

31. Some such doctrine as this the great apostle also teaches us in his Epistle to the Corinthians, when he says, *"When I was a child, I spoke as a child, I understood as a child, I thought as a child; but when I became a man I put away childish things* 1 Corinthians 13:11 *"*; not that the soul which arises in the man is different from that which we know to be in the boy, and the childish intellect fails while the manly intellect takes its being in us; but that the same soul displays its imperfect condition in the one, its perfect state in the other.

32. For we say that those things are alive which spring up and grow, and no one would deny that all things that participate in life and natural motion are animate, yet at the same time one cannot say that such life partakes of a perfect soul—for though a certain animate operation exists in plants, it does not attain to the motions of sense; and on the other hand, though a certain further animate power exists in the brutes, neither does this attain perfection, since it does not contain in itself the grace of reason and intelligence.

33. And even so we say that the true and perfect soul is the human soul, recognized by every operation; and anything else that shares in life we call animate by a sort of customary misuse of language, because in these cases the soul does not exist in a perfect condition, but only certain parts of the operation of the soul, which in man also (according to Moses' mystical account of man's origin) we learn to have accrued when he made himself like this sensuous world. Thus Paul, advising those who were able to hear him to lay hold on perfection, indicates also the mode in which they may attain that object, telling them that they must *"put off the old man,"* and put on the man *"which is renewed after the image of Him that created him* Colossians 3:9-10 *."*

On the Soul and the Resurrection

Basil, great among the saints, had departed from this life to God; and the impulse to mourn for him was shared by all the churches. But his sister the Teacher was still living; and so I journeyed to her , yearning for an interchange of sympathy over the loss of her brother. My soul was right sorrow-stricken by this grievous blow, and I sought for one who could feel it equally, to mingle my tears with. But when we were in each other's presence the sight of the Teacher awakened all my pain; for she too was lying in a state of prostration even unto death. Well, she gave in to me for a little while, like a skilful driver, in the ungovernable violence of my grief; and then she tried to check me by speaking, and to correct with the curb of her reasonings the disorder of my soul. She quoted the Apostle's words about the duty of not being *"grieved for them that sleep"*; because only *"men without hope"* have such feelings. With a heart still fermenting with my pain, I asked—

How can that ever be practised by mankind? There is such an instinctive and deep-seated abhorrence of death in all! Those who look on a death-bed can hardly bear the sight; and those whom death approaches recoil from him all they can. Why, even the law that controls us puts death highest on the list of crimes, and highest on the list of punishments. By what device, then, can we bring ourselves to regard as nothing a departure from life even in the case of a stranger, not to mention that of relations, when so be they cease to live? We see before us the whole course of human life aiming at this one thing, viz. how we may continue in this life; indeed it is for this that houses have been invented by us to live in; in order that our bodies may not be prostrated in their environment by cold or heat. Agriculture, again, what is it but the providing of our sustenance? In fact all thought about how we are to go on living is occasioned by the fear of dying. Why is medicine so honoured among men? Because it is thought to carry on the combat with death to a certain extent by its methods. Why do we have corslets, and long shields, and greaves, and helmets, and all the defensive armour, and inclosures of fortifications, and iron-barred gates, except that we fear to die? Death then being naturally so terrible to us, how can it be easy for a survivor to obey this command to remain unmoved over friends departed?

Why, what is the special pain you feel, asked the Teacher, in the mere necessity itself of dying? This common talk of unthinking persons is no sufficient accusation.

What! Is there no occasion for grieving, I replied to her, when we see one who so lately lived and spoke becoming all of a sudden lifeless and motionless, with the sense of every bodily organ extinct, with no sight or hearing in operation, or any other faculty of apprehension that sense possesses; and if you apply fire or steel to him, even if you were to plunge a sword into the body, or cast it to the beasts of prey, or if you bury it beneath a mound, that dead man is alike unmoved at any treatment? Seeing, then, that this change is observed in all these ways, and that principle of life, whatever it might be, disappears all at once out of sight, as the flame of an extinguished lamp which burnt on it the moment before neither remains upon the wick nor passes to some other place, but completely disappears, how can such a change be borne without emotion by one who has no clear ground to rest upon? We *hear* the departure of the spirit, we *see* the shell that is left; but of the part that has been separated we are ignorant, both as to its nature, and as to the place whither it has fled; for neither earth, nor air, nor water, nor any other element can show as residing within itself this force that has left the body, at whose withdrawal a corpse only remains, ready for dissolution.

Whilst I was thus enlarging on the subject, the Teacher signed to me with her hand , and said: Surely what alarms and disturbs your mind is not the thought that the soul, instead of lasting for ever, ceases with the body's dissolution!

I answered rather audaciously, and without due consideration of what I said, for my passionate grief had not yet given me back my judgment. In fact, I said that the Divine utterances seemed to me like mere commands compelling us to believe that the soul lasts for ever; not, however, that we were led by them to this belief by any reasoning. Our mind within us appears slavishly to accept the opinion enforced, but not to acquiesce with a spontaneous impulse. Hence our sorrow over the departed is all the more grievous; we do not exactly know whether this vivifying principle is anything by itself; where it is, or how it is; whether, in fact, it exists in any way at all anywhere. This uncertainty about the real state of the case balances the opinions on either side; many adopt the one view, many the other; and indeed there are certain persons, of no small philosophical reputation among the Greeks, who have held and maintained this which I have just said.

Away, she cried, with that pagan nonsense! For therein the inventor of lies fabricates false theories only to harm the Truth. Observe this, and nothing else; that such a view about the soul amounts to nothing less than the abandoning of virtue, and seeking the pleasure of the moment only; the life of eternity, by which alone virtue claims the advantage, must be despaired of.

And pray how, I asked, are we to get a firm and unmovable belief in the soul's continuance? I, too, am sensible of the fact that human life will be bereft of the most beautiful ornament that life has to give, I mean virtue, unless an undoubting confidence with regard to this be established within us. What, indeed, has virtue to stand upon in the case of those persons who conceive of this present life as the limit of their existence, and hope for nothing beyond?

Well, replied the Teacher, we must seek where we may get a beginning for our discussion upon this point; and if you please, let the defence of the opposing views be undertaken by yourself; for I see that your mind is a little inclined to accept such a brief. Then, after the conflicting belief has been stated, we shall be able to look for the truth.

When she made this request, and I had deprecated the suspicion that I was making the objections in real earnest, instead of only wishing to get a firm ground for the belief about the soul by calling into court first what is aimed against this view, I began—

Would not the defenders of the opposite belief say this: that the body, being composite, must necessarily be resolved into that of which it is composed? And when the coalition of elements in the body ceases, each of those elements naturally gravitates towards its kindred element with the irresistible bias of like to like; the heat in us will thus unite with heat, the earthy with the solid, and each of the other elements also will pass towards its like. Where, then, will the soul be after that? If one affirm that it is in those elements, one will be obliged to admit that it is identical with them, for this fusion could not possibly take place between two things of different natures. But this being granted, the soul must necessarily be viewed as a complex thing, fused as it is with qualities so opposite. But the complex is not simple, but must be classed with the composite, and the composite is necessarily dissoluble; and dissolution means the destruction of the compound; and the destructible is not immortal, else the flesh itself, resolvable as it is into its constituent elements, might so be called immortal. If, on the other hand, the soul is something other than these elements, where can our reason suggest a place for it to be, when it is thus, by virtue of its alien nature, not to be discovered in those elements, and there is no other place in the world, either, where it may continue, in harmony with its own peculiar character, to exist? But, if a thing can be found nowhere, plainly it has no existence.

The Teacher sighed gently at these words of mine, and then said; Maybe these were the objections, or such as these, that the Stoics and Epicureans collected at Athens made in answer to the Apostle. I hear that Epicurus carried his theories in this very direction. The framework of things was to his mind a fortuitous and mechanical affair, without a Providence penetrating its operations; and, as a piece with this, he thought that human life was like a bubble, existing only as long as the breath within was held in by the enveloping substance, inasmuch as our body was a mere membrane, as it were, encompassing a breath; and that on the collapse of the inflation the imprisoned essence was extinguished. To him the visible was the limit of existence; he made our senses the only means of our apprehension of things; he completely closed the eyes of his soul, and was incapable of seeing anything in the intelligible and immaterial world, just as a man, who is imprisoned in a cabin whose walls and roof obstruct the view outside, remains without a glimpse of all the wonders of the sky. Verily, everything in the universe that is seen to be an object of sense is as an earthen wall, forming in itself a barrier between the narrower souls and that intelligible world which is ready for their contemplation; and it is the earth and water and fire alone that such behold; whence comes each of these elements, in what and by what they are encompassed, such souls because of their narrowness cannot detect. While the sight of a garment suggests to any one the weaver of it, and the thought of the shipwright comes at the sight of the ship, and the hand of the builder is brought to the mind of him who sees the building, these little souls gaze upon the world, but their eyes are blind to Him whom all this that we see around us makes manifest; and so they propound their clever and pungent doctrines about the soul's evanishment;— body from elements, and elements from body, and, besides, the impossibility of the soul's self-existence (if it is not to be one of these elements, or lodged in one); for if these opponents suppose that by virtue of the soul not being akin to the elements it is nowhere after death, they must propound, to begin with, the absence of the soul from the fleshly life as well, seeing that the body itself is nothing but a concourse of those elements; and so they must not tell us that the soul is to be found there either, independently vivifying their compound. If it is not possible for the soul to exist *after* death, though the elements do, then, I say, according to this teaching our life as well is proved to be nothing else but death. But if on the other hand they do not make the existence of the soul now in the body a question for doubt, how can they maintain its evanishment when the body is resolved into its elements? Then, secondly, they must employ an equal audacity against the God in this Nature too. For how can they assert that the intelligible and immaterial Unseen can be dissolved and diffused into the wet and the soft, as also into the hot and the dry, and so hold together the universe in existence through being, though not of a kindred nature with the things which it penetrates, yet not thereby incapable of so penetrating them? Let them, therefore, remove from their system the very Deity Who upholds the world.

That is the very point, I said, upon which our adversaries cannot fail to have doubts; viz. that all things depend on God and are encompassed by Him, or, that there is any divinity at all transcending the physical world.

It would be more fitting, she cried, to be silent about such doubts, and not to deign to make any answer to such foolish and wicked propositions; for there is a Divine precept forbidding us to answer a fool in his folly; and he must be a fool, as the Prophet declares, who says that there is no God. But since one needs must speak, I will urge upon you an argument which is not mine nor that of any human being (for it would then be of small value, whosoever spoke it), but an argument which the whole Creation enunciates by the medium of its wonders to the audience of the eye, with a skilful and artistic utterance that reaches the heart. The Creation proclaims outright the Creator; for the very heavens, as the Prophet says, declare the glory of God with their unutterable words. We see the universal harmony in the wondrous sky and on the wondrous earth; how elements essentially opposed to each other are all woven together in an ineffable union to serve one common end, each contributing its particular force to maintain the whole; how the unmingling and mutually repellent do not fly apart from each other by virtue of their peculiarities, any more than they are destroyed, when compounded, by such contrariety; how those elements which are naturally buoyant move downwards, the heat of the sun, for instance, descending in the rays, while the bodies which possess weight are lifted by becoming rarefied in vapour, so that water contrary to its nature ascends, being conveyed through the air to the upper regions; how too that fire of the firmament so penetrates the earth that even its abysses feel the heat; how the moisture of the rain infused into the soil generates, one though it be by nature, myriads of differing germs, and animates in due proportion each subject of its influence; how very swiftly the polar sphere revolves, how the orbits within it move the contrary way, with all the eclipses, and conjunctions, and measured intervals of the planets. We see all this with the piercing eyes of mind, nor can we fail to be taught by means of such a spectacle that a Divine power, working with skill and method, is manifesting itself in this actual world, and, penetrating each portion, combines those portions with the whole and completes the whole by the portions, and encompasses the universe with a single all-controlling force, self-centred and self-contained, never ceasing from its motion, yet never altering the position which it holds.

And pray how, I asked, does this belief in the existence of God prove along with it the existence of the human soul? For God, surely, is not the same thing as the soul, so that, if the one were believed in, the other must necessarily be believed in.

She replied: It has been said by wise men that man is a little world in himself and contains all the elements which go to complete the universe. If this view is a true one (and so it seems), we perhaps shall need no other ally than it to establish the truth of our conception of the soul. And our conception of it is this; that it exists, with a rare and peculiar nature of its own, independently of the body with its gross texture. We get our exact knowledge of this outer world from the apprehension of our senses, and these sensational operations themselves lead us on to the understanding of the super-sensual world of fact and thought, and our eye thus becomes the interpreter of that almighty wisdom which is visible in the universe, and points in itself to the Being Who encompasses it. Just so, when we look to our inner world, we find no slight grounds there also, in the known, for conjecturing the unknown; and the unknown there also is that which, being the object of thought and not of sight, eludes the grasp of sense.

I rejoined, Nay, it may be very possible to infer a wisdom transcending the universe from the skilful and artistic designs observable in this harmonized fabric of physical nature; but, as regards the soul, what knowledge is possible to those who would trace, from any indications the body has to give, the unknown through the known?

Most certainly, the Virgin replied, the soul herself, to those who wish to follow the wise proverb and know themselves, is a competent instructress; of the fact, I mean, that she is an immaterial and spiritual thing, working and moving in a way corresponding to her peculiar nature, and evincing these peculiar emotions through the organs of the body. For this bodily organization exists the same even in those who have just been reduced by death to the state of corpses, but it remains without motion or action because the force of the soul is no longer in it. It moves only when there is sensation in the organs, and not only that, but the mental force by means of that sensation penetrates with its own impulses and moves whither it will all those organs of sensation.

What then, I asked, is the soul? Perhaps there may be some possible means of delineating its nature; so that we may have some comprehension of this subject, in the way of a sketch.

Its definition, the Teacher replied, has been attempted in different ways by different writers, each according to his own bent; but the following is our opinion about it. The soul is an essence created, and living, and intellectual, transmitting from itself to an organized and sentient body the power of living and of grasping objects of sense, as long as a natural constitution capable of this holds together.

Saying this she pointed to the physician who was sitting to watch her state, and said: There is a proof of what I say close by us. How, I ask, does this man, by putting his fingers to feel the pulse, hear in a manner, through this sense of touch, Nature calling loudly to him and telling him of her peculiar pain; in fact, that the disease in the body is an inflammatory one , and that the malady originates in this or that internal organ; and that there is such and such a degree of fever? How too is he taught by the agency of the eye other facts of this kind, when he looks to see the posture of the patient and watches the wasting of the flesh? As, too, the state of the complexion, pale somewhat and bilious, and the gaze of the eyes, as is the case with those in pain, involuntarily inclining to sadness, indicate the internal condition, so the ear gives information of the like, ascertaining the nature of the malady by the shortness of the breathing and by the groan that comes with it. One might say that even the sense of smell in the expert is not incapable of detecting the kind of disorder, but that it notices the secret suffering of the vitals in the particular quality of the breath. Could this be so if there were not a certain force of intelligence present in each organ of the senses? What would our hand have taught us of itself, without thought conducting it from feeling to understanding the subject before it? What would the ear, as separate from mind, or the eye or the nostril or any other organ have helped towards the settling of the question, all by themselves? Verily, it is most true what one of heathen culture is recorded to have said, that it is the mind that sees and the mind that hears. Else, if you will not allow this to be true, you must tell me why, when you look at the sun, as you have been trained by your instructor to look at him, you assert that he is not in the breadth of his disc of the size he appears to the many, but that he exceeds by many times the measure of the entire earth. Do you not confidently maintain that it is so, because you have arrived by reasoning through phenomena at the conception of such and such a movement, of such distances of time and space, of such causes of eclipse? And when you look at the waning and waxing moon you are taught other truths by the visible figure of that heavenly body, viz. that it is in itself devoid of light, and that it revolves in the circle nearest to the earth, and that it is lit by light from the sun; just as is the case with mirrors, which, receiving the sun upon them, do not reflect rays of their own, but those of the sun, whose light is given back from their smooth flashing surface. Those who see this, but do not examine it, think that the light comes from the moon herself. But that this is not the case is proved by this; that when she is diametrically facing the sun she has the whole of the disc that looks our way illuminated; but, as she traverses her own circle of revolution quicker from moving in a narrower space, she herself has completed this more than twelve times before the sun has once travelled round his; whence it happens that her substance is not always covered with light. For her position facing him is not maintained in the frequency of her revolutions; but, while this position causes the whole side of the moon which looks to us to be illumined, directly she moves sideways her hemisphere which is turned to us necessarily becomes partially shadowed, and only that which is turned to him meets his embracing rays; the brightness, in fact, keeps on retiring from that which can no longer see the sun to that which still sees him, until she passes right across the sun's disc and receives his rays upon her hinder part; and then the fact of her being in herself totally devoid of light and splendour causes the side turned to us to be invisible while the further hemisphere is all in light; and this is called the completion of her waning. But when again, in her own revolution, she has passed the sun and she is transverse to his rays, the side which was dark just before begins to shine a little, for the rays move from the illumined part to that so lately invisible. You see what the eye does teach; and yet it would never of itself have afforded this insight, without something that looks through the eyes and uses the data of the senses as mere guides to penetrate from the apparent to the unseen. It is needless to add the methods of geometry that lead us step by step through visible delineations to truths that lie out of sight, and countless other instances which all prove that apprehension is the work of an intellectual essence deeply seated in our nature, acting through the operation of our bodily senses.

But what, I asked, if, insisting on the great differences which, in spite of a certain quality of matter shared alike by all elements in their visible form, exist between each particular kind of matter (motion, for instance, is not the same in all, some moving up, some down; nor form, nor quality either), some one were to say that there was in the same manner incorporated in, and belonging to, these elements a certain force as well which effects these intellectual insights and operations by a purely natural effort of their own (such effects, for instance, as we often see produced by the mechanists, in whose hands matter, combined according to the rules of Art, thereby imitates Nature, exhibiting resemblance not in figure alone but even in motion, so that when the piece of mechanism sounds in its resonant part it mimics a human voice, without, however, our being able to perceive anywhere any mental force working out the particular figure, character, sound, and movement); suppose, I say, we were to affirm that all this was produced as well in the organic machine of our natural bodies, without any intermixture of a special thinking substance, but owing simply to an inherent motive power of the elements within us accomplishing by itself these operations— to nothing else, in fact, but an impulsive movement working for the cognition of the object before us; would not then the fact stand proved of the absolute nonexistence of that intellectual and impalpable Being, the soul, which you talk of?

Your instance, she replied, and your reasoning upon it, though belonging to the counter-argument, may both of them be made allies of our statement, and will contribute not a little to the confirmation of its truth.

Why, how can you say that?

Because, you see, so to understand, manipulate, and dispose the soulless matter, that the art which is stored away in such mechanisms becomes almost like a soul to this material, in all the various ways in which it mocks movement, and figure, and voice, and so on, may be turned into a proof of there being something in man whereby he shows an innate fitness to think out within himself, through the contemplative and inventive faculties, such thoughts, and having prepared such mechanisms in theory, to put them into practice by manual skill, and exhibit in matter the product of his mind. First, for instance, he saw, by dint of thinking, that to produce any sound there is need of some wind; and then, with a view to produce wind in the mechanism, he previously ascertained by a course of reasoning and close observation of the nature of elements, that there is no vacuum at all in the world, but that the lighter is to be considered a vacuum only by comparison with the heavier; seeing that the air itself, taken as a separate subsistence, is crowded quite full. It is by an abuse of language that a jar is said to be *"empty"*; for when it is empty of any liquid it is none the less, even in this state, full, in the eyes of the experienced. A proof of this is that a jar when put into a pool of water is not immediately filled, but at first floats on the surface, because the air it contains helps to buoy up its rounded sides; till at last the hand of the drawer of the water forces it down to the bottom, and, when there, it takes in water by its neck; during which process it is shown not to have been empty even before the water came; for there is the spectacle of a sort of combat going on in the neck between the two elements, the water being forced by its weight into the interior, and therefore streaming in; the imprisoned air on the other hand being straitened for room by the gush of the water along the neck, and so

Selected Works

rushing in the contrary direction; thus the water is checked by the strong current of air, and gurgles and bubbles against it. Men observed this, and devised in accordance with this property of the two elements a way of introducing air to work their mechanism. They made a kind of cavity of some hard stuff, and prevented the air in it from escaping in any direction; and then introduced water into this cavity through its mouth, apportioning the quantity of water according to requirement; next they allowed an exit in the opposite direction to the air, so that it passed into a pipe placed ready to hand, and in so doing, being violently constrained by the water, became a blast; and this, playing on the structure of the pipe, produced a note. Is it not clearly proved by such visible results that there is a mind of some kind in man, something other than that which is visible, which, by virtue of an invisible thinking nature of its own, first prepares by inward invention such devices, and then, when they have been so matured, brings them to the light and exhibits them in the subservient matter? For if it were possible to ascribe such wonders, as the theory of our opponents does, to the actual constitution of the elements, we should have these mechanisms building themselves spontaneously; the bronze would not wait for the artist, to be made into the likeness of a man, but would become such by an innate force; the air would not require the pipe, to make a note, but would sound spontaneously by its own fortuitous flux and motion; and the jet of the water upwards would not be, as it now is, the result of an artificial pressure forcing it to move in an unnatural direction, but the water would rise into the mechanism of its own accord, finding in that direction a natural channel. But if none of these results are produced spontaneously by elemental force, but, on the contrary, each element is employed at will by artifice; and if artifice is a kind of movement and activity of mind, will not the very consequences of what has been urged by way of objection show us Mind as something other than the thing perceived?

That the thing perceived, I replied, is not the same as the thing not perceived, I grant; but I do not discover any answer to our question in such a statement; it is not yet clear to me what we are to think that thing not-perceived to be; all I have been shown by your argument is that it is not anything material; and I do not yet know the fitting name for it. I wanted especially to know what it is, not what it is not.

We do learn, she replied, much about many things by this very same method, inasmuch as, in the very act of saying a thing is *"not so and so,"* we by implication interpret the very nature of the thing in question. For instance, when we say a *"guileless,"* we indicate a good man; when we say *"unmanly,"* we have expressed that a man is a coward; and it is possible to suggest a great many things in like fashion, wherein we either convey the idea of goodness by the negation of badness , or *vice versâ*. Well, then, if one thinks so with regard to the matter now before us, one will not fail to gain a proper conception of it. The question is—What are we to think of Mind in its very essence? Now granted that the inquirer has had his doubts set at rest as to the existence of the thing in question, owing to the activities which it displays to us, and only wants to know what it is, he will have adequately discovered it by being told that it is not that which our senses perceive, neither a colour, nor a form, nor a hardness, nor a weight, nor a quantity, nor a cubic dimension, nor a point, nor anything else perceptible in matter; supposing, that is, that there does exist a something beyond all these.

Here I interrupted her discourse: If you leave all these out of the account I do not see how you can possibly avoid cancelling along with them the very thing which you are in search of. I cannot at present conceive to what, as apart from these, the perceptive activity is to cling. For on all occasions in investigating with the scrutinizing intellect the contents of the world, we must, so far as we put our hand at all on what we are seeking, inevitably touch, as blind men feeling along the walls for the door, some one of those things aforesaid; we must come on colour, or form, or quantity, or something else on your list; and when it comes to saying that the thing is none of them, our feebleness of mind induces us to suppose that it does not exist at all.

Shame on such absurdity! said she, indignantly interrupting. A fine conclusion this narrow-minded, grovelling view of the world brings us to! If all that is not cognizable by sense is to be wiped out of existence, the all-embracing Power that presides over things is admitted by this same assertion not to be; once a man has been told about the non-material and invisible nature of the Deity, he must perforce with such a premise reckon it as absolutely non-existent. If, on the other hand, the absence of such characteristics in His case does not constitute any limitation of His existence, how can the Mind of man be squeezed out of existence along with this withdrawal one by one of each property of matter?

Well, then, I retorted, we only exchange one paradox for another by arguing in this way; for our reason will be reduced to the conclusion that the Deity and the Mind of man are identical, if it be true that neither can be thought of, except by the withdrawal of all the data of sense.

Say not so, she replied; to talk so also is blasphemous. Rather, as the Scripture tells you, say that the one is *like* the other. For that which is *"made in the image"* of the Deity necessarily possesses a likeness to its prototype in every respect; it resembles it in being intellectual, immaterial, unconnected with any notion of weight , and in eluding any measurement of its dimensions ; yet as regards its own peculiar nature it is something different from that other. Indeed, it would be no longer an *"image,"* if it were altogether identical with that other; but where we have *A* in that uncreate prototype we have *a* in the image; just as in a minute particle of glass, when it happens to face the light, the complete disc of the sun is often to be seen, not represented thereon in proportion to its proper size, but so far as the minuteness of the particle admits of its being represented at all. Thus do the reflections of those ineffable qualities of Deity shine forth within the narrow limits of our nature; and so our reason, following the leading of these reflections, will not miss grasping the Mind in its essence by clearing away from the question all corporeal qualities; nor on the other hand will it bring the pure and infinite Existence to the level of that which is perishable and little; it will regard this essence of the Mind as an object of thought only, since it is the *"image"* of an Existence which is such; but it will not pronounce this image to be identical with the prototype. Just, then, as we have no doubts, owing to the display of a Divine mysterious wisdom in the universe, about a Divine Being and a Divine Power existing in it all which secures its continuance (though if you required a definition of that Being you would therein find the Deity completely sundered from every object in creation, whether of sense or thought, while in these last, too, natural distinctions are admitted), so, too, there is nothing strange in the soul's separate existence as a substance (whatever we may think that substance to be) being no hindrance to her actual existence, in spite of the elemental atoms of the world not harmonizing with her in the definition of her being. In the case of our living bodies, composed as they are from the blending of these atoms, there is no sort of communion, as has been just said, on the score of substance, between the simplicity and invisibility of the soul, and the grossness of those bodies; but, notwithstanding that, there is not a doubt that there is in them the soul's vivifying influence exerted by a law which it is beyond the human understanding to comprehend. Not even then, when those atoms have again been dissolved into themselves, has that bond of a vivifying influence vanished; but as, while the framework of the body still holds together, each individual part is possessed of a soul which penetrates equally every component member, and one could not call that soul hard and resistent though blended with the solid, nor humid, or cold, or the reverse, though it transmits life to all and each of such parts, so, when that framework is dissolved, and has returned to its kindred elements, there is nothing against probability that that simple and incomposite essence which has once for all by some inexplicable law grown with the growth of the bodily framework should continually remain beside the atoms with which it has been blended, and should in no way be sundered from a union once formed. For it does not follow that because the composite is dissolved the incomposite must be dissolved with it.

That those atoms, I rejoined, should unite and again be separated, and that this constitutes the formation and dissolution of the body, no one would deny. But we have to consider this. There are great intervals between these atoms; they differ from each other, both in position, and also in qualitative distinctions and peculiarities. When, indeed, these atoms have all converged upon the given subject, it is reasonable that that intelligent and undimensional essence which we call the soul should cohere with that which is so united; but once these atoms are separated from each other, and have gone whither their nature impels them, what is to become of the soul when her vessel is thus scattered in many directions? As a sailor, when his ship has been wrecked and gone to pieces, cannot float upon all the pieces at once which have been scattered this way and that over the surface of the sea (for he seizes any bit that comes to hand, and lets all the rest drift away), in the same way the soul, being by nature incapable of dissolution along with the atoms, will, if she finds it hard to be parted from the body altogether, cling to some one of them; and if we take this view, consistency will no more allow us to regard her as immortal for living in one atom than as mortal for not living in a number of them.

But the intelligent and undimensional, she replied, is neither contracted nor diffused (contraction and diffusion being a property of body only); but by virtue of a nature which is formless and bodiless it is present with the body equally in the contraction and in the diffusion of its atoms, and is no more narrowed by the compression which attends the uniting of the atoms than it is abandoned by them when they wander off to their kindred, however wide the interval is held to be which we observe between alien atoms. For instance, there is a great difference between the buoyant and light as contrasted with the heavy and solid; between the hot as contrasted with the cold; between the humid as contrasted with its opposite; nevertheless it is no strain to an intelligent essence to be present in each of those elements to which it has once cohered; this blending with opposites does not split it up. In locality, in peculiar qualities, these elemental atoms are held to be far removed from each other; but an undimensional nature finds it no labour to cling to what is locally divided, seeing that even now it is possible for the mind at once to contemplate the heavens above us and to extend its busy scrutiny beyond the horizon, nor is its contemplative power at all distracted by these excursions into distances so great. There is nothing, then, to hinder the soul's presence in the body's atoms, whether fused in union or decomposed in dissolution. Just as in the amalgam of gold and silver a certain methodical force is to be observed which has fused the metals, and if the one be afterwards smelted out of the other, the law of this method nevertheless continues to reside in each, so that while the amalgam is separated this method does not suffer division along with it (for you cannot make fractions out of the indivisible), in the same way this intelligent essence of the soul is observable in the concourse of the atoms, and does not undergo division when they are dissolved; but it remains with them, and even in their separation it is co-extensive with them, yet not itself dissevered nor discounted into sections to accord with the number of the atoms. Such a condition belongs to the material and spacial world, but that which is intelligent and undimensional is not liable to the circumstances of space. Therefore the soul exists in the actual atoms which she has once animated, and there is no force to tear her away from her cohesion with them. What cause for melancholy, then, is there herein, that the visible is exchanged for the invisible; and wherefore is it that your mind has conceived such a hatred of death?

Upon this I recurred to the definition which she had previously given of the soul, and I said that to my thinking her definition had not indicated distinctly enough all the powers of the soul which are a matter of observation. It declares the soul to be an intellectual essence which imparts to the organic body a force of life by which the senses operate. Now the soul is not thus operative only in our scientific and speculative intellect; it does not produce results in that world only, or employ the organs of sense only for this their natural work. On the contrary, we observe in our nature many emotions of desire and many of anger; and both these exist in us as qualities of our kind, and we see both of them in their manifestations displaying further many most subtle differences. There are many states, for instance, which are occasioned by desire; many others which on the other hand proceed from anger; and none of them are of the body; but that which is not of the body is plainly intellectual. Now our definition exhibits the soul as something intellectual; so that one of two alternatives, both absurd, must emerge when we follow out this view to this end; either anger and desire are both second souls in us, and a plurality of souls must take the place of the single soul, or the thinking faculty in us cannot be regarded as a soul either (if *they* are not), the intellectual element adhering equally to all of them and stamping them all as souls, or else excluding every one of them equally from the specific qualities of soul.

You are quite justified, she replied, in raising this question, and it has ere this been discussed by many elsewhere; namely, what we are to think of the principle of desire and the principle of anger within us. Are they consubstantial with the soul, inherent in the soul's very self from her first organization , or are they something different, accruing to us afterwards? In fact, while all equally allow that these principles are to be detected in the soul, investigation has not yet discovered exactly what we are to think of them so as to gain some fixed belief with regard to them. The generality of men still fluctuate in their opinions about this, which are as erroneous as they are numerous. As for ourselves, if the Gentile philosophy, which deals methodically with all these points, were really adequate for a demonstration, it would certainly be superfluous to add a discussion on the soul to those speculations. But while the latter proceeded, on the subject of the soul, as far in the direction of supposed consequences as the thinker pleased, we are not entitled to such licence, I mean that of affirming what we please; we make the Holy Scriptures the rule and the measure of every tenet; we necessarily fix our eyes upon that, and approve that alone which may be made to harmonize with the intention of those writings. We must therefore neglect the Platonic chariot and the pair of horses of dissimilar forces yoked to it, and their driver, whereby the philosopher allegorizes these facts about the soul; we must neglect also all that is said by the philosopher who succeeded him and who followed out probabilities by rules of art , and diligently investigated the very question now before us, declaring that the soul was mortal by reason of these two principles; we must neglect all before and since their time, whether they philosophized in prose or in verse, and we will adopt, as the guide of our reasoning, the Scripture, which lays it down as an axiom that there is no excellence in the soul which is not a property as well of the Divine nature. For he who declares the soul to be God's likeness asserts that anything foreign to Him is outside the limits of the soul; similarity cannot be retained in those qualities which are diverse from the original. Since, then, nothing of the kind we are considering is included in the conception of the Divine nature, one would be reasonable in surmising that such things are not consubstantial with the soul either. Now to seek to build up our doctrine by rule of dialectic and the science which draws and destroys conclusions, involves a species of discussion which we shall ask to be excused from, as being a weak and questionable way of demonstrating truth. Indeed, it is clear to every one that that subtle dialectic possesses a force that may be turned both ways, as well for the overthrow of truth as for the detection of falsehood; and so we begin to suspect even truth itself when it is advanced in company with such a kind of artifice, and to think that the very ingenuity of it is trying to bias our judgment and to upset the truth. If on the other hand any one will accept a discussion which is in a naked unsyllogistic form, we will speak upon these points by making our study of them so far as we can follow the chain of Scriptural tradition. What is it, then, that we assert? We say that the fact of the reasoning animal man being capable of understanding and knowing is most surely attested by those outside our faith; and that this definition would never have sketched our nature so, if it had viewed anger and desire and all such-like emotions as consubstantial with that nature. In any other case, one would not give a definition of the subject in hand by putting a generic instead of a specific quality; and so, as the principle of desire and the principle of anger are observed equally in rational and irrational natures, one could not rightly mark the specific quality by means of this generic one. But how can that which, in defining a nature, is superfluous and worthy of exclusion be treated as a part of that nature, and, so, available for falsifying the definition? Every definition of an essence looks to the specific quality of the subject in hand; and whatever is outside that speciality is set aside as having nothing to do with the required definition. Yet, beyond question, these faculties of anger and desire are allowed to be common to all reasoning and brute natures; anything common is not identical with that which is peculiar; it is imperative therefore that we should not range these faculties among those whereby humanity is exclusively meant: but just as one may perceive the principle of sensation, and that of nutrition and growth in man, and yet not shake thereby the given definition of his soul (for the quality A being in the soul does not prevent the quality B being in it too), so, when one detects in humanity these emotions of anger and desire, one cannot on that account fairly quarrel with this definition, as if it fell short of a full indication of man's nature.

What then, I asked the Teacher, are we to think about this? For I cannot yet see how we can fitly repudiate faculties which are actually within us.

You see, she replied, there is a battle of the reason with them and a struggle to rid the soul of them; and there are men in whom this struggle has ended in success; it was so with Moses, as we know; he was superior both to anger and to desire; the history testifying of him in both respects, that he was meek beyond all men (and by meekness it indicates the absence of all anger and a mind quite devoid of resentment), and that he desired none of those things about which we see the desiring faculty in the generality so active. This could not have been so, if these faculties were nature, and were referable to the contents of man's essence. For it is impossible for one who has come quite outside of his nature to be in Existence at all. But if Moses was at one and the same time in Existence and not in these conditions, then it follows that these conditions are something other than nature and not nature itself. For if, on the one hand, that is truly nature in which the essence of the being is found, and, on the other, the removal of these conditions is in our power, so that their removal not only does no harm, but is even beneficial to the nature, it is clear that these conditions are to be numbered among externals, and are affections, rather than the essence, of the nature; for the essence is that thing only which it is. As for anger, most think it a fermenting of the blood round the heart; others an eagerness to inflict pain in return for a previous pain; we would take it to be the impulse to hurt one who has provoked us. But none of these accounts of it tally with the definition of the soul. Again, if we were to define what desire is in itself, we should call it a seeking for that which is wanting, or a longing for pleasurable enjoyment, or a pain at not possessing that upon which the heart is set, or a state with regard to some pleasure which there is no opportunity of enjoying. These and such-like descriptions all indicate desire, but they have no connection with the definition of the soul. But it is so with regard to all those other conditions also which we see to have some relation to the soul, those, I mean, which are mutually opposed to each other, such as cowardice and courage, pleasure and pain, fear and contempt, and so on; each of them seems akin to the principle of desire or to that of anger, while they have a separate definition to mark their own peculiar nature. Courage and contempt, for instance, exhibit a certain phase of the irascible impulse; the dispositions arising from cowardice and fear exhibit on the other hand a diminution and weakening of that same impulse. Pain, again, draws its material both from anger and desire. For the impotence of anger, which consists in not being able to punish one who has first given pain, becomes itself pain; and the despair of getting objects of desire and the absence of things upon which the heart is set create in the mind this same sullen state. Moreover, the opposite to pain, I mean the sensation of pleasure , like pain, divides itself between anger and desire; for pleasure is the leading motive of them both. All these conditions, I say, have some relation to the soul, and yet they are not the soul , but only like warts growing out of the soul's thinking part, which are reckoned as parts of it because they adhere to it, and yet are not that actual thing which the soul is in its essence.

And yet, I rejoined to the virgin, we see no slight help afforded for improvement to the virtuous from all these conditions. Daniel's desire was his glory; and Phineas' anger pleased the Deity. We have been told, too, that fear is the beginning of wisdom, and learned from Paul that salvation is the goal of the *"sorrow after a godly sort."* The

Gospel bids us have a contempt for danger; and the *"not being afraid with any amazement"* is nothing else but a describing of courage, and this last is numbered by Wisdom among the things that are good. In all this Scripture shows that such conditions are not to be considered weaknesses; weaknesses would not have been so employed for putting virtue into practice.

I think, replied the Teacher, that I am myself responsible for this confusion arising from different accounts of the matter; for I did not state it as distinctly as I might have, by introducing a certain order of consequences for our consideration. Now, however, some such order shall, as far as it is possible, be devised, so that our essay may advance in the way of logical sequence and so give no room for such contradictions. We declare, then, that the speculative, critical, and world-surveying faculty of the soul is its peculiar property by virtue of its very nature , and that thereby the soul preserves within itself the image of the divine grace; since our reason surmises that divinity itself, whatever it may be in its inmost nature, is manifested in these very things—universal supervision and the critical discernment between good and evil. But all those elements of the soul which lie on the border-land and are capable from their peculiar nature of inclining to either of two opposites (whose eventual determination to the good or to the bad depends on the kind of use they are put to), anger, for instance, and fear, and any other such-like emotion of the soul divested of which human nature cannot be studied— all these we reckon as accretions from without, because in the Beauty which is man's prototype no such characteristics are to be found. Now let the following statement be offered as a mere exercise (in interpretation). I pray that it may escape the sneers of cavilling hearers. Scripture informs us that the Deity proceeded by a sort of graduated and ordered advance to the creation of man. After the foundations of the universe were laid, as the history records, man did not appear on the earth at once; but the creation of the brutes preceded his, and the plants preceded them. Thereby Scripture shows that the vital forces blended with the world of matter according to a gradation; first, it infused itself into insensate nature; and in continuation of this advanced into the sentient world; and then ascended to intelligent and rational beings. Accordingly, while all existing things must be either corporeal or spiritual, the former are divided into the animate and inanimate. By animate, I mean possessed of life: and of the things possessed of life, some have it with sensation, the rest have no sensation. Again, of these sentient things, some have reason, the rest have not. Seeing, then, that this life of sensation could not possibly exist apart from the matter which is the subject of it, and the intellectual life could not be embodied, either, without growing in the sentient, on this account the creation of man is related as coming last, as of one who took up into himself every single form of life, both that of plants and that which is seen in brutes. His nourishment and growth he derives from vegetable life; for even in vegetables such processes are to be seen when aliment is being drawn in by their roots and given off in fruit and leaves. His sentient organization he derives from the brute creation. But his faculty of thought and reason is incommunicable , and is a peculiar gift in our nature, to be considered by itself. However, just as this nature has the instinct acquisitive of the necessaries to material existence— an instinct which, when manifested in us men, we call Appetite— and as we admit this appertans to the vegetable form of life, since we can notice it there too like so many impulses working naturally to satisfy themselves with their kindred aliment and to issue in germination, so all the peculiar conditions of the brute creation are blended with the intellectual part of the soul. To them, she continued, belongs anger; to them belongs fear; to them all those other opposing activities within us; everything except the faculty of reason and thought. That alone, the choice product, as has been said, of all our life, bears the stamp of the Divine character. But since, according to the view which we have just enunciated, it is not possible for this reasoning faculty to exist in the life of the body without existing by means of sensations, and since sensation is already found subsisting in the brute creation, necessarily as it were, by reason of this one condition, our soul has touch with the other things which are knit up with it ; and these are all those phænomena within us that we call *"passions"*; which have not been allotted to human nature for any bad purpose at all (for the Creator would most certainly be the author of evil, if in *them*, so deeply rooted as they are in our nature, any necessities of wrongdoing were found), but according to the use which our free will puts them to, these emotions of the soul become the instruments of virtue or of vice. They are like the iron which is being fashioned according to the volition of the artificer, and receives whatever shape the idea which is in his mind prescribes, and becomes a sword or some agricultural implement. Supposing, then, that our reason, which is our nature's choicest part, holds the dominion over these imported emotions (as Scripture allegorically declares in the command to men to rule over the brutes), none of them will be active in the ministry of evil; fear will only generate within us obedience , and anger fortitude, and cowardice caution; and the instinct of desire will procure for us the delight that is Divine and perfect. But if reason drops the reins and is dragged behind like a charioteer who has got entangled in his car, then these instincts are changed into fierceness, just as we see happens among the brutes. For since reason does not preside over the natural impulses that are implanted in them, the more irascible animals, under the generalship of their anger, mutually destroy each other; while the bulky and powerful animals get no good themselves from their strength, but become by their want of reason slaves of that which has reason. Neither are the activities of their desire for pleasure employed on any of the higher objects; nor does any other instinct to be observed in them result in any profit to themselves. Thus too, with ourselves, if these instincts are not turned by reasoning into the right direction, and if our feelings get the mastery of our mind, the man is changed from a reasoning into an unreasoning being, and from godlike intelligence sinks by the force of these passions to the level of the brute.

Much moved by these words, I said: To any one who reflects indeed, your exposition, advancing as it does in this consecutive manner, though plain and unvarnished, bears sufficiently upon it the stamp of correctness and hits the truth. And to those who are expert only in the technical methods of proof a mere demonstration suffices to convince; but as for ourselves, we were agreed that there is something more trustworthy than any of these artificial conclusions, namely, that which the teachings of Holy Scripture point to: and so I deem that it is necessary to inquire, in addition to what has been said, whether this inspired teaching harmonizes with it all.

And who, she replied, could deny that truth is to be found only in that upon which the seal of Scriptural testimony is set? So, if it is necessary that something from the Gospels should be adduced in support of our view, a study of the Parable of the Wheat and Tares will not be here out of place. The Householder there sowed good seed; (and we are plainly the *"house"*). But the *"enemy,"* having watched for the time when men slept, sowed that which was useless in that which was good for food, setting the tares in the very middle of the wheat. The two kinds of seed grew up together; for it was not possible that seed put into the very middle of the wheat should fail to grow up with it. But the Superintendent of the field forbids the servants to gather up the useless crop, on account of their growing at the very root of the contrary sort; so as not to root up the nutritious along with that foreign growth. Now we think that Scripture means by the good seed the corresponding impulses of the soul, each one of which, if only they are cultured for good, necessarily puts forth the fruit of virtue within us. But since there has been scattered among these the bad seed of the error of judgment as to the true Beauty which is alone in its intrinsic nature such, and since this last has been thrown into the shade by the growth of delusion which springs up along with it (for the active principle of desire does not germinate and increase in the direction of that natural Beauty which was the object of its being sown in us, but it has changed its growth so as to move towards a bestial and unthinking state, this very error as to Beauty carrying its impulse towards this result; and in the same way the seed of anger does not steel us to be brave, but only arms us to fight with our own people; and the power of loving deserts its intellectual objects and becomes completely mad for the immoderate enjoyment of pleasures of sense; and so in like manner our other affections put forth the worse instead of the better growths),— on account of this the wise Husbandman leaves this growth that has been introduced among his seed to remain there, so as to secure our not being altogether stripped of better hopes by desire having been rooted out along with that good-for-nothing growth. If our nature suffered such a mutilation, what will there be to lift us up to grasp the heavenly delights? If love is taken from us, how shall we be united to God? If anger is to be extinguished, what arms shall we possess against the adversary? Therefore the Husbandman leaves those bastard seeds within us, not for them always to overwhelm the more precious crop, but in order that the land itself (for so, in his allegory, he calls the heart) by its native inherent power, which is that of reasoning, may wither up the one growth and may render the other fruitful and abundant: but if that is not done, then he commissions the fire to mark the distinction in the crops. If, then, a man indulges these affections in a due proportion and holds them in his own power instead of being held in theirs, employing them for an instrument as a king does his subjects' many hands, then efforts towards excellence more easily succeed for him. But should he become theirs, and, as when any slaves mutiny against their master, get enslaved by those slavish thoughts and ignominiously bow before them; a prey to his natural inferiors, he will be forced to turn to those employments which his imperious masters command. This being so, we shall not pronounce these emotions of the soul, which lie in the power of their possessors for good or ill, to be either virtue or vice. But, whenever their impulse is towards what is noble, then they become matter for praise, as his desire did to Daniel, and his anger to Phineas, and their grief to those who nobly mourn. But if they incline to baseness, then these are, and they are called, bad passions.

She ceased after this statement and allowed the discussion a short interval, in which I reviewed mentally all that had been said; and reverting to that former course of proof in her discourse, that it was not impossible that the soul after the body's dissolution should reside in its atoms, I again addressed her. Where is that much-talked-of and renowned Hades , then? The word is in frequent circulation both in the intercourse of daily life, and in the writings of the heathens and in our own; and all think that into it, as into a place of safe-keeping, souls migrate from here. Surely you would not call your atoms that Hades.

Clearly, replied the Teacher, you have not quite attended to the argument. In speaking of the soul's migration from the seen to the unseen, I thought I had omitted nothing as regards the question about Hades. It seems to me that, whether in the heathen or in the Divine writings, this word for a place in which souls are said to be means nothing else but a transition to that Unseen world of which we have no glimpse.

And how, then, I asked, is it that some think that by the underworld is meant an actual place, and that it harbours within itself the souls that have at last flitted away from human life, drawing them towards itself as the right receptacle for such natures?

Well, replied the Teacher, our doctrine will be in no ways injured by such a supposition. For if it *is* true, what you say , and also that the vault of heaven prolongs itself so uninterruptedly that it encircles all things with itself, and that the earth and its surroundings are poised in the middle, and that the motion of all the revolving bodies is round this fixed and solid centre, then, I say, there is an absolute necessity that, whatever may happen to each one of the atoms on the upper side of the earth, the same will happen on the opposite side, seeing that one single substance encompasses its entire bulk. As, when the sun shines *above* the earth, the shadow is spread over its lower part, because its spherical shape makes it impossible for it to be clasped all round at one and the same time by the rays, and necessarily, on whatever side the sun's rays may fall on some particular point of the globe, if we follow a straight diameter, we shall find shadow upon the opposite point, and so, continuously, at the opposite end of the direct line of the rays shadow moves round that globe, keeping pace with the sun, so that equally in their turn both the upper half and the under half of the earth are in light and darkness; so, by this analogy, we have reason to be certain that, whatever in our hemisphere is observed to befall the atoms, the same will befall them in that other. The environment of the atoms being one and the same on every side of the earth, I deem it right neither to contradict nor yet to favour those who raise the objection that we must regard either this or the lower region as assigned to the souls released. As long as this objection does not shake our central doctrine of the existence of those souls after the life in the flesh, there need be no controversy about the whereabouts to our mind, holding as we do that place is a property of body only, and that soul, being immaterial, is by no necessity of its nature detained in any place.

But what, I asked, if your opponent should shield himself behind the Apostle, where he says that every reasoning creature, in the restitution of all things, is to look towards Him Who presides over the whole? In that passage in the Epistle to the Philippians Philippians 2:10 he makes mention of certain things that are *"under the earth" "every knee shall bow"* to Him *"of things in heaven, and things in earth, and things under the earth."*

We shall stand by our doctrine, answered the Teacher, even if we should hear them adducing these words. For the existence of the soul (after death) we have the assent of our opponent, and so we do not make an objection as to the place, as we have just said.

But if some were to ask the meaning of the Apostle in this utterance, what is one to say? Would you remove all signification of place from the passage?

I do not think, she replied, that the divine Apostle divided the intellectual world into localities, when he named part as in heaven, part as on earth, and part as under the earth. There are three states in which reasoning creatures can be: one from the very first received an immaterial life, and we call it the angelic: another is in union with the flesh, and we call it the human: a third is released by death from fleshly entanglements, and is to be found in souls pure and simple. Now I think that the divine Apostle in his deep wisdom looked to this, when he revealed the future concord of all these reasoning beings in the work of goodness; and that he puts the unembodied angel-world *"in heaven,"* and that still involved with a body *"on earth,"* and that released from a body *"under the earth"*; or, indeed, if there is any other world to be classed under that which is possessed of reason (it is not left out); and whether any one choose to call this last *"demons"* or *"spirits,"* or anything else of the kind, we shall not care. We certainly believe, both because of the prevailing opinion, and still more of Scripture teaching, that there exists another world of beings besides, divested of such bodies as ours are, who are opposed to that which is good and are capable of hurting the lives of men, having by an act of will lapsed from the nobler view , and by this revolt from goodness personified in themselves the contrary principle; and this world is what, some say, the Apostle adds to the number of the *"things under the earth,"* signifying in that passage that when evil shall have been some day annihilated in the long revolutions of the ages, nothing shall be left outside the world of goodness, but that even from those evil spirits shall rise in harmony the confession of Christ's Lordship. If this is so, then no one can compel us to see any spot of the underworld in the expression, *"things under the earth"*; the atmosphere spreads equally over every part of the earth, and there is not a single corner of it left unrobed by this circumambient air.

When she had finished, I hesitated a moment, and then said: I am not yet satisfied about the thing which we have been inquiring into; after all that has been said my mind is still in doubt; and I beg that our discussion may be allowed to revert to the same line of reasoning as before , omitting only that upon which we are thoroughly agreed. I say this, for I think that all but the most stubborn controversialists will have been sufficiently convinced by our debate not to consign the soul after the body's dissolution to annihilation and nonentity, nor to argue that because it differs substantially from the atoms it is impossible for it to exist anywhere in the universe; for, however much a being that is intellectual and immaterial may fail to coincide with these atoms, it is in no ways hindered (so far) from existing in them; and this belief of ours rests on two facts: firstly, on the soul's existing in our bodies in this present life, though fundamentally different from them: and secondly, on the fact that the Divine being, as our argument has shown, though distinctly something other than visible and material substances, nevertheless pervades each one among all existences, and by this penetration of the whole keeps the world in a state of being; so that following these analogies we need not think that the soul, either, is out of existence, when she passes from the world of forms to the Unseen. But how, I insisted, after the united whole of the atoms has assumed , owing to their mixing together, a form quite different— the form in fact with which the soul has been actually domesticated— by what mark, when this form, as we should have expected, is effaced along with the resolution of the atoms, shall the soul follow along (them), now that that familiar form ceases to persist?

She waited a moment and then said: Give me leave to invent a fanciful simile in order to illustrate the matter before us: even though that which I suppose may be outside the range of possibility. Grant it possible, then, in the art of painting not only to mix opposite colours, as painters are always doing, to represent a particular tint , but also to separate again this mixture and to restore to each of the colours its natural dye. If then white, or black, or red, or golden colour, or any other colour that has been mixed to form the given tint, were to be again separated from that union with another and remain by itself, we suppose that our artist will none the less remember the actual nature of that colour, and that in no case will he show forgetfulness, either of the red, for instance, or the black, if after having become quite a different colour by composition with each other they each return to their natural dye. We suppose, I say, that our artist remembers the manner of the mutual blending of these colours, and so knows what sort of colour was mixed with a given colour and what sort of colour was the result, and how, the other colour being ejected from the composition, (the original colour) in consequence of such release resumed its own peculiar hue; and, supposing it were required to produce the same result again by composition, the process will be all the easier from having been already practised in his previous work. Now, if reason can see any analogy in this simile, we must search the matter in hand by its light. Let the soul stand for this Art of the painter ; and let the natural atoms stand for the colours of his art; and let the mixture of that tint compounded of the various dyes, and the return of these to their native state (which we have been allowed to assume), represent respectively the concourse, and the separation of the atoms. Then, as we assume in the simile that the painter's Art tells him the actual dye of each colour, when it has returned after mixing to its proper hue, so that he has an exact knowledge of the red, and of the black, and of any other colour that went to form the required tint by a specific way of uniting with another kind— a knowledge which includes its appearance both in the mixture, and now when it is in its natural state, and in the future again, supposing all the colours were mixed over again in like fashion— so, we assert, does the soul know the natural peculiarities of those atoms whose concourse makes the frame of the body in which it has itself grown, even after the scattering of those atoms. However far from each other their natural propensity and their inherent forces of repulsion urge them, and debar each from mingling with its opposite, none the less will the soul be near each by its power of recognition, and will persistently cling to the familiar atoms, until their concourse after this division again takes place in the same way, for that fresh formation of the dissolved body which will properly be, and be called, resurrection.

You seem, I interrupted, in this passing remark to have made an excellent defence of the faith in the Resurrection. By it, I think, the opponents of this doctrine might be gradually led to consider it not as a thing absolutely impossible that the atoms should again coalesce and form the same man as before.

That is very true, the Teacher replied. For we may hear these opponents urging the following difficulty. *"The atoms are resolved, like to like, into the universe; by what device, then, does the warmth, for instance, residing in such and such a man, after joining the universal warmth, again dissociate itself from this connection with its kindred , so as to form this man who is being 'remoulded'? For if the identical individual particle does not return and only something that is homogeneous but not identical is fetched, you will have something else in the place of that first thing, and such a process will cease to be a resurrection and will be merely the creation of a new man. But if the same man is to return into himself, he must be the same entirely, and regain his original formation in every single atom of his elements."*

Then to meet such an objection, I rejoined, the above opinion about the soul will, as I said, avail; namely, that she remains after dissolution in those very atoms in which she first grew up, and, like a guardian placed over private property, does not abandon them when they are mingled with their kindred atoms, and by the subtle ubiquity of her intelligence makes no mistake about them, with all their subtle minuteness, but diffuses herself along with those which belong to herself when they are being mingled with their kindred dust, and suffers no exhaustion in keeping up with the whole number of them when they stream back into the universe, but remains with them, no matter in what direction or in what fashion Nature may arrange them. But should the signal be given by the All-disposing Power for these scattered atoms to combine again, then, just as when every one of the various ropes that hang from one block answer at one and the same moment to the pull from that centre, so, following this force of the soul which acts upon the various atoms, all these, once so familiar with each other, rush simultaneously together and form the cable of the body by means of the soul, each single one of them being wedded to its former neighbour and embracing an old acquaintance.

The following illustration also, the Teacher went on, might be very properly added to those already brought forward, to show that the soul has not need of much teaching in order to distinguish its own from the alien among the atoms. Imagine a potter with a supply of clay; and let the supply be a large one; and let part of it have been already moulded to form finished vessels, while the rest is still waiting to be moulded; and suppose the vessels themselves not to be all of similar shape, but one to be a jug, for instance, and another a wine-jar, another a plate, another a cup or any other useful vessel; and further, let not one owner possess them all, but let us fancy for each a special owner. Now as long as these vessels are unbroken they are of course recognizable by their owners, and none the less so, even should they be broken in pieces; for from those pieces each will know, for instance, that this belongs to a jar , and, again, what sort of fragment belongs to a cup. And if they are plunged again into the unworked clay, the discernment between what has been already worked and that clay will be a more unerring one still. The individual man is as such a vessel; he has been moulded out of the universal matter, owing to the concourse of his atoms; and he exhibits in a form peculiarly his own a marked distinction from his kind; and when that form has gone to pieces the soul that has been mistress of this particular vessel will have an exact knowledge of it, derived even from its fragments; nor will she leave this property, either, in the common blending with all the other fragments, or if it be plunged into the still formless part of the matter from which the atoms have come ; she always remembers her own as it was when compact in bodily form, and after dissolution she never makes any mistake about it, led by marks still clinging to the remains.

I applauded this as well devised to bring out the natural features of the case before us; and I said: It is very well to speak like this and to believe that it is so; but suppose some one were to quote against it our Lord's narrative about those who are in hell, as not harmonizing with the results of our inquiry, how are we to be prepared with an answer?

The Teacher answered: The expressions of that narrative of the Word are certainly material; but still many hints are interspersed in it to rouse the skilled inquirer to a more discriminating study of it. I mean that He Who parts the good from the bad by a great gulf, and makes the man in torment crave for a drop to be conveyed by a finger, and the man who has been ill-treated in this life rest on a patriarch's bosom, and Who relates their previous death and consignment to the tomb, takes an intelligent searcher of His meaning far beyond a superficial interpretation. For what sort of eyes has the Rich Man to lift up in hell, when he has left his bodily eyes in that tomb? And how can a disembodied spirit feel any flame? And what sort of tongue can he crave to be cooled with the drop of water, when he has lost his tongue of flesh? What is the finger that is to convey to him this drop? What sort of place is the *"bosom"* of repose? The bodies of both of them are in the tomb, and their souls are disembodied, and do not consist of parts either; and so it is impossible to make the framework of the narrative correspond with the truth, if we understand it literally; we can do that only by translating each detail into an equivalent in the world of ideas. Thus we must think of the gulf as that which parts ideas which may not be confounded from running together, not as a chasm of the earth. Such a chasm, however vast it were, could be traversed with no difficulty by a disembodied intelligence; since intelligence can in no time be wherever it will.

What then, I asked, *are* the fire and the gulf and the other features in the picture? Are they not that which they are said to be?

I think, she replied, that the Gospel signifies by means of each of them certain doctrines with regard to our question of the soul. For when the patriarch first says to the Rich Man, *"You in your lifetime received your good things,"* and in the same way speaks of the Poor Man, that he, namely, has done his duty in bearing his share of life's evil things, and then, after that, adds with regard to the gulf that it is a barrier between them, he evidently by such expressions intimates a very important truth; and, to my thinking, it is as follows. Once man's life had but one character; and by that I mean that it was to be found only in the category of the good and had no contact with evil. The first of God's commandments attests the truth of this; that, namely, which gave to man unstinted enjoyment of all the blessings of Paradise, forbidding only that which was a mixture of good and evil and so composed of contraries, but making death the penalty for transgressing in that particular. But man, acting freely by a voluntary impulse, deserted the lot that was unmixed with evil, and drew upon himself that which was a mixture of contraries. Yet Divine Providence did not leave that recklessness of ours without a corrective. Death indeed, as the fixed penalty for breaking the law, necessarily fell upon its transgressors; but God divided the life of man into two parts, namely, this present life, and that *"out of the body"* hereafter; and He placed on the first a limit of the briefest possible time, while He prolonged the other into eternity; and in His love for man He gave him his choice, to have the one or the other of those things, good or evil, I mean, in which of the two parts he liked: either in this short and transitory life, or in those endless ages, whose limit is infinity. Now these expressions *"good"* and *"evil"* are equivocal; they are used in two senses, one relating to mind and the other to sense; some classify as good whatever is pleasant to feeling: others are confident that only that which is perceptible by intelligence is good and deserves that name. Those, then, whose reasoning powers have never been exercised and who have never had a glimpse of the better way soon use up on gluttony in this fleshly life the dividend of good which their constitution can claim, and they reserve none of it for the after life; but those who by a discreet and sober-minded calculation economize the powers of living are afflicted by things painful to sense here, but they reserve their good for the succeeding life, and so their happier lot is lengthened out to last as long as that eternal life. This, in my opinion, is the *"gulf"*; which is not made by the parting of the earth, but by those decisions in this life which result in a separation into opposite characters. The man who has once chosen pleasure in this life, and has not cured his inconsiderateness by repentance, places the land of the good beyond his own reach; for he has dug against himself the yawning impassable abyss of a necessity that nothing can break through. This is the reason, I think, that the name of Abraham's bosom is given to that good situation of the soul in which Scripture makes the athlete of endurance repose. For it is related of this patriarch first, of all up to that time born, that he exchanged the enjoyment of the present for the hope of the future; he was stripped of all the surroundings in which his life at first was passed, and resided among foreigners, and thus purchased by present annoyance future blessedness. As then figuratively we call a particular circuit of the ocean a *"bosom,"* so does Scripture seem to me to express the idea of those measureless blessings above by the word *"bosom,"* meaning a place into which all virtuous voyagers of this life are, when they have put in from hence, brought to anchor in the waveless harbour of that gulf of blessings. Meanwhile the denial of these blessings which they witness becomes in the others a flame, which burns the soul and causes the craving for the refreshment of one drop out of that ocean of blessings wherein the saints are affluent; which nevertheless they do not get. If, too, you consider the *"tongue,"* and the *"eye,"* and the *"finger,"* and the other names of bodily organs, which occur in the conversation between those disembodied souls, you will be persuaded that this conjecture of ours about them chimes in with the opinion we have already stated about the soul. Look closely into the meaning of those words. For as the concourse of atoms forms the substance of the entire body, so it is reasonable to think that the same cause operates to complete the substance of each member of the body. If, then, the soul is present with the atoms of the body when they are again mingled with the universe, it will not only be cognizant of the entire mass which once came together to form the whole body, and will be present with it, but, besides that, will not fail to know the particular materials of each one of the members, so as to remember by what divisions among the atoms our limbs were completely formed. There is, then, nothing improbable in supposing that what is present in the complete mass is present also in each division of the mass. If one, then, thinks of those atoms in which each detail of the body potentially inheres, and surmises that Scripture means a *"finger"* and a *"tongue"* and an *"eye"* and the rest as existing, after dissolution, only in the sphere of the soul, one will not miss the probable truth.

Moreover, if each detail carries the mind away from a material acceptation of the story, surely the *"hell"* which we have just been speaking of cannot reasonably be thought a place so named; rather we are there told by Scripture about a certain unseen and immaterial situation in which the soul resides. In this story of the Rich and the Poor Man we are taught another doctrine also, which is intimately connected with our former discoveries. The story makes the sensual pleasure-loving man, when he sees that his own case is one that admits of no escape, evince forethought for his relations on earth; and when Abraham tells him that the life of those still in the flesh is not unprovided with a guidance, for they may find it at hand, if they will, in the Law and the Prophets, he still continues entreating that Just Patriarch, and asks that a sudden and convincing message, brought by some one risen from the dead, may be sent to them.

What then, I asked, is the doctrine here?

Why, seeing that Lazarus' soul is occupied with his present blessings and turns round to look at nothing that he has left, while the rich man is still attached, with a cement as it were, even after death, to the life of feeling, which he does not divest himself of even when he has ceased to live, still keeping as he does flesh and blood in his thoughts (for in his entreaty that his kindred may be exempted from his sufferings he plainly shows that he is not freed yet from fleshly feeling)—in such details of the story (she continued) I think our Lord teaches us this; that those still living in the flesh must as much as ever they can separate and free themselves in a way from its attachments by virtuous conduct, in order that after death they may not need a second death to cleanse them from the remnants that are owing to this cement of the flesh, and, when once the bonds are loosed from around the soul, her soaring up to the Good may be swift and unimpeded, with no anguish of the body to distract her. For if any one becomes wholly and thoroughly carnal in thought, such an one, with every motion and energy of the soul absorbed in fleshly desires, is not parted from such attachments, even in the disembodied state; just as those who have lingered long in noisome places do not part with the unpleasantness contracted by that lengthened stay, even when they pass into a sweet atmosphere. So it is that, when the change is made into the impalpable Unseen, not even then will it be possible for the lovers of the flesh to avoid dragging away with them under any circumstances some fleshly foulness; and thereby their torment will be intensified, their soul having been materialized by such surroundings. I think too that this view of the matter harmonizes to a certain extent with the assertion made by some persons that around their graves shadowy phantoms of the departed are often seen. If this is really so, an inordinate attachment of that particular soul to the life in the flesh is proved to have existed, causing it to be unwilling, even when expelled from the flesh, to fly clean away and to admit the complete change of its form into the impalpable; it remains near the frame even after the dissolution of the frame, and though now outside it, hovers regretfully over the place where its material is and continues to haunt it.

Then, after a moment's reflection on the meaning of these latter words, I said: I think that a contradiction now arises between what you have said and the result of our former examination of the passions. For if, on the one hand, the activity of such movements within us is to be held as arising from our kinship with the brutes, such movements I mean as were enumerated in our previous discussion , anger, for instance, and fear, desire of pleasure, and so on, and, on the other hand, it was affirmed that virtue consists in the good employment of these movements, and vice in their bad employment, and in addition to this we discussed the actual contribution of each of the other passions to a virtuous life, and found that through desire above all we are brought nearer God, drawn up, by its chain as it were, from earth towards Him—I think (I said) that that part of the discussion is in a way opposed to that which we are now aiming at.

How so? She asked.

Why, when every unreasoning instinct is quenched within us after our purgation, this principle of desire will not exist any more than the other principles; and this being removed, it looks as if the striving after the better way would also cease, no other emotion remaining in the soul that can stir us up to the appetence of Good.

To that objection, she replied, we answer this. The speculative and critical faculty is the property of the soul's godlike part; for it is by these that we grasp the Deity also. If, then whether by forethought here, or by purgation hereafter, our soul becomes free from any emotional connection with the brute creation, there will be nothing to impede its contemplation of the Beautiful; for this last is essentially capable of attracting in a certain way every being that looks towards it. If, then, the soul is purified of every vice, it will most certainly be in the sphere of Beauty. The Deity is in very substance Beautiful; and to the Deity the soul will in its state of purity have affinity, and will embrace It as like itself. Whenever this happens, then, there will be no longer need of the impulse of Desire to lead the way to the Beautiful. Whoever passes his time in darkness, he it is who will be under the influence of a desire for the light; but whenever he comes into the light, then enjoyment takes the place of desire, and the power to enjoy renders desire useless and out of date. It will therefore be no detriment to our participation in the Good, that the soul should be free from such emotions, and turning back upon herself should know herself accurately what her actual nature is, and should behold the Original Beauty reflected in the mirror and in the figure of her own beauty. For truly herein consists the real assimilation to the Divine; viz. in making our own life in some degree a copy of the Supreme Being. For a Nature like that, which transcends all thought and is far removed from all that we observe within ourselves, proceeds in its existence in a very different manner to what we do in this present life. Man, possessing a constitution whose law it is to be moving, is carried in that particular direction whither the impulse of his will directs: and so his soul is not affected in the same way towards what lies before it , as one may say, as to what it has left behind; for hope leads the forward movement, but it is memory that succeeds that movement when it has advanced to the attainment of the hope; and if it is to something intrinsically good that hope thus leads on the soul, the print that this exercise of the will leaves upon the memory is a bright one; but if hope has seduced the soul with some phantom only of the Good, and the excellent Way has been missed, then the memory that succeeds what has happened becomes shame, and an intestine war is thus waged in the soul between memory and hope, because the last has been such a bad leader of the will. Such in fact is the state of mind that shame gives expression to; the soul is stung as it were at the result; its remorse for its ill-considered attempt is a whip that makes it feel to the quick, and it would bring in oblivion to its aid against its tormentor. Now in our case nature, owing to its being indigent of the Good, is aiming always at this which is still wanting to it, and this aiming at a still missing thing is this very habit of Desire, which our constitution displays equally, whether it is baulked of the real Good, or wins that which it is good to win. But a nature that surpasses every idea that we can form of the Good and transcends all other power, being in no want of anything that can be regarded as good, is itself the plenitude of every good; it does not move in the sphere of the good by way of participation in it only, but it is itself the substance of the Good (whatever we imagine the Good to be); it neither gives scope for any rising hope (for hope manifests activity in the direction of something absent; but *"what a man has, why does he yet hope for?"* as the Apostle asks), nor is it in want of the activity of the memory for the knowledge of things; that which is actually seen has no need of being remembered. Since, then, this Divine nature is beyond any particular good , and to the good the good is an object of love, it follows that when It looks within Itself , It wishes for what It contains and contains that which It wishes, and admits nothing external. Indeed there is nothing external to It, with the sole exception of evil, which, strange as it may seem to say, possesses an existence in not existing at all. For there is no other origin of evil except the negation of the existent, and the truly-existent forms the substance of the Good. That therefore which is not to be found in the existent must be in the non-existent. Whenever the soul, then, having divested itself of the multifarious emotions incident to its nature, gets its Divine form and, mounting above Desire, enters within that towards which it was once incited by that Desire, it offers no harbour within itself either for hope or for memory. It holds the object of the one; the other is extruded from the consciousness by the occupation in enjoying all that is good: and thus the soul copies the life that is above, and is conformed to the peculiar features of the Divine nature; none of its habits are left to it except that of love, which clings by natural affinity to the Beautiful. For this is what love is; the inherent affection towards a chosen object. When, then, the soul, having become simple and single in form and so perfectly godlike, finds that perfectly simple and immaterial good which is really worth enthusiasm and love , it attaches itself to it and blends with it by means of the movement and activity of love, fashioning itself according to that which it is continually finding and grasping. Becoming by this assimilation to the Good all that the nature of that which it participates is, the soul will consequently, owing to there being no lack of any good in that thing itself which it participates, be itself also in no lack of anything, and so will expel from within the activity and the habit of Desire; for this arises only when the thing missed is not found. For this teaching we have the authority of God's own Apostle, who announces a subduing and a ceasing of all other activities, even for the good, which are within us, and finds no limit for love alone. Prophecies, he says, shall fail; forms of knowledge shall cease; but *"charity never fails;"* which is equivalent to its being always as it is: and though he says that faith and hope have endured so far by the side of love, yet again he prolongs its date beyond theirs, and with good reason too; for hope is in operation only so long as the enjoyment of the things hoped for is not to be had; and faith in the same way is a support in the uncertainty about the things hoped for; for so he defines it— *"the substance of things hoped for"*; but when the thing hoped for actually comes, then all other faculties are reduced to quiescence , and love alone remains active, finding nothing to succeed itself. Love, therefore, is the foremost of all excellent achievements and the first of the commandments of the law. If ever, then, the soul reach this goal, it will be in no need of anything else; it will embrace that plenitude of things which are, whereby alone it seems in any way to preserve within itself the stamp of God's actual blessedness. For the life of the Supreme Being is love, seeing that the Beautiful is necessarily lovable to those who recognize it, and the Deity does recognize it, and so this recognition becomes love, that which He recognizes being essentially beautiful. This True Beauty the insolence of satiety cannot touch ; and no satiety interrupting this continuous capacity to love the Beautiful, God's life will have its activity in love; which life is thus in itself beautiful, and is essentially of a loving disposition towards the Beautiful, and receives no check to this activity of love. In fact, in the Beautiful no limit is to be found so that love should have to cease with any limit of the Beautiful. This last can be ended only by its opposite; but when you have a good, as here, which is in its essence incapable of a change for the worse, then that good will go on unchecked into infinity. Moreover, as every being is capable of attracting its like, and humanity is, in a way, like God, as bearing within itself some resemblances to its Prototype, the soul is by a strict necessity attracted to the kindred Deity. In fact what belongs to God must by all means and at any cost be preserved for Him. If, then, on the one hand, the soul is unencumbered with superfluities and no trouble connected with the body presses it down, its advance towards Him Who draws it to Himself is sweet and congenial. But suppose , on the other hand, that it has been transfixed with the nails of propension so as to be held down to a habit connected with material things—a case like that of those in the ruins caused by earthquakes, whose bodies are crushed by the mounds of rubbish; and let us imagine by way of illustration that these are not only pressed down by the weight of the ruins, but have been pierced as well with some spikes and splinters discovered with them in the rubbish. What then, would naturally be the plight of those bodies, when they were being dragged by relatives from the ruins to receive the holy rites of burial, mangled and torn entirely, disfigured in the most direful manner conceivable, with the nails beneath the heap harrowing them by the very violence necessary to pull them out?— Such I think is the plight of the soul as well when the Divine force, for God's very love of man, drags that which belongs to Him from the ruins of the irrational and material. Not in hatred or revenge for a wicked life, to my thinking, does God bring upon sinners those painful dispensations; He is only claiming and drawing to Himself whatever, to please Him, came into existence. But while He for a noble end is attracting the soul to Himself, the Fountain of all Blessedness, it is the occasion necessarily to the being so attracted of a state of torture. Just as those who refine gold from the dross which it contains not only get this base alloy to melt in the fire, but are obliged to melt the pure gold along with the alloy, and then while this last is being consumed the gold remains, so, while evil is being consumed in the purgatorial fire, the soul that is welded to this evil must inevitably be in the fire too, until the spurious material alloy is consumed and annihilated by this fire. If a clay of the more tenacious kind is deeply plastered round a rope, and then the end of the rope is put through a narrow hole, and then some one on the further side violently pulls it by that end, the result must be that, while the rope itself obeys the force exerted, the clay that has been plastered upon it is scraped off it with this violent pulling and is left outside the hole, and, moreover, is the cause why the rope does not run easily through the passage, but has to undergo a violent tension at the hands of the puller. In such a manner, I think, we may figure to ourselves the agonized struggle of that soul which has wrapped itself up in earthy material passions, when God is drawing it, His own one, to Himself, and the foreign matter, which has somehow grown into its substance, has to be scraped from it by main force, and so occasions it that keen intolerable anguish.

Then it seems, I said, that it is not punishment chiefly and principally that the Deity, as Judge, afflicts sinners with; but He operates, as your argument has shown, only to get the good separated from the evil and to attract it into the communion of blessedness.

That, said the Teacher, is my meaning; and also that the agony will be measured by the amount of evil there is in each individual. For it would not be reasonable to think that the man who has remained so long as we have supposed in evil known to be forbidden, and the man who has fallen only into moderate sins, should be tortured to the same amount in the judgment upon their vicious habit; but according to the quantity of material will be the longer or shorter time that that agonizing flame will be burning; that is, as long as there is fuel to feed it. In the case of the man who has acquired a heavy weight of material, the consuming fire must necessarily be very searching; but where that which the fire has to feed upon has spread less far, there the penetrating fierceness of the punishment is mitigated, so far as the subject itself, in the amount of its evil, is diminished. In any and every case evil must be removed out of existence, so that, as we said above, the absolutely non-existent should cease to be at all. Since it is not in its nature that evil should exist outside the will, does it not follow that when it shall be that every will rests in God, evil will be reduced to complete annihilation, owing to no receptacle being left for it?

But, said I, what help can one find in this devout hope, when one considers the greatness of the evil in undergoing torture even for a single year; and if that intolerable anguish be prolonged for the interval of an age, what grain of comfort is left from any subsequent expectation to him whose purgation is thus commensurate with an entire age?

Why , either we must plan to keep the soul absolutely untouched and free from any stain of evil; or, if our passionate nature makes that quite impossible, then we must plan that our failures in excellence consist only in mild and easily-curable derelictions. For the Gospel in its teaching distinguishes between a debtor of ten thousand talents and a debtor of five hundred pence, and of fifty pence and of a farthing , which is *"the uttermost"* of coins; it proclaims that God's just judgment reaches to all, and enhances the payment necessary as the weight of the debt increases, and on the other hand does not overlook the very smallest debts. But the Gospel tells us that this payment of debts was not effected by the refunding of money, but that the indebted man was delivered to the tormentors until he should pay the whole debt; and that means nothing else than paying in the coin of torment the inevitable recompense, the recompense, I mean, that consists in taking the share of pain incurred during his lifetime, when he inconsiderately chose mere pleasure, undiluted with its opposite; so that having put off from him all that foreign growth which sin is, and discarded the shame of any debts, he might stand in liberty and fearlessness. Now liberty is the coming up to a state which owns no master and is self-regulating; it is that with which we were gifted by God at the beginning, but which has been obscured by the feeling of shame arising from indebtedness. Liberty too is in all cases one and the same essentially; it has a natural attraction to itself. It follows, then, that as everything that is free will be united with its like, and as virtue is a thing that has no master, that is, is free, everything that is free will be united with virtue. But, further, the Divine Being is the fountain of all virtue. Therefore, those who have parted with evil will be united with Him; and so, as the Apostle says, God will be *"all in all"*; for this utterance seems to me plainly to confirm the opinion we have already arrived at, for it means that God will be instead of all other things, and in all. For while our present life is active among a variety of multiform conditions, and the things we have relations with are numerous, for instance, time, air, locality, food and drink, clothing, sunlight, lamplight, and other necessities of life, none of which, many though they be, are God—that blessed state which we hope for is in need of none of these things, but the Divine Being will become all, and instead of all, to us, distributing Himself proportionately to every need of that existence. It is plain, too, from the Holy Scripture that God becomes, to those who deserve it, locality, and home, and clothing, and food, and drink, and light, and riches, and dominion, and everything thinkable and nameable that goes to make our life happy. But He that becomes *"all"* things will be *"in all"* things too; and herein it appears to me that Scripture teaches the complete annihilation of evil. If, that is, God will be *"in all"* existing things, evil; plainly, will not then be among them; for if any one was to assume that it did exist then, how will the belief that God will be *"in all"* be kept intact? The excepting of that one thing, evil, mars the comprehensiveness of the term *"all."* But He that will be *"in all"* will never be in that which does not exist.

What then, I asked, are we to say to those whose hearts fail at these calamities?

We will say to them, replied the Teacher, this. *"It is foolish, good people, for you to fret and complain of the chain of this fixed sequence of life's realities; you do not know the goal towards which each single dispensation of the universe is moving. You do not know that all things have to be assimilated to the Divine Nature in accordance with the artistic plan of their author, in a certain regularity and order. Indeed, it was for this that intelligent beings came into existence; namely, that the riches of the Divine blessings should not lie idle. The All-creating Wisdom fashioned these souls, these receptacles with free wills, as vessels as it were, for this very purpose, that there should be some capacities able to receive His blessings and become continually larger with the inpouring of the stream. Such are the wonders that the participation in the Divine blessings works: it makes him into whom they come larger and more capacious; from his capacity to receive it gets for the receiver an actual increase in bulk as well, and he never stops enlarging. The fountain of blessings wells up unceasingly, and the partaker's nature, finding nothing superfluous and without a use in that which it receives, makes the whole influx an enlargement of its own proportions, and becomes at once more wishful to imbibe the nobler nourishment and more capable of containing it; each grows along with each, both the capacity which is nursed in such abundance of blessings and so grows greater, and the nurturing supply which comes on in a flood answering to the growth of those increasing powers. It is likely, therefore, that this bulk will mount to such a magnitude as there is no limit to check, so that we should not grow into it. With such a prospect before us, are you angry that our nature is advancing to its goal along the path appointed for us? Why, our career cannot be run there-ward, except that which weighs us down, I mean this encumbering load of earthiness, be shaken off the soul; nor can we be domiciled in Purity with the corresponding part of our nature, unless we have cleansed ourselves by a better training from the habit of affection which we have contracted in life towards this earthiness. But if there be in you any clinging to this body , and the being unlocked from this darling thing give you pain, let not this, either, make you despair. You will behold this bodily envelopment, which is now dissolved in death, woven again out of the same atoms, not indeed into this organization with its gross and heavy texture, but with its threads worked up into something more subtle and ethereal, so that you will not only have near you that which you love, but it will be restored to you with a brighter and more entrancing beauty."*

But it somehow seems to me now, I said, that the doctrine of the Resurrection necessarily comes on for our discussion; a doctrine which I think is even at first sight true as well as credible , as it is told us in Scripture; so that that will not come in question between us: but since the weakness of the human understanding is strengthened still farther by any arguments that are intelligible to us, it would be well not to leave this part of the subject, either, without philosophical examination. Let us consider, then, what ought to be said about it.

As for the thinkers, the Teacher went on, outside our own system of thought, they have, with all their diverse ways of looking at things, one in one point, another in another, approached and touched the doctrine of the Resurrection: while they none of them exactly coincide with us, they have in no case wholly abandoned such an expectation. Some indeed make human nature vile in their comprehensiveness, maintaining that a soul becomes alternately that of a man and of something irrational; that it transmigrates into various bodies, changing at pleasure from the man into fowl, fish, or beast, and then returning to human kind. While some extend this absurdity even to trees and shrubs, so that they consider their wooden life as corresponding and akin to humanity, others of them hold only thus much— that the soul exchanges one man for another man, so that the life of humanity is continued always by means of the same souls, which, being exactly the same in number, are being born perpetually first in one generation, then in another. As for ourselves, we take our stand upon the tenets of the Church, and assert that it will be well to accept only so much of these speculations as is sufficient to show that those who indulge in them are to a certain extent in accord with the doctrine of the Resurrection. Their statement, for instance, that the soul after its release from this body insinuates itself into certain other bodies is not absolutely out of harmony with the revival which we hope for. For our view, which maintains that the body, both now, and again in the future, is composed of the atoms of the universe, is held equally by these heathens. In fact, you cannot imagine any constitution of the body independent of a concourse of these atoms. But the divergence lies in this: we assert that the same body again as before, composed of the same atoms, is compacted around the soul; they suppose that the soul alights on other bodies, not only rational, but irrational and even insensate; and while all are agreed that these bodies which the soul resumes derive their substance from the atoms of the universe, they part company from us in thinking that they are not made out of identically the same atoms as those which in this mortal life grew around the soul. Let then, this external testimony stand for the fact that it is not contrary to probability that the soul should again inhabit a body; after that however, it is incumbent upon us to make a survey of the inconsistencies of their position, and it will be easy thus, by means of the consequences that arise as we follow out the consistent view, to bring the truth to light. What, then, is to be said about these theories? This that those who would have it that the soul migrates into natures divergent from each other seem to me to obliterate all natural distinctions; to blend and confuse together, in every possible respect, the rational, the irrational, the sentient, and the insensate; if, that is, all these are to pass into each other, with no distinct natural order secluding them from mutual transition. To say that one and the same soul, on account of a particular environment of body, is at one time a rational and intellectual soul, and that then it is caverned along with the reptiles, or herds with the birds, or is a beast of burden, or a carnivorous one, or swims in the deep; or even drops down to an insensate thing, so as to strike out roots or become a complete tree, producing buds on branches, and from those buds a flower, or a thorn, or a fruit edible or noxious— to say this, is nothing short of making all things the same and believing that one single nature runs through all beings; that there is a connection between them which blends and confuses hopelessly all the marks by which one could be distinguished from another. The philosopher who asserts that the same thing may be born in anything intends no less than that all things are to be one; when the observed differences in things are for him no obstacle to mixing together things which are utterly incongruous. He makes it necessary that, even when one sees one of the creatures that are venom-darting or carnivorous, one should regard it, in spite of appearances, as of the same tribe, nay even of the same family, as oneself. With such beliefs a man will look even upon hemlock as not alien to his own nature, detecting, as he does, humanity in the plant. The grape-bunch itself, produced though it be by cultivation for the purpose of sustaining life, he will not regard without suspicion; for it too comes from a plant : and we find even the fruit of the ears of grain upon which we live are plants; how, then, can one put in the sickle to cut them down; and how can one squeeze the bunch, or pull up the thistle from the field, or gather flowers, or hunt birds, or set fire to the logs of the funeral pyre: it being all the while uncertain whether we are not laying violent hands on kinsmen, or ancestors, or fellow-country-men, and whether it is not through the medium of some body of theirs that the fire is being kindled, and the cup mixed, and the food prepared? To think that in the case of any single one of these things a soul of a man has become a plant or animal , while no marks are stamped upon them to indicate what sort of plant or animal it is that has been a man, and what sort has sprung from other beginnings—such a conception as this will dispose him who has entertained it to feel an equal amount of interest in everything: he must perforce either harden himself against actual human beings who are in the land of the living, or, if his nature inclines him to love his kindred, he will feel alike towards every kind of life, whether he meet it in reptiles or in wild beasts. Why, if the holder of such an opinion go into a thicket of trees, even then he will regard the trees as a crowd of men. What sort of life will his be, when he has to be tender towards everything on the ground of kinship, or else hardened towards mankind on account of his seeing no difference between them and the other creatures? From what has been already said, then, we must reject this theory: and there are many other considerations as well which on the grounds of mere consistency lead us away from it. For I have heard persons who hold these opinions saying that whole nations of souls are hidden away somewhere in a realm of their own, living a life analogous to that of the embodied soul; but such is the fineness and buoyancy of their substance that they themselves' roll round along with the revolution of the universe; and that these souls, having individually lost their wings through some gravitation towards evil, become embodied; first this takes place in men; and after that, passing from a human life, owing to brutish affinities of their passions, they are reduced to the level of brutes; and, leaving that, drop down to this insensate life of pure nature which you have been hearing so much of; so that that inherently fine and buoyant thing that the soul is first becomes weighted and downward tending in consequence of some vice, and so migrates to a human body; then its reasoning powers are extinguished, and it goes on living in some brute; and then even this gift of sensation is withdrawn, and it changes into the insensate plant life; but after that mounts up again by the same gradations until it is restored to its place in heaven. Now this doctrine will at once be found, even after a very cursory survey, to have no coherency with itself. For, first, seeing that the soul is to be dragged down from its life in heaven, on account of evil there, to the condition of a tree, and is then from this point, on account of virtue exhibited there, to return to heaven, their theory will be unable to decide which is to have the preference, the life in heaven, or the life in the tree. A circle, in fact, of the same sequences will be perpetually traversed, where the soul, at whatever point it may be, has no resting-place. If it thus lapses from the disembodied state to the embodied, and thence to the insensate, and then springs back to the disembodied, an inextricable confusion of good and evil must result in the minds of those who thus teach. For the life in heaven will no more preserve its blessedness (since evil can touch heaven's denizens), than the life in trees will be devoid of virtue (since it is from this, they say, that the rebound of the soul towards the good begins, while from there it begins the evil life again). Secondly, seeing that the soul as it moves round in heaven is there entangled with evil and is in consequence dragged down to live in mere matter, from whence, however, it is lifted again into its residence on high, it follows that those philosophers establish the very contrary of their own views; they establish, namely, that the life in matter is the purgation of evil, while that undeviating revolution along with the stars is the foundation and cause of evil in every soul: if it is here that the soul by means of virtue grows its wing and then soars upwards, and there that those wings by reason of evil fall off, so that it descends and clings to this lower world and is commingled with the grossness of material nature. But the untenableness of this view does not stop even in this, namely, that it contains assertions diametrically opposed to each other. Beyond this, their fundamental conception itself cannot stand secure on every side. They say, for instance, that a heavenly nature is unchangeable. How then, can there be room for any weakness in the unchangeable? If, again, a lower nature is subject to infirmity, how in the midst of this infirmity can freedom from it be achieved? They attempt to amalgamate two things that can never be joined together: they descry strength in weakness, passionlessness in passion. But even to this last view they are not faithful throughout; for they bring home the soul from its material life to that very place whence they had exiled it because of evil there, as though the life in that place was quite safe and uncontaminated; apparently quite forgetting the fact that the soul was weighted with evil *there*, before it plunged down into this lower world. The blame thrown on the life here below, and the praise of the things in heaven, are thus interchanged and reversed; for that which was once blamed conducts in their opinion to the brighter life, while that which was taken for the better state gives an impulse to the soul's propensity to evil. Expel, therefore, from among the doctrines of the Faith all erroneous and shifting suppositions about such matters! We must not follow, either, as though they had hit the truth those who suppose that souls pass from women's bodies to live in men, or, reversely, that souls that have parted with men's bodies exist in women: or even if they only say that they pass from men into men, or from women into women. As for the former theory, not only has it been rejected for being shifting and illusory, and for landing us in opinions diametrically opposed to each other; but it must be rejected also because it is a godless theory, maintaining as it does that nothing among the things in nature is brought into existence without deriving its peculiar constitution from evil as its source. If, that is, neither men nor plants nor cattle can be born unless some soul from above has fallen into them, and if this fall is owing to some tendency to evil, then they evidently think that evil controls the creation of all beings. In some mysterious way, too, both events are to occur at once; the birth of the man in consequence of a marriage, and the fall of the soul (synchronizing as it must with the proceedings at that marriage). A greater absurdity even than this is involved: if, as is the fact, the large majority of the brute creation copulate in the spring, are we, then, to say that the spring brings it about that evil is engendered in the revolving world above, so that, at one and the same moment, *there* certain souls are impregnated with evil and so fall, and *here* certain brutes conceive? And what are we to say about the husbandman who sets the vine-shoots in the soil? How does his hand manage to have covered in a human soul along with the plant, and how does the moulting of wings last simultaneously with his employment in planting? The same absurdity, it is to be observed, exists in the other of the two theories as well; in the direction, I mean, of thinking that the soul must be anxious about the intercourses of those living in wedlock, and must be on the look-out for the times of bringing forth, in order that it may insinuate itself into the bodies then produced. Supposing the man refuses the union, or the woman keeps herself clear of the necessity of becoming a mother, will evil then fail to weigh down that particular soul? Will it be marriage, in consequence, that sounds up above the first note of evil in the soul, or will this reversed state invade the soul quite independently of any marriage?

But then, in this last case, the soul will have to wander about in the interval like a houseless vagabond, lapsed as it has from its heavenly surroundings, and yet, as it may happen in some cases, still without a body to receive it. But how, after that, can they imagine that the Deity exercises any superintendence over the world, referring as they do the beginnings of human lives to this casual and meaningless descent of a soul. For all that follows must necessarily accord with the beginning; and so, if a life begins in consequence of a chance accident, the whole course of it becomes at once a chapter of accidents, and the attempt to make the whole world depend on a Divine power is absurd, when it is made by these men, who deny to the individualities in it a birth from the fiat of the Divine Will and refer the several origins of beings to encounters that come of evil, as though there could never have existed such a thing as a human life, unless a vice had struck, as it were, its leading note. If the beginning is like that, a sequel will most certainly be set in motion in accordance with that beginning. None would dare to maintain that what is fair can come out of what is foul, any more than from good can come its opposite. We expect fruit in accordance with the nature of the seed. Therefore this blind movement of chance is to rule the whole of life, and no Providence is any more to pervade the world.

Nay, even the forecasting by our calculations will be quite useless; virtue will lose its value; and to turn from evil will not be worth the while. Everything will be entirely under the control of the driver, Chance; and our lives will differ not at all from vessels devoid of ballast, and will drift on waves of unaccountable circumstances, now to this, now to that incident of good or of evil. The treasures of virtue will never be found in those who owe their constitution to causes quite contrary to virtue. If God really superintends our life, then, confessedly, evil cannot begin it. But if we do owe our birth to evil, then we must go on living in complete uniformity with it. Thereby it will be shown that it is folly to talk about the *"houses of correction"* which await us after this life is ended, and the *"just recompenses,"* and all the other things there asserted, and believed in too, that tend to the suppression of vice: for how can a man, owing, as he does, his birth to evil, be outside its pale? How can he, whose very nature has its rise in a vice, as they assert, possess any deliberate impulse towards a life of virtue? Take any single one of the brute creation; it does not attempt to speak like a human being, but in using the natural kind of utterance sucked in, as it were, with its mother's milk, it deems it no loss to be deprived of articulate speech. Just in the same way those who believe that a vice was the origin and the cause of their being alive will never bring themselves to have a longing after virtue, because it will be a thing quite foreign to their nature. But, as a fact, they who by reflecting have cleansed the vision of their soul do all of them desire and strive after a life of virtue. Therefore it is by that fact clearly proved that vice is not prior in time to the act of beginning to live, and that our nature did not thence derive its source, but that the all-disposing wisdom of God was the Cause of it: in short, that the soul issues on the stage of life in the manner which is pleasing to its Creator, and then (but not before), by virtue of its power of willing, is free to choose that which is to its mind, and so, whatever it may wish to be, becomes that very thing. We may understand this truth by the example of the eyes. To see is their natural state; but to fail to see results to them either from choice or from disease. This unnatural state may supervene instead of the natural, either by wilful shutting of the eyes or by deprivation of their sight through disease. With the like truth we may assert that the soul derives its constitution from God, and that, as we cannot conceive of any vice in Him, it is removed from any necessity of being vicious; that nevertheless, though this is the condition in which it came into being, it can be attracted of its own free will in a chosen direction, either wilfully shutting its eyes to the Good, or letting them be damaged by that insidious foe whom we have taken home to live with us, and so passing through life in the darkness of error; or, reversely, preserving undimmed its sight of the Truth and keeping far away from all weaknesses that could darken it. — But then some one will ask, *"When and how did it come into being?"* Now as for the question, how any single thing came into existence, we must banish it altogether from our discussion. Even in the case of things which are quite within the grasp of our understanding and of which we have sensible perception, it would be impossible for the speculative reason to grasp the *"how"* of the production of the phenomenon; so much so, that even inspired and saintly men have deemed such questions insoluble. For instance, the Apostle says, *"Through faith we understand that the worlds were framed by the word of God, so that things which are seen are not made of things which do appear* Hebrews 11:3 *."* He would not, I take it, have spoken like that, if he had thought that the question could be settled by any efforts of the reasoning powers. While the Apostle affirms that it is an object of his faith that it was by the will of God that the world itself and all which is therein was framed (whatever this *"world"* be that involves the idea of the whole visible and invisible creation), he has on the other hand left out of the investigation the *"how"* of this framing. Nor do I think that this point can ever be reached by any inquirers. The question presents, on the face of it, many insuperable difficulties. How, for instance, can a world of movement come from one that is at rest? How from the simple and undimensional that which shows dimension and compositeness? Did it come actually out of the Supreme Being? But the fact that this world presents a difference in kind to that Being militates against such a supposition. Did it then come from some other quarter? Yet Faith can contemplate nothing as quite outside the Divine Nature; for we should have to believe in two distinct and separate Principles, if outside the Creative Cause we are to suppose something else, which the Artificer, with all His skill, has to put under contribution for the formative processes of the Universe. Since, then, the Cause of all things is one, and one only, and yet the existences produced by that Cause are not of the same nature as its transcendent quality, an inconceivability of equal magnitude arises in both our suppositions, *i.e.* both that the creation comes straight out of the Divine Being, and that the universe owes its existence to some cause other than Him; for if created things are to be of the same nature as God, we must consider Him to be invested with the properties belonging to His creation; or else a world of matter, outside the circle of God's substance, and equal, on the score of the absence in it of all beginning, to the eternity of the Self-existent One, will have to be ranged against Him: and this is in fact what the followers of Manes, and some of the Greek philosophers who held opinions of equal boldness with his, did imagine; and they raised this imagination into a system. In order, then, to avoid falling into either of these absurdities, which the inquiry into the origin of things involves, let us, following the example of the Apostle, leave the question of the *"how"* in each created thing, without meddling with it at all, but merely observing incidentally that the movement of God's Will becomes at any moment that He pleases a fact, and the intention becomes at once realized in Nature ; for Omnipotence does not leave the plans of its far-seeing skill in the state of unsubstantial wishes: and the actualizing of a wish is Substance. In short, the whole world of existing things falls into two divisions: *i.e.* that of the intelligible, and that of the corporeal: and the intelligible creation does not, to begin with, seem to be in any way at variance with a spiritual Being, but on the contrary to verge closely upon Him, exhibiting as it does that absence of tangible form and of dimension which we rightly attribute to His transcendent nature. The corporeal creation, on the other hand, must certainly be classed among specialities that have nothing in common with the Deity; and it does offer this supreme difficulty to the Reason; namely, that the Reason cannot see *how* the visible comes out of the invisible, *how* the hard solid comes out of the intangible, *how* the finite comes out of the infinite, *how* that which is circumscribed by certain proportions, where the idea of quantity comes in, can come from that which has no size, no proportions, and so on through each single circumstance of body. But even about this we can say so much: *i.e.* that not one of those things which we attribute to body is itself body; neither figure, nor colour, nor weight, nor extension, nor quantity, nor any other qualifying notion whatever; but every one of them is a category; it is the combination of them all into a single whole that constitutes body. Seeing, then, that these several qualifications which complete the particular body are grasped by thought alone, and not by sense, and that the Deity is a thinking being, what trouble can it be to such a thinking agent to produce the thinkables whose mutual combination generates *for us* the substance of that body? All this discussion, however, lies outside our present business. The previous question was—If some souls exist anterior to their bodies, *when* and *how* do they come into existence? And of this question, again, the part about the *how*, has been left out of our examination and has not been meddled with, as presenting impenetrable difficulties. There remains the question of the *when* of the soul's commencement of existence: it follows immediately on that which we have already discussed. For if we were to grant that the soul has lived previous to its body in some place of resort peculiar to itself, then we cannot avoid seeing some force in all that fantastic teaching lately discussed, which would explain the soul's habitation of the body as a consequence of some vice. Again, on the other hand, no one who can reflect will imagine an after-birth of the soul, *i.e.* that it is younger than the moulding of the body; for every one can see for himself that not one among all the things that are inanimate or soulless possesses any power of motion or of growth; whereas there is no question about that which is bred in the uterus both growing and moving from place to place. It remains therefore that we must think that the point of commencement of existence is one and the same for body and soul. Also we affirm that, just as the earth receives the sapling from the hands of the husbandman and makes a tree of it, without itself imparting the power of growth to its nursling, but only lending it, when placed within itself, the impulse to grow, in this very same way that which is secreted from a man for the planting of a man is itself to a certain extent a living being as much gifted with a soul and as capable of nourishing itself as that from which it comes. If this offshoot, in its diminutiveness, cannot contain at first all the activities and the movements of the soul, we need not be surprised; for neither in the seed of grain is there visible all at once the ear. How indeed could anything so large be crowded into so small a space? But the earth keeps on feeding it with its congenial aliment, and so the grain becomes the ear, without changing its nature while in the clod, but only developing it and bringing it to perfection under the stimulus of that nourishment. As, then, in the case of those growing seeds the advance to perfection is a graduated one , so in man's formation the forces of his soul show themselves in proportion to the size to which his body has attained. They dawn first in the fœtus, in the shape of the power of nutrition and of development: after that, they introduce into the organism that has come into the light the gift of perception: then, when this is reached, they manifest a certain measure of the reasoning faculty, like the fruit of some matured plant, not growing all of it at once, but in a continuous progress along with the shooting up of that plant. Seeing, then, that that which is secreted from one living being to lay the foundations of another living being cannot itself be dead (for a state of deadness arises from the privation of life, and it cannot be that privation should precede the having), we grasp from these considerations the fact that in the compound which results from the joining of both (soul and body) there is a simultaneous passage of both into existence; the one does not come first, any more than the other comes after. But as to the number of souls, our reason must necessarily contemplate a stopping some day of its increase; so that Nature's stream may not flow on for ever, pouring forward in her successive births and never staying that onward movement. The reason for our race having some day to come to a standstill is as follows, in our opinion: since every intellectual reality is fixed in a plenitude of its own, it is reasonable to expect that humanity also will arrive at a goal (for in this respect also humanity is not to be parted from the intellectual world); so that we are to believe that it will not be visible for ever only in defect, as it is now: for this continual addition of after generations indicates that there is something deficient in our race.

Whenever, then, humanity shall have reached the plenitude that belongs to it, this on-streaming movement of production will altogether cease; it will have touched its destined bourn, and a new order of things quite distinct from the present precession of births and deaths will carry on the life of humanity. If there is no birth, it follows necessarily that there will be nothing to die. Composition must precede dissolution (and by composition I mean the coming into this world by being born); necessarily, therefore, if this synthesis does not precede, no dissolution will follow. Therefore, if we are to go upon probabilities, the life after this is shown to us beforehand as something that is fixed and imperishable, with no birth and no decay to change it.

The Teacher finished her exposition; and to the many persons sitting by her bedside the whole discussion seemed now to have arrived at a fitting conclusion. Nevertheless, fearing that if the Teacher's illness took a fatal turn (such as did actually happen), we should have no one among us to answer the objections of the unbelievers to the Resurrection , I still insisted.

The argument has not yet touched the most vital of all the questions relating to our Faith. I mean, that the inspired Writings, both in the New and in the Old Testament, declare most emphatically not only that, when our race has completed the ordered chain of its existence as the ages lapse through their complete circle , this current streaming onward as generation succeeds generation will cease altogether, but also that then, when the completed Universe no longer admits of further increase, all the souls in their entire number will come back out of their invisible and scattered condition into tangibility and light, the identical atoms (belonging to each soul) reassembling together in the same order as before; and this reconstitution of human life is called, in these Writings which contain God's teaching, the Resurrection, the entire movement of the atoms receiving the same term as the raising up of that which is actually prostrate on the ground.

But, said she, which of these points has been left unnoticed in what has been said?

Why, the actual doctrine of the Resurrection, I replied.

And yet, she answered, much in our long and detailed discussion pointed to that.

Then are you not aware, I insisted, of all the objections, a very swarm of them, which our antagonists bring against us in connection with that hope of yours?

And I at once tried to repeat all the devices hit upon by their captious champions to upset the doctrine of the Resurrection.

She, however, replied, First, I think, we must briefly run over the scattered proclamations of this doctrine in Holy Scripture; they shall give the finishing touch to our discourse. Observe, then, that I can hear David, in the midst of his praises in the Divine Songs, saying at the end of the hymnody of the hundred and third (104th) Psalm, where he has taken for his theme God's administration of the world, *"You shall take away their breath, and they shall die, and return to their dust: You shall send forth Your Spirit, and they shall be created: and You shall renew the face of the earth."* He says that a power of the Spirit which works in all vivifies the beings into whom it enters, and deprives those whom He abandons of their life. Seeing, then, that the dying is declared to occur at the Spirit's departure, and the renewal of these dead ones at His appearance, and seeing moreover that in the order of the statement the death of those who are to be thus renewed comes first, we hold that in these words that mystery of the Resurrection is proclaimed to the Church, and that David in the spirit of prophecy expressed this very gift which you are asking about. You will find this same prophet in another place also saying that *"the God of the world, the Lord of everything that is, has showed Himself to us, that we may keep the Feast among the decorators;"* by that mention of *"decoration"* with boughs, he means the Feast of Tabernacle-fixing, which, in accordance with Moses' injunction, has been observed from of old. That lawgiver, I take it, adopting a prophet's spirit, predicted therein things still to come; for though the decoration was always going on it was never finished. The truth indeed was foreshadowed under the type and riddle of those Feasts that were always occurring, but the true Tabernacle-fixing was not yet come; and on this account *"the God and Lord of the whole world,"* according to the Prophet's declaration, *"has showed Himself to us, that the Tabernacle-fixing of this our tenement that has been dissolved may be kept for human kind";* a material decoration, that is, may be begun again by means of the concourse of our scattered atoms. For that word πυκασμὸς in its peculiar meaning signifies the Temple-circuit and the decoration which completes it. Now this passage from the Psalms runs as follows: *"God and Lord has showed Himself to us; keep the Feast among the decorators even unto the horns of the altar;"* and this seems to me to proclaim in metaphors the fact that one single feast is to be kept by the whole rational creation, and that in that assembly of the saints the inferiors are to join the dance with their superiors. For in the case of the fabric of that Temple which was the Type it was not allowed to all who were on the outside of its circuit to come within, but everything that was Gentile and alien was prohibited from entering; and of those, further, who had entered, all were not equally privileged to advance towards the centre; but only those who had consecrated themselves by a holier manner of life, and by certain sprinklings; and, again, not every one among these last might set foot within the interior of the Temple; the priests alone had the right of entering within the Curtain, and that only for the service of the sanctuary; while even to the priests the darkened shrine of the Temple, where stood the beautiful Altar with its jutting horns, was forbidden, except to one of them, who held the highest office of the priesthood, and who once a year, on a stated day, and unattended, passed within it, carrying an offering more than usually sacred and mystical. Such being the differences in connection with this Temple which you know of, it was clearly a representation and an imitation of the condition of the spirit-world, the lesson taught by these material observances being this, that it is not the whole of the rational creation that can approach the temple of God, or, in other words, the adoration of the Almighty; but that those who are led astray by false persuasions are outside the precinct of the Deity; and that from the number of those who by virtue of this adoration have been preferred to the rest and admitted within it, some by reason of sprinklings and purifications have still further privileges; and again among these last those who have been consecrated priests have privileges further still, even to being admitted to the mysteries of the interior. And, that one may bring into still clearer light the meaning of the allegory, we may understand the Word here as teaching this, that among all the Powers endued with reason some have been fixed like a Holy Altar in the inmost shrine of the Deity; and that again of these last some jut forward like horns, for their eminence, and that around them others are arranged first or second, according to a prescribed sequence of rank; that the race of man, on the contrary, on account of indwelling evil was excluded from the Divine precinct, but that purified with lustral water it re-enters it; and, since all the further barriers by which our sin has fenced us off from the things within the veil are in the end to be taken down, whenever the time comes that the tabernacle of our nature is as it were to be fixed up again in the Resurrection, and all the inveterate corruption of sin has vanished from the world, then a universal feast will be kept around the Deity by those who have decorated themselves in the Resurrection; and one and the same banquet will be spread for all, with no differences cutting off any rational creature from an equal participation in it; for those who are now excluded by reason of their sin will at last be admitted within the Holiest places of God's blessedness, and will bind themselves to the horns of the Altar there, that is, to the most excellent of the transcendental Powers. The Apostle says the same thing more plainly when he indicates the final accord of the whole Universe with the Good: *"That"* to Him *"every knee should bow, of things in heaven, and things in earth, and things under the earth: And that every tongue should confess that Jesus Christ is Lord, to the glory of God the Father"*: instead of the *"horns,"* speaking of that which is angelic and *"in heaven,"* and by the other terms signifying ourselves, the creatures whom we think of next to that; one festival of united voices shall occupy us all; that festival shall be the confession and the recognition of the Being Who truly Is. One might (she proceeded) select many other passages of Holy Scripture to establish the doctrine of the Resurrection. For instance, Ezekiel leaps in the spirit of prophecy over all the intervening time, with its vast duration; he stands, by his powers of foresight, in the actual moment of the Resurrection, and, as if he had really gazed on what is still to come, brings it in his description before our eyes. He saw a mighty plain Ezekiel 37:1-10, unfolded to an endless distance before him, and vast heaps of bones upon it flung at random, some this way, some that; and then under an impulse from God these bones began to move and group themselves with their fellows that they once owned, and adhere to the familiar sockets, and then clothe themselves with muscle, flesh, and skin (which was the process called *"decorating"* in the poetry of the Psalms); a Spirit in fact was giving life and movement to everything that lay there. But as regards our Apostle's description of the wonders of the Resurrection, why should one repeat it, seeing that it can easily be found and read?

How, for instance, *"with a shout"* and the *"sound of trumpets"* (in the language of the Word) all dead and prostrate things shall be *"changed in the twinkling of an eye"* into immortal beings. The expressions in the Gospels also I will pass over; for their meaning is quite clear to every one; and our Lord does not declare in word alone that the bodies of the dead shall be raised up again; but He shows in action the Resurrection itself, making a beginning of this work of wonder from things more within our reach and less capable of being doubted. First, that is, He displays His life-giving power in the case of the deadly forms of disease, and chases those maladies by one word of command; then He raises a little girl just dead; then He makes a young man, who is already being carried out, sit up on his bier, and delivers him to his mother; after that He calls forth from his tomb the four-days-dead and already decomposed Lazarus, vivifying the prostrate body with His commanding voice; then after three days He raises from the dead His own human body, pierced though it was with the nails and spear, and brings the print of those nails and the spear-wound to witness to the Resurrection. But I think that a detailed mention of these things is not necessary; for no doubt about them lingers in the minds of those who have accepted the written accounts of them.

But that, said I, was not the point in question. Most of your hearers will assent to the fact that there will some day be a Resurrection, and that man will be brought before the incorruptible tribunal ; on account both of the Scripture proofs, and also of our previous examination of the question. But still the question remains : Is the state which we are to expect to be like the present state of the body? Because if so, then, as I was saying , men had better avoid hoping for any Resurrection at all. For if our bodies are to be restored to life again in the same sort of condition as they are in when they cease to breathe, then all that man can look forward to in the Resurrection is an unending calamity. For what spectacle is more piteous than when in extreme old age our bodies shrivel up and change into something repulsive and hideous, with the flesh all wasted in the length of years, the skin dried up about the bones till it is all in wrinkles, the muscles in a spasmodic state from being no longer enriched with their natural moisture, and the whole body consequently shrunk, the hands on either side powerless to perform their natural work, shaken with an involuntary trembling? What a sight again are the bodies of persons in a long consumption! They differ from bare bones only in giving the appearance of being covered with a worn-out veil of skin. What a sight too are those of persons swollen with the disease of dropsy! What words could describe the unsightly disfigurement of sufferers from leprosy? Gradually over all their limbs and organs of sensation rottenness spreads and devours them. What words could describe that of persons who have been mutilated in earthquake, battle, or by any other visitation, and live on in such a plight for a long time before their natural deaths? Or of those who from an injury have grown up from infancy with their limbs awry! What can one say of them? What is one to think about the bodies of newborn infants who have been either exposed, or strangled, or died a natural death, if they are to be brought to life again just such as they were? Are they to continue in that infantine state? What condition could be more miserable than that? Or are they to come to the flower of their age? Well, but what sort of milk has Nature got to suckle them again with? It comes then to this: that, if our bodies are to live again in every respect the same as before, this thing that we are expecting is simply a calamity; whereas if they are not the same, the person raised up will be another than he who died. If, for instance, a little boy was buried, but a grown man rises again, or reversely, how can we say that the dead in his very self is raised up, when he has had some one substituted for him by virtue of this difference in age? Instead of the child, one sees a grown-up man. Instead of the old man, one sees a person in his prime. In fact, instead of the one person another entirely. The cripple is changed into the able-bodied man; the consumptive sufferer into a man whose flesh is firm; and so on of all possible cases, not to enumerate them for fear of being prolix. If, then, the body will not come to life again just such in its attributes as it was when it mingled with the earth, that dead body will not rise again; but on the contrary the earth will be formed into another man. How, then, will the Resurrection affect myself, when instead of me some one else will come to life? Some one else, I say; for how could I recognize myself when, instead of what was once myself, I see some one not myself? It cannot really be I, unless it is in every respect the same as myself. Suppose, for instance, in this life I had in my memory the traits of some one; say he was bald, had prominent lips, a somewhat flat nose, a fair complexion, grey eyes, white hair, wrinkled skin; and then went to look for such an one, and met a young man with a fine head of hair, an aquiline nose, a dark complexion, and in all other respects quite different in his type of countenance; am I likely in seeing the latter to think of the former? But why dwell longer on these the less forcible objections to the Resurrection, and neglect the strongest one of all? For who has not heard that human life is like a stream, moving from birth to death at a certain rate of progress, and then only ceasing from that progressive movement when it ceases also to exist? This movement indeed is not one of spacial change; our bulk never exceeds itself; but it makes this advance by means of internal alteration; and as long as this alteration is that which its name implies, it never remains at the same stage (from moment to moment); for how can that which is being altered be kept in any sameness? The fire on the wick, as far as appearance goes, certainly seems always the same, the continuity of its movement giving it the look of being an uninterrupted and self-centred whole; but in reality it is always passing itself along and never remains the same; the moisture which is extracted by the heat is burnt up and changed into smoke the moment it has burst into flame and this alterative force effects the movement of the flame, working by itself the change of the subject-matter into smoke; just, then, as it is impossible for one who has touched that flame twice on the same place, to touch twice the very same flame (for the speed of the alteration is too quick; it does not wait for that second touch, however rapidly it may be effected; the flame is always fresh and new; it is always being produced, always transmitting itself, never remaining at one and the same place), a thing of the same kind is found to be the case with the constitution of our body. There is influx and afflux going on in it in an alterative progress until the moment that it ceases to live; as long as it is living it has no stay; for it is either being replenished, or it is discharging in vapour, or it is being kept in motion by both of these processes combined. If, then, a particular man is not the same even as he was yesterday , but is made different by this transmutation, when so be that the Resurrection shall restore our body to life again, that single man will become a crowd of human beings, so that with his rising again there will be found the babe, the child, the boy, the youth, the man, the father, the old man, and all the intermediate persons that he once was. But further ; chastity and profligacy are both carried on in the flesh; those also who endure the most painful tortures for their religion, and those on the other hand who shrink from such, both one class and the other reveal their character in relation to fleshly sensations; how, then, can justice be done at the Judgment ?

Or take the case of one and the same man first sinning and then cleansing himself by repentance, and then, it might so happen, relapsing into his sin; in such a case both the defiled and the undefiled body alike undergoes a change, as his nature changes, and neither of them continue to the end the same; which body, then, is the profligate to be tortured in? In that which is stiffened with old age and is near to death? But this is not the same as that which did the sin. In that, then, which defiled itself by giving way to passion? But where is the old man, in that case? This last, in fact, will not rise again, and the Resurrection will not do a complete work; or else he will rise, while the criminal will escape. Let me say something else also from among the objections made by unbelievers to this doctrine. No part, they urge, of the body is made by nature without a function. Some parts, for instance, are the efficient causes within us of our being alive; without them our life in the flesh could not possibly be carried on; such are the heart, liver, brain, lungs, stomach, and the other vitals; others are assigned to the activities of sensation; others to those of handing and walking ; others are adapted for the transmission of a posterity. Now if the life to come is to be in exactly the same circumstances as this, the supposed change in us is reduced to nothing; but if the report is true, as indeed it is, which represents marriage as forming no part of the economy of that after-life, and eating and drinking as not then preserving its continuance, what use will there be for the members of our body, when we are no longer to expect in that existence any of the activities for which our members now exist? If, for the sake of marriage, there are now certain organs adapted for marriage, then, whenever the latter ceases to be, we shall not need those organs: the same may be said of the hands for working with, the feet for running with, the mouth for taking food with, the teeth for grinding it with, the organs of the stomach for digesting, the evacuating ducts for getting rid of that which has become superfluous. When therefore, all those operations will be no more how or wherefore will their instruments exist? So that necessarily, if the things that are not going to contribute in any way to that other life are not to surround the body, none of the parts which at present constitute the body would exist either. That life , then, will be carried on by other instruments; and no one could call such a state of things a Resurrection, where the particular members are no longer present in the body, owing to their being useless to that life. But if on the other hand our Resurrection will be represented in every one of these; then the Author of the Resurrection will fashion things in us of no use and advantage to that life. And yet we must believe, not only that there is a Resurrection, but also that it will not be an absurdity. We must, therefore, listen attentively to the explanation of this, so that, for every part of this truth we may have its probability saved to the last.

When I had finished, the Teacher thus replied, You have attacked the doctrines connected with the Resurrection with some spirit, in the way of rhetoric as it is called; you have coursed round and round the truth with plausibly subversive arguments; so much so, that those who have not very carefully considered this mysterious truth might possibly be affected in their view of it by the likelihood of those arguments, and might think that the difficulty started against what has been advanced was not altogether beside the point. But, she proceeded, the truth does not lie in these arguments, even though we may find it impossible to give a rhetorical answer to them, couched in equally strong language. The true explanation of all these questions is still stored up in the hidden treasure-rooms of Wisdom, and will not come to the light until that moment when we shall be taught the mystery of the Resurrection by the reality of it; and then there will be no more need of phrases to explain the things which we now hope for. Just as many questions might be started for debate among people sitting up at night as to the kind of thing that sunshine is, and then the simple appearing of it in all its beauty would render any verbal description superfluous, so every calculation that tries to arrive conjecturally at the future state will be reduced to nothingness by the object of our hopes, when it comes upon us. But since it is our duty not to leave the arguments brought against us in any way unexamined, we will expound the truth as to these points as follows. First let us get a clear notion as to the scope of this doctrine; in other words, what is the end that Holy Scripture has in view in promulgating it and creating the belief in it. Well, to sketch the outline of so vast a truth and to embrace it in a definition, we will say that the Resurrection is "*the reconstitution of our nature in its original form.*" But in that form of life, of which God Himself was the Creator, it is reasonable to believe that there was neither age nor infancy nor any of the sufferings arising from our present various infirmities, nor any kind of bodily affliction whatever. It is reasonable, I say, to believe that God was the Creator of none of these things, but that man was a thing divine before his humanity got within reach of the assault of evil; that then, however, with the inroad of evil, all these afflictions also broke in upon him. Accordingly a life that is free from evil is under no necessity whatever of being passed amidst the things that result from evil. It follows that when a man travels through ice he must get his body chilled; or when he walks in a very hot sun that he must get his skin darkened; but if he has kept clear of the one or the other, he escapes these results entirely, both the darkening and the chilling; no one, in fact, when a particular cause was removed, would be justified in looking for the effect of that particular cause. Just so our nature, becoming passional, had to encounter all the necessary results of a life of passion: but when it shall have started back to that state of passionless blessedness, it will no longer encounter the inevitable results of evil tendencies. Seeing, then, that all the infusions of the life of the brute into our nature were not in us before our humanity descended through the touch of evil into passions, most certainly, when we abandon those passions, we shall abandon all their visible results. No one, therefore, will be justified in seeking in that other life for the consequences in us of any passion. Just as if a man, who, clad in a ragged tunic, has divested himself of the garb, feels no more its disgrace upon him, so we too, when we have cast off that dead unsightly tunic made from the skins of brutes and put upon us (for I take the *"coats of skins"* to mean that conformation belonging to a brute nature with which we were clothed when we became familiar with passionate indulgence), shall, along with the casting off of that tunic, fling from us all the belongings that were round us of that skin of a brute; and such accretions are sexual intercourse, conception, parturition, impurities, suckling, feeding, evacuation, gradual growth to full size, prime of life, old age, disease, and death. If that skin is no longer round us, how can its resulting consequences be left behind within us? It is folly, then, when we are to expect a different state of things in the life to come, to object to the doctrine of the Resurrection on the ground of something that has nothing to do with it. I mean, what has thinness or corpulence, a state of consumption or of plethora, or any other condition supervening in a nature that is ever in a flux, to do with the other life, stranger as it is to any fleeting and transitory passing such as that? One thing, and one thing only, is required for the operation of the Resurrection; viz. that a man should have lived, by being born; or, to use rather the Gospel words, that *"a man should be born into the world"*; the length or briefness of the life, the manner, this or that, of the death, is an irrelevant subject of inquiry in connection with that operation. Whatever instance we take, howsoever we suppose this to have been, it is all the same; from these differences in life there arises no difficulty, any more than any facility, with regard to the Resurrection. He who has once begun to live must necessarily go on having once lived , after his intervening dissolution in death has been repaired in the Resurrection.

As to the *how* and the *when* of his dissolution, what do *they* matter to the Resurrection? Consideration of such points belongs to another line of inquiry altogether. For instance, a man may have lived in bodily comfort, or in affliction, virtuously or viciously, renowned or disgraced; he may have passed his days miserably, or happily. These and such-like results must be obtained from the length of his life and the manner of his living; and to be able to pass a judgment on the things done in his life, it will be necessary for the judge to scrutinize his indulgences, as the case may be, or his losses, or his disease, or his old age, or his prime, or his youth, or his wealth, or his poverty: how well or ill a man, placed in either of these, concluded his destined career; whether he was the recipient of many blessings, or of many ills in a length of life; or tasted neither of them at all, but ceased to live before his mental powers were formed. But whenever the time come that God shall have brought our nature back to the primal state of man, it will be useless to talk of such things then, and to imagine that objections based upon such things can prove God's power to be impeded in arriving at His end. His end is one, and one only; it is this: when the complete whole of our race shall have been perfected from the first man to the last—some having at once in this life been cleansed from evil, others having afterwards in the necessary periods been healed by the Fire, others having in their life here been unconscious equally of good and of evil—to offer to every one of us participation in the blessings which are in Him, which, the Scripture tells us, *"eye has not seen, nor ear heard,"* nor thought ever reached. But this is nothing else, as I at least understand it, but to be in God Himself; for the Good which is above hearing and eye and heart must be that Good which transcends the universe. But the difference between the virtuous and the vicious life led at the present time will be illustrated in this way; viz. in the quicker or more tardy participation of each in that promised blessedness. According to the amount of the ingrained wickedness of each will be computed the duration of his cure. This cure consists in the cleansing of his soul, and that cannot be achieved without an excruciating condition, as has been expounded in our previous discussion. But any one would more fully comprehend the futility and irrelevancy of all these objections by trying to fathom the depths of our Apostle's wisdom. When explaining this mystery to the Corinthians, who, perhaps, themselves were bringing forward the same objections to it as its impugners today bring forward to overthrow our faith, he proceeds on his own authority to chide the audacity of their ignorance, and speaks thus: *"You will say, then, to me, How are the dead raised up, and with what body do they come? You fool, that which you sow is not quickened, except it die; And that which you sow, you sow not that body that shall be, but bare grain, it may chance of wheat or of some other grain; But God gives it a body as it has pleased Him."* In that passage, as it seems to me, he gags the mouths of men who display their ignorance of the fitting proportions in Nature, and who measure the Divine power by their own strength, and think that only so much is possible to God as the human understanding can take in, but that what is beyond it surpasses also the Divine ability. For the man who had asked the Apostle, *"how are the dead raised up?"* evidently implies that it is impossible when once the body's atoms have been scattered that they should again come in concourse together; and this being impossible, and no other possible form of body, besides that arising from such a concourse, being left, he, after the fashion of clever controversialists, concludes the truth of what he wants to prove, by a species of syllogism, thus: If a body is a concourse of atoms, and a second assemblage of these is impossible, what sort of body will those get who rise again? This conclusion, involved seemingly in this artful contrivance of premises, the Apostle calls *"folly,"* as coming from men who failed to perceive in other parts of the creation the masterliness of the Divine power. For, omitting the sublimer miracles of God's hand, by which it would have been easy to place his hearer in a dilemma (for instance he might have asked *"how or whence comes a heavenly body, that of the sun for example, or that of the moon, or that which is seen in the constellations; whence the firmament, the air, water, the earth?"*), he, on the contrary, convicts the objectors of inconsiderateness by means of objects which grow alongside of us and are very familiar to all. *"Does not even husbandry teach you,"* he asks, *"that the man who in calculating the transcendent powers of the Deity limits them by his own is a fool?"* Whence do seeds get the bodies that spring up from them? What precedes this springing up? Is it not a death that precedes? At least, if the dissolution of a compacted whole is a death; for indeed it cannot be supposed that the seed would spring up into a shoot unless it had been dissolved in the soil, and so become spongy and porous to such an extent as to mingle its own qualities with the adjacent moisture of the soil, and thus become transformed into a root and shoot; not stopping even there, but changing again into the stalk with its intervening knee-joints that gird it up like so many clasps, to enable it to carry with figure erect the ear with its load of grain. Where, then, were all these things belonging to the grain before its dissolution in the soil? And yet this result sprang from that grain; if that grain had not existed first, the ear would not have arisen. Just, then, as the *"body"* of the ear comes to light out of the seed, God's artistic touch of power producing it all out of that single thing, and just as it is neither entirely the same thing as that seed nor something altogether different, so (she insisted) by these miracles performed on seeds you may now interpret the mystery of the Resurrection. The Divine power, in the superabundance of Omnipotence, does not only restore you that body once dissolved, but makes great and splendid additions to it, whereby the human being is furnished in a manner still more magnificent.

"It is sown," he says, *"in corruption; it is raised in incorruption: it is sown in weakness; it is raised in power: it is sown in dishonour; it is raised in glory: it is sown a natural body; it is raised a spiritual body."* The grain of wheat, after its dissolution in the soil, leaves behind the slightness of its bulk and the peculiar quality of its shape, and yet it has not left and lost itself, but, still self-centred, grows into the ear, though in many points it has made an advance upon itself, viz. in size, in splendour, in complexity, in form. In the same fashion the human being deposits in death all those peculiar surroundings which it has acquired from passionate propensities; dishonour, I mean, and corruption and weakness and characteristics of age; and yet the human being does not lose itself. It changes into an ear of grain as it were; into incorruption, that is, and glory and honour and power and absolute perfection; into a condition in which its life is no longer carried on in the ways peculiar to mere nature, but has passed into a spiritual and passionless existence. For it is the peculiarity of the natural body to be always moving on a stream, to be always altering from its state for the moment and changing into something else; but

none of these processes, which we observe not in man only but also in plants and brutes will be found remaining in the life that shall be then. Further, it seems to me that the words of the Apostle in every respect harmonize with our own conception of what the Resurrection is. They indicate the very same thing that we have embodied in our own definition of it, wherein we said that the Resurrection is no other thing than *"the re-constitution of our nature in its original form."* For, whereas we learn from Scripture in the account of the first Creation, that first the earth brought forth *"the green herb"* (as the narrative says), and that then from this plant seed was yielded, from which, when it was shed on the ground, the same form of the original plant again sprang up, the Apostle, it is to be observed, declares that this very same thing happens in the Resurrection also; and so we learn from him the fact, not only that our humanity will be then changed into something nobler, but also that what we have therein to expect is nothing else than that which was at the beginning. In the beginning, we see, it was not an ear rising from a grain, but a grain coming from an ear, and, after that, the ear grows round the grain: and so the order indicated in this similitude clearly shows that all that blessed state, which arises for us by means of the Resurrection is only a return to our pristine state of grace. We too, in fact, were once in a fashion a full ear ; but the burning heat of sin withered us up, and then on our dissolution by death the earth received us: but in the spring of the Resurrection she will reproduce this naked grain of our body in the form of an ear, tall, well-proportioned, and erect, reaching to the heights of heaven, and, for blade and beard, resplendent in incorruption, and with all the other godlike marks. For *"this corruptible must put on incorruption"*; and this incorruption and glory and honour and power are those distinct and acknowledged marks of Deity which once belonged to him who was created in God's image, and which we hope for hereafter. The first man Adam, that is, was the first ear; but with the arrival of evil human nature was diminished into a mere multitude ; and, as happens to the grain on the ear, each individual man was denuded of the beauty of that primal ear, and mouldered in the soil: but in the Resurrection we are born again in our original splendour; only instead of that single primitive ear we become the countless myriads of ears in the cornfields. The virtuous life as contrasted with that of vice is distinguished thus: those who while living have by virtuous conduct exercised husbandry on themselves are at once revealed in all the qualities of a perfect ear,

Selected Works

while those whose bare grain (that is the forces of their natural soul) has become through evil habits degenerate, as it were, and hardened by the weather (as the so-called *"hornstruck"* seeds, according to the experts in such things, grow up), will, though they live again in the Resurrection, experience very great severity from their Judge, because they do not possess the strength to shoot up into the full proportions of an ear, and thereby become that which we were before our earthly fall. The remedy offered by the Overseer of the produce is to collect together the tares and the thorns, which have grown up with the good seed, and into whose bastard life all the secret forces that once nourished its root have passed, so that it not only has had to remain without its nutriment, but has been choked and so rendered unproductive by this unnatural growth. When from the nutritive part within them everything that is the reverse or the counterfeit of it has been picked out, and has been committed to the fire that consumes everything unnatural, and so has disappeared, then in this class also their humanity will thrive and will ripen into fruit-bearing, owing to such husbandry, and some day after long courses of ages will get back again that universal form which God stamped upon us at the beginning. Blessed are they, indeed, in whom the full beauty of those ears shall be developed directly they are born in the Resurrection. Yet we say this without implying that any merely bodily distinctions will be manifest between those who have lived virtuously and those who have lived viciously in this life, as if we ought to think that one will be imperfect as regards his material frame, while another will win perfection as regards it. The prisoner and the free, here in this present world, are just alike as regards the constitutions of their two bodies; though as regards enjoyment and suffering the gulf is wide between them. In this way, I take it, should we reckon the difference between the good and the bad in that intervening time. For the perfection of bodies that rise from that sowing of death is, as the Apostle tells us, to consist in incorruption and glory and honour and power; but any diminution in such excellences does not denote a corresponding bodily mutilation of him who has risen again, but a withdrawal and estrangement from each one of those things which are conceived of as belonging to the good. Seeing, then, that one or the other of these two diametrically opposed ideas, I mean good and evil, must any way attach to us, it is clear that to say a man is not included in the good is a necessary demonstration that he is included in the evil. But then, in connection with evil, we find no honour, no glory, no incorruption, no power; and so we are forced to dismiss all doubt that a man who has nothing to do with these last-mentioned things must be connected with their opposites, viz. with weakness, with dishonour, with corruption, with everything of that nature, such as we spoke of in the previous parts of the discussion, when we said how many were the passions, sprung from evil, which are so hard for the soul to get rid of, when they have infused themselves into the very substance of its entire nature and become one with it. When such, then, have been purged from it and utterly removed by the healing processes worked out by the Fire, then every one of the things which make up our conception of the good will come to take their place; incorruption, that is, and life, and honour, and grace, and glory, and everything else that we conjecture is to be seen in God, and in His Image, man as he was made.

The Great Catechism
The Trinity

Prologue and Chapter 1.— The belief in God rests on the art and wisdom displayed in the order of the world: the belief in the *Unity* of God, on the *perfection* that must belong to Him in respect of power, goodness, wisdom, etc. Still, the Christian who combats polytheism has need of care lest in contending against Hellenism he should fall unconsciously into Judaism. For God has a Logos: else He would be without reason. And this Logos cannot be merely an attribute of God. We are led to a more exalted conception of the Logos by the consideration that in the measure in which God is greater than we, all His predicates must also be higher than those which belong to us. Our logos is limited and transient; but the subsistence of the Divine Logos must be indestructible; and at the same time living, since the rational cannot be lifeless, like a stone. It must also have an independent life, not a participated life, else it would lose its simplicity; and, as living, it must also have the faculty of will. This will of the Logos must be equalled by his power: for a mixture of choice and impotence would, again, destroy the simplicity. His will, as being Divine, must be also good. From this ability and will to work there follows the realization of the good; hence the bringing into existence of the wisely and artfully adjusted world. But since, still further, the logical conception of the Word is in a certain sense a relative one, it follows that together with the Word He Who speaks it, *i.e.* the Father of the Word, must be recognized as existing. Thus the mystery of the faith avoids equally the absurdity of Jewish monotheism, and that of heathen polytheism. On the one hand, we say that the Word has *life and activity*; on the other, we affirm that we find in the Λόγος, whose existence is derived from the Father, *all* the attributes of the Father's nature.

Chapter II.— By the analogy of human breath, which is nothing but inhaled and exhaled fire, *i.e.* an object foreign to us, is demonstrated the community of the Divine Spirit with the essence of God, and yet the independence of Its existence.

Chapter III.— From the Jewish doctrine, then, the unity of the Divine nature has been retained: from Hellenism the distinction into hypostases.

Chapter IV.— The Jew convicted from Scripture.

Reasonableness of the Incarnation.

Chapters V. and VI.— God created the world by His reason and wisdom; for He cannot have proceeded irrationally in that work; but His reason and wisdom are, as above shown, not to be conceived as a spoken word, or as the mere possession of knowledge, but as a personal and willing potency. If the entire world was created by this second Divine hypostasis, then certainly was man also thus created; yet not in view of any necessity, but *from superabounding love*, that there might exist a being who should participate in the Divine perfections. If man was to be receptive of these, it was necessary that his nature should contain an element akin to God; and, in particular, that he should be immortal. Thus, then, man was created in the image of God. He could not therefore be without the gifts of freedom, independence, self-determination; and his participation in the Divine gifts was consequently made dependent on his virtue. Owing to this *freedom* he could decide in favour of evil, which cannot have its origin in the Divine will, but only in our inner selves, where it arises in the form of a deviation from good, and so a privation of it. Vice is opposed to virtue only as the absence of the better. Since, then, all that is created is subject to change, it was possible that, in the first instance, one of the created spirits should turn his eye away from the good, and become envious, and that from this envy should arise a leaning towards badness, which should, in natural sequence, prepare the way for all other evil. He seduced the first men into the folly of turning away from goodness, *by disturbing the Divinely ordered harmony between their sensuous and intellectual natures*; and guilefully tainting their wills with evil.

Chapters VII. and VIII.— God did not, on account of His foreknowledge of the evil that would result from man's creation, leave man uncreated; for it was better to bring back sinners to original grace by the way of repentance and physical suffering than not to create man at all. The raising up of the fallen was a work befitting the Giver of life, Who is the wisdom and power of God; and for this purpose He became man.

Chapter IX.— The Incarnation was not unworthy of Him; for *only evil brings degradation*.

Chapter X.— The objection that the finite cannot contain the infinite, and that therefore the human nature could not receive into itself the Divine, is founded on the false supposition that the Incarnation of the Word means that the infinity of God was contained in the limits of the flesh, as in a vessel.— Comparison of the flame and wick.

Chapters XI., XII., XIII.— For the rest, the manner in which the Divine nature was united to the human surpasses our power of comprehension; although we are not permitted to doubt the fact of that union in Jesus, *on account of the miracles which He wrought.* The supernatural character of those miracles bears witness to their Divine origin.

Chapters XIV., XV., XVI., XVII.— The scheme of the Incarnation is still further drawn out, to show that this way for man's salvation was preferable to a single fiat of God's will. Christ took human *weakness* upon Him; but it was physical, not moral, weakness. In other words the Divine goodness did not change to its opposite, which is only vice. In Him soul and body were united, and then separated, according to the course of nature; but after He had thus purged human life, He reunited them *upon a more general scale*, for all, and for ever, in the Resurrection.

Chapter XVIII.— The ceasing of demon-worship, the Christian martyrdoms, and the devastation of Jerusalem, are accepted by some as proofs of the Incarnation—

Chapters XIX., XX.— But not by the Greek and the Jew. To return, then, to its *reasonableness*. Whether we regard the goodness, the power, the wisdom, or the justice of God, it displays a combination of all these acknowledged attributes, which, if one be wanting, cease to be Divine. It is therefore true to the Divine perfection.

Chapters XXI., XXII., XXIII.— What, then, is the *justice* in it? We must remember that man was necessarily created subject to change (to better or to worse). Moral beauty was to be the direction in which his free will was to move; but then he was deceived, to his ruin, by an illusion of that beauty. After we had thus *freely* sold ourselves to the deceiver, He who of His goodness sought to restore us to liberty could not, because He was just too, for this end have recourse to measures of arbitrary violence. It was necessary therefore that a ransom should be paid, which should exceed in value that which was to be ransomed; and hence it was necessary that the Son of God should surrender Himself to the power of death. God's *justice* then impelled Him to choose a method of exchange, as His *wisdom* was seen in executing it.

Chapters XXIV., XXV.— But how about the *power?* That was more conspicuously displayed in Deity descending to lowliness, than in all the natural wonders of the universe. It was like flame being made to stream downwards. Then, after such a birth, Christ conquered death.

Chapter XXVI.— A certain deception was indeed practised upon the Evil one, by concealing the Divine nature within the human; but for the latter, as himself a deceiver, it was only a just recompense that he should be deceived himself: the great adversary must himself at last find that what has been done is just and salutary, when he also shall experience the benefit of the Incarnation. He, as well as humanity, will be purged.

Chapters XXVII., XXVIII.— A patient, to be healed, must be *touched*; and humanity had to be touched by Christ. It was not in *"heaven"*; so only through the Incarnation could it be healed.— It was, besides, no more inconsistent with His Divinity to assume a human than a *"heavenly"* body; all created beings are on a level beneath Deity. Even *"abundant honour"* is due to the instruments of human birth.

Chapters XXIX., XXX., XXXI.— As to the delay of the Incarnation, it was necessary that human degeneracy should have reached the lowest point, before the work of salvation could enter in. That, however, grace through faith has not come to all must be laid to the account of human freedom; if God were to break down our opposition by violent means, the praise-worthiness of human conduct would be destroyed.

Chapter XXXII.— Even the death on the Cross was sublime: for it was the culminating and necessary point in that scheme of Love in which death was to be followed by blessed resurrection for the whole *"lump"* of humanity: and the Cross itself has a mystic meaning.

The Sacraments.

Chapters XXXIII., XXXIV., XXXV., XXXVI.— The saving nature of Baptism depends on three things; Prayer, Water, and Faith. 1. It is shown how Prayer secures the Divine Presence. God is a God of truth; and He has promised to come (as Miracles prove that He has come already) if invoked *in a particular way*. 2. It is shown how the

Deity gives life from water. In human generation, even without prayer, He gives life from a small beginning. In a higher generation He transforms matter, not into soul, but into spirit. 3. Human freedom, as evinced in faith and repentance, is also necessary to Regeneration. Being thrice dipped in the water is our earliest mortification; coming out of it is a forecast of the ease with which the pure shall rise in a *blessed* resurrection: the whole process is an imitation of Christ.

Chapter XXXVII.— The Eucharist unites the body, as Baptism the soul, to God. Our bodies, having received poison, need an Antidote; and only by eating and drinking can it enter. One Body, the receptacle of Deity, is this Antidote, thus received. But how can it enter whole into each one of the Faithful? This needs an illustration. Water gives its own body to a skin-bottle. So nourishment (bread and wine) by becoming flesh and blood gives bulk to the human frame: the nourishment is the body. Just as in the case of other men, our Saviour's nourishment (bread and wine) was His Body; but these, nourishment and Body, were in Him changed into the Body of God by the Word indwelling. So now repeatedly the bread and wine, sanctified by the Word (the sacred Benediction), is *at the same time* changed into the Body of that Word; and this Flesh is disseminated among all the Faithful.

Chapters XXXVIII., XXXIX.— It is essential for Regeneration to believe that the Son and the Spirit are not created spirits, but of like nature with God the Father; for he who would make his salvation dependent (in the baptismal Invocation) on anything created would trust to an imperfect nature, and one itself needing a saviour.

Chapter XL.— He alone has truly become a child of God who gives evidence of his regeneration by putting away from himself all vice.

On the Baptism of Christ

A Sermon for the Day of the Lights.

Now I recognize my own flock: today I behold the wonted figure of the Church, when, turning with aversion from the occupation even of the cares of the flesh, you come together in your undiminished numbers for the service of God— when the people crowds the house, coming within the sacred sanctuary, and when the multitude that can find no place within fills the space outside in the precincts like bees. For of them some are at their labours within, while others outside hum around the hive. So do, my children: and never abandon this zeal. For I confess that I feel a shepherd's affections, and I wish, when I am set upon this watchtower, to see the flock gathered round about the mountain's foot: and when it so happens to me, I am filled with wonderful earnestness, and work with pleasure at my sermon, as the shepherds do at their rustic strains. But when things are otherwise, and you are straying in distant wanderings, as you did but lately, the last Lord's Day, I am much troubled, and glad to be silent; and I consider the question of flight from hence, and seek for the Carmel of the prophet Elijah, or for some rock without inhabitant; for men in depression naturally choose loneliness and solitude. But now, when I see you thronging here with all your families, I am reminded of the prophetic saying, which Isaiah proclaimed from afar off, addressing by anticipation the Church with her fair and numerous children:— *"Who are these that fly as a cloud, and as doves with their young to me"*? Yes, and he adds moreover this also, *"The place is too strait for me; give place that I may dwell* Isaiah 49:20 *."* For these predictions the power of the Spirit made with reference to the populous Church of God, which was afterwards to fill the whole world from end to end of the earth.

The time, then, has come, and bears in its course the remembrance of holy mysteries, purifying man—mysteries which purge out from soul and body even that sin which is hard to cleanse away, and which bring us back to that fairness of our first estate which God, the best of artificers, impressed upon us. Therefore it is that you, the initiated people, are gathered together; and you bring also that people who have not made trial of them, leading, like good fathers, by careful guidance, the uninitiated to the perfect reception of the faith. I for my part rejoice over both—over you that are initiated, because you are enriched with a great gift: over you that are uninitiated, because you have a fair expectation of hope— remission of what is to be accounted for, release from bondage, close relation to God, free boldness of speech, and in place of servile subjection equality with the angels. For these things, and all that follow from them, the grace of Baptism secures and conveys to us. Therefore let us leave the other matters of the Scriptures for other occasions, and abide by the topic set before us, offering, as far as we may, the gifts that are proper and fitting for the feast: for each festival demands its own treatment. So we welcome a marriage with wedding songs; for mourning we bring the due offering with funeral strains; in times of business we speak seriously, at times of festivity we relax the concentration and strain of our minds; but each time we keep free from disturbance by things that are alien to its character.

Christ, then, was born as it were a few days ago— He Whose generation was before all things, sensible and intellectual. Today He is baptized by John that He might cleanse him who was defiled, that He might bring the Spirit from above, and exalt man to heaven, that he who had fallen might be raised up and he who had cast him down might be put to shame. And marvel not if God showed so great earnestness in our cause: for it was with care on the part of him who did us wrong that the plot was laid against us; it is with forethought on the part of our Maker that we are saved. And he, that evil charmer, framing his new device of sin against our race, drew along his serpent train, a disguise worthy of his own intent, entering in his impurity into what was like himself—dwelling, earthly and mundane as he was in will, in that creeping thing. But Christ, the repairer of his evil-doing, assumes manhood in its fullness, and saves man, and becomes the type and figure of us all, to sanctify the first-fruits of every action, and leave to His servants no doubt in their zeal for the tradition. Baptism, then, is a purification from sins, a remission of trespasses, a cause of renovation and regeneration. By regeneration, understand regeneration conceived in thought, not discerned by bodily sight. For we shall not, according to the Jew Nicodemus and his somewhat dull intelligence, change the old man into a child, nor shall we form anew him who is wrinkled and gray-headed to tenderness and youth, if we bring back the man again into his mother's womb: but we do bring back, by royal grace, him who bears the scars of sin, and has grown old in evil habits, to the innocence of the babe. For as the child new-born is free from accusations and from penalties, so too the child of regeneration has nothing for which to answer, being released by royal bounty from accountability. And this gift it is not the water that bestows (for in that case it were a thing more exalted than all creation), but the command of God, and the visitation of the Spirit that comes sacramentally to set us free. But water serves to express the cleansing. For since we are wont by washing in water to render our body clean when it is soiled by dirt or mud, we therefore apply it also in the sacramental action, and display the spiritual brightness by that which is subject to our senses. Let us however, if it seems well, persevere in enquiring more fully and more minutely concerning Baptism, starting, as from the fountain-head, from the Scriptural declaration, *"Unless a man be born of water and of the Spirit, he cannot enter into the kingdom of God."* Why are both named, and why is not the Spirit alone accounted sufficient for the completion of Baptism? Man, as we know full well, is compound, not simple: and therefore the cognate and similar medicines are assigned for healing to him who is twofold and conglomerate:— for his visible body, water, the sensible element—for his soul, which we cannot see, the Spirit invisible, invoked by faith, present unspeakably. For *"the Spirit breathes where He wills, and you hear His voice, but canst not tell whence He comes or whither He goes."* He blesses the body that is baptized, and the water that baptizes. Despise not, therefore, the Divine laver, nor think lightly of it, as a common thing, on account of the use of water. For the power that operates is mighty, and wonderful are the things that are wrought thereby. For this holy altar, too, by which I stand, is stone, ordinary in its nature, nowise different from the other slabs of stone that build our houses and adorn our pavements; but seeing that it was consecrated to the service of God, and received the benediction, it is a holy table, an altar undefiled, no longer touched by the hands of all, but of the priests alone, and that with reverence. The bread again is at first common bread, but when the sacramental action consecrates it, it is called, and becomes, the Body of Christ. So with the sacramental oil; so with the wine: though before the benediction they are of little value, each of them, after the sanctification bestowed by the Spirit, has its several operation. The same power of the word, again, also makes the priest venerable and honourable, separated, by the new blessing bestowed upon him, from his community with the mass of men. While but yesterday he was one of the mass, one of the people, he is suddenly rendered a guide, a president, a teacher of righteousness, an instructor in hidden mysteries; and this he does without being at all changed in body or in form; but, while continuing to be in all appearance the man he was before, being, by some unseen power and grace, transformed in respect of his unseen soul to the higher condition. And so there are many things, which if you consider you will see that their appearance is contemptible, but the things they accomplish are mighty: and this is especially the case when you collect from the ancient history instances cognate and similar to the subject of our inquiry. The rod of Moses was a hazel wand. And what is that, but common wood that every hand cuts and carries, and fashions to what use it chooses, and casts as it will into the fire? But when God was pleased to accomplish by that rod those wonders, lofty, and passing the power of language to express, the wood was changed into a serpent. And again, at another time, he smote the waters, and now made the water blood, now made to issue forth a countless brood of frogs: and again he divided the sea, severed to its depths without flowing together again. Likewise the mantle of one of the prophets, though it was but a goat's skin, made Elisha renowned in the whole world. And the wood of the Cross is of saving efficacy for all men, though it is, as I am informed, a piece of a poor tree, less valuable than most trees are. So a bramble bush showed to Moses the manifestation of the presence of God: so the remains of Elisha raised a dead man to life; so clay gave sight to him that was blind from the womb. And all these things, though they were matter without soul or sense, were made the means for the performance of the great marvels wrought by them, when they received the power of God. Now by a similar train of reasoning, water also, though it is nothing else than water, renews the man to spiritual regeneration , when the grace from above hallows it. And if any one answers me again by raising a difficulty, with his questions and doubts, continually asking and inquiring how water and the sacramental act that is performed therein regenerate, I most justly reply to him, *"Show me the mode of that generation which is after the flesh, and I will explain to you the power of regeneration in the soul."* You will say perhaps, by way of giving an account of the matter, *"It is the cause of the seed which makes the man."* Learn then from us in return, that hallowed water cleanses and illuminates the man. And if you again object to me your *"How?"* I shall more vehemently cry in answer, *"How does the fluid and formless substance become a man?"* and so the argument as it advances will be exercised on everything through all creation. How does heaven exist? How earth? How sea?

How every single thing? For everywhere men's reasoning, perplexed in the attempt at discovery, falls back upon this syllable *"how,"* as those who cannot walk fall back upon a seat. To speak concisely, everywhere the power of God and His operation are incomprehensible and incapable of being reduced to rule, easily producing whatever He wills, while concealing from us the minute knowledge of His operation. Hence also the blessed David, applying his mind to the magnificence of creation, and filled with perplexed wonder in his soul, spoke that verse which is sung by all, *"O Lord, how manifold are Your works: in wisdom have You made them all."* The wisdom he perceived: but the art of the wisdom he could not discover. Let us then leave the task of searching into what is beyond human power, and seek rather that which shows signs of being partly within our comprehension:— what is the reason why the cleansing is effected by water? And to what purpose are the three immersions received? That which the fathers taught, and which our mind has received and assented to, is as follows:— We recognize four elements, of which the world is composed, which every one knows even if their names are not spoken; but if it is well, for the sake of the more simple, to tell you their names, they are fire and air, earth and water. Now our God and Saviour, in fulfilling the Dispensation for our sakes, went beneath the fourth of these, the earth, that He might raise up life from thence. And we in receiving Baptism, in imitation of our Lord and Teacher and Guide, are not indeed buried in the earth (for this is the shelter of the body that is entirely dead, covering the infirmity and decay of our nature), but coming to the element akin to earth, to water, we conceal ourselves in that as the Saviour did in the earth: and by doing this thrice we represent for ourselves that grace of the Resurrection which was wrought in three days: and this we do, not receiving the sacrament in silence, but while there are spoken over us the Names of the Three Sacred Persons on Whom we believed, in Whom we also hope, from Whom comes to us both the fact of our present and the fact of our future existence. It may be you are offended, thou who contendest boldly against the glory of the Spirit, and that you grudge to the Spirit that veneration wherewith He is reverenced by the godly. Leave off contending with me: resist, if you can, those words of the Lord which gave to men the rule of the Baptismal invocation. What says the Lord's command? *"Baptizing them in the Name of the Father and of the Son and of the Holy Ghost* Matthew 28:19 *."* How in the Name of the Father? Because He is the primal cause of all things. How in the Name of the Son? Because He is the Maker of the Creation. How in the Name of the Holy Ghost? Because He is the power perfecting all. We bow ourselves therefore before the Father, that we may be sanctified: before the Son also we bow, that the same end may be fulfilled: we bow also before the Holy Ghost, that we may be made what He is in fact and in Name. There is not a distinction in the sanctification, in the sense that the Father sanctifies more, the Son less, the Holy Spirit in a less degree than the other Two. Why then do you divide the Three Persons into fragments of different natures, and make Three Gods, unlike one to another, while from all thou dost receive one and the same grace?

As, however, examples always render an argument more vivid to the hearers, I propose to instruct the mind of the blasphemers by an illustration, explaining, by means of earthly and lowly matters, those matters which are great, and invisible to the senses. If it befell you to be enduring the misfortune of captivity among enemies, to be in bondage and in misery, to be groaning for that ancient freedom which thou once had— and if all at once three men, who were notable men and citizens in the country of your tyrannical masters, set you free from the constraint that lay upon you, giving your ransom equally, and dividing the charges of the money in equal shares among themselves, would you not then, meeting with this favour, look upon the three alike as benefactors, and make repayment of the ransom to them in equal shares, as the trouble and the cost on your behalf was common to them all— if, that is, thou were a fair judge of the benefit done to you? This we may see, so far as illustration goes , for our aim at present is not to render a strict account of the Faith. Let us return to the present season, and to the subject it sets before us.

I find that not only do the Gospels, written after the Crucifixion, proclaim the grace of Baptism, but, even before the Incarnation of our Lord, the ancient Scripture everywhere prefigured the likeness of our regeneration; not clearly manifesting its form, but fore-showing, in dark sayings, the love of God to man. And as the Lamb was proclaimed by anticipation, and the Cross was foretold by anticipation, so, too, was Baptism shown forth by action and by word. Let us recall its types to those who love good thoughts— for the festival season of necessity demands their recollection.

Hagar, the handmaid of Abraham (whom Paul treats allegorically in reasoning with the Galatians), being sent forth from her master's house by the anger of Sarah— for a servant suspected in regard to her master is a hard thing for lawful wives to bear— was wandering in desolation to a desolate land with her babe Ishmael at her breast. And when she was in straits for the needs of life, and was herself near unto death, and her child yet more sore for the water in the skin was spent (since it was not possible that the Synagogue, she who once dwelt among the figures of the perennial Fountain, should have all that was needed to support life), an angel unexpectedly appears, and shows her a well of living water, and drawing thence, she saves Ishmael. Behold, then, a sacramental type: how from the very first it is by the means of living water that salvation comes to him that was perishing— water that was not before, but was given as a boon by an angel's means. Again, at a later time, Isaac— the same for whose sake Ishmael was driven with his mother from his father's home— was to be wedded. Abraham's servant is sent to make the match, so as to secure a bride for his master, and finds Rebekah at the well: and a marriage that was to produce the race of Christ had its beginning and its first covenant in water. Yes, and Isaac himself also, when he was ruling his flocks, dug wells at all parts of the desert, which the aliens stopped and filled up , for a type of all those impious men of later days who hindered the grace of Baptism, and talked loudly in their struggle against the truth. Yet the martyrs and the priests overcame them by digging the wells, and the gift of Baptism over-flowed the whole world. According to the same force of the text, Jacob also, hastening to seek a bride, met Rachel unexpectedly at the well. And a great stone lay upon the well, which a multitude of shepherds were wont to roll away when they came together, and then gave water to themselves and to their flocks. But Jacob alone rolls away the stone, and waters the flocks of his spouse. The thing is, I think, a dark saying, a shadow of what should come. For what is the stone that is laid but Christ Himself? For of Him Isaiah says, *"And I will lay in the foundations of Sion a costly stone, precious, elect :"* and Daniel likewise, *"A stone was cut out without hands ,"* that is, Christ was born without a man. For as it is a new and marvellous thing that a stone should be cut out of the rock without a hewer or stone-cutting tools, so it is a thing beyond all wonder that an offspring should appear from an unwedded Virgin. There was lying, then, upon the well the spiritual stone, Christ, concealing in the deep and in mystery the laver of regeneration which needed much time— as it were a long rope— to bring it to light. And none rolled away the stone save Israel, who is mind seeing God. But he both draws up the water and gives drink to the sheep of Rachel; that is, he reveals the hidden mystery, and gives living water to the flock of the Church. Add to this also the history of the three rods of Jacob. For from the time when the three rods were laid by the well, Laban the polytheist thenceforth became poor, and Jacob became rich and wealthy in herds. Now let Laban be interpreted of the devil, and Jacob of Christ. For after the institution of Baptism Christ took away all the flock of Satan and Himself grew rich. Again, the great Moses, when he was a goodly child, and yet at the breast, falling under the general and cruel decree which the hard-hearted Pharaoh made against the men-children, was exposed on the banks of the river — not naked, but laid in an ark, for it was fitting that the Law should typically be enclosed in a coffer. And he was laid near the water; for the Law, and those daily sprinklings of the Hebrews which were a little later to be made plain in the perfect and marvellous Baptism, are near to grace. Again, according to the view of the inspired Paul, the people itself, by passing through the Red Sea, proclaimed the good tidings of salvation by water. The people passed over, and the Egyptian king with his host was engulfed, and by these actions this Sacrament was foretold. For even now, whenever the people is in the water of regeneration, fleeing from Egypt, from the burden of sin, it is set free and saved; but the devil with his own servants (I mean, of course, the spirits of evil), is choked with grief, and perishes, deeming the salvation of men to be his own misfortune.

Even these instances might be enough to confirm our present position; but the lover of good thoughts must yet not neglect what follows. The people of the Hebrews, as we learn, after many sufferings, and after accomplishing their weary course in the desert, did not enter the land of promise until it had first been brought, with Joshua for its guide and the pilot of its life, to the passage of the Jordan. But it is clear that Joshua also, who set up the twelve stones in the stream, was anticipating the coming of the twelve disciples, the ministers of Baptism. Again, that marvellous sacrifice of the old Tishbite, that passes all human understanding, what else does it do but prefigure in action the Faith in the Father, the Son, and the Holy Ghost, and redemption? For when all the people of the Hebrews had trodden underfoot the religion of their fathers, and fallen into the error of polytheism, and their king Ahab was deluded by idolatry, with Jezebel, of ill-omened name, as the wicked partner of his life, and the vile prompter of his impiety, the prophet, filled with the grace of the Spirit, coming to a meeting with Ahab, withstood the priests of Baal in a marvellous and wondrous contest in the sight of the king and all the people; and by proposing to them the task of sacrificing the bullock without fire, he displayed them in a ridiculous and wretched plight, vainly praying and crying aloud to gods that were not. At last, himself invoking his own and the true God, he accomplished the test proposed with further exaggerations and additions. For he did not simply by prayer bring down the fire from heaven upon the wood when it was dry, but exhorted and enjoined the attendants to bring abundance of water. And when he had thrice poured out the barrels upon the cleft wood, he kindled at his prayer the fire from out of the water, that by the contrariety of the elements, so concurring in friendly cooperation, he might show with superabundant force the power of his own God. Now herein, by that wondrous sacrifice, Elijah clearly proclaimed to us the sacramental rite of Baptism that should afterwards be instituted. For the fire was kindled by water thrice poured upon it, so that it is clearly shown that where the mystic water is, there is the kindling, warm, and fiery Spirit, that burns up the ungodly, and illuminates the faithful. Yes, and yet again his disciple Elisha, when Naaman the Syrian, who was diseased with leprosy, had come to him as a suppliant, cleanses the sick man by washing him in Jordan , clearly indicating what should come, both by the use of water generally, and by the dipping in the river in particular. For Jordan alone of rivers, receiving in itself the first-fruits of sanctification and benediction, conveyed in its channel to the whole world, as it were from some fount in the type afforded by itself, the grace of Baptism. These then are indications in deed and act of regeneration by Baptism. Let us for the rest consider the prophecies of it in words and language. Isaiah cried saying, *"Wash you, make you clean, put away evil from your souls ;"* and David, *"Draw near to Him and be enlightened, and your faces shall not be ashamed."* And Ezekiel, writing more clearly and plainly than them both, says, *"And I will sprinkle clean water upon you, and you shall be cleansed: from all your filthiness, and from all your idols, will I cleanse you. A new heart also will I give you, and a new spirit will I give you: and I will take away the stony heart out of your flesh, and I will give you an heart of flesh, and my Spirit will I put within you."* Most manifestly also does

Zechariah prophesy of Joshua , who was clothed with the filthy garment (to wit, the flesh of a servant, even ours), and stripping him of his ill-favoured raiment adorns him with the clean and fair apparel; teaching us by the figurative illustration that verily in the Baptism of Jesus all we, putting off our sins like some poor and patched garment, are clothed in the holy and most fair garment of regeneration. And where shall we place that oracle of Isaiah, which cries to the wilderness, *"Be glad, O thirsty wilderness: let the desert rejoice and blossom as a lily: and the desolate places of Jordan shall blossom and shall rejoice "*? For it is clear that it is not to places without soul or sense that he proclaims the good tidings of joy: but he speaks, by the figure of the desert, of the soul that is parched and unadorned, even as David also, when he says, *"My soul is unto You as a thirsty land ,"* and, *"My soul is thirsty for the mighty, for the living God. "* So again the Lord says in the Gospels, *"If any man thirst, let him come unto Me and drink ;"* and to the woman of Samaria, *"Whosoever drinks of this water shall thirst again: but whosoever drinks of the water that I shall give him shall never thirst* John 4:13-14 *."* And *"the excellency of Carmel"* Isaiah 35:2 is given to the soul that bears the likeness to the desert, that is, the grace bestowed through the Spirit. For since Elijah dwelt in Carmel, and the mountain became famous and renowned by the virtue of him who dwelt there, and since moreover John the Baptist, illustrious in the spirit of Elijah, sanctified the Jordan, therefore the prophet foretold that *"the excellency of Carmel"* should be given to the river. And *"the glory of Lebanon* Isaiah 35:2 *,"* from the similitude of its lofty trees, he transfers to the river. For as great Lebanon presents a sufficient cause of wonder in the very trees which it brings forth and nourishes, so is the Jordan glorified by regenerating men and planting them in the Paradise of God: and of them, as the words of the Psalmist say, ever blooming and bearing the foliage of virtues, *"the leaf shall not wither ,"* and God shall be glad, receiving their fruit in due season, rejoicing, like a good planter, in his own works. And the inspired David, foretelling also the voice which the Father uttered from heaven upon the Son at His Baptism, that He might lead the hearers, who till then had looked upon that low estate of His Humanity which was perceptible by their senses, to the dignity of nature that belongs to the Godhead, wrote in his book that passage, *"The voice of the Lord is upon the waters, the voice of the Lord in majesty. "* But here we must make an end of the testimonies from the Divine Scriptures: for the discourse would extend to an infinite length if one should seek to select every passage in detail, and set them forth in a single book.

But do ye all, as many as are made glad, by the gift of regeneration, and make your boast of that saving renewal, show me, after the sacramental grace, the change in your ways that should follow it, and make known by the purity of your conversation the difference effected by your transformation for the better. For of those things which are before our eyes nothing is altered: the characteristics of the body remain unchanged, and the mould of the visible nature is nowise different. But there is certainly need of some manifest proof, by which we may recognize the new-born man, discerning by clear tokens the new from the old. And these I think are to be found in the intentional motions of the soul, whereby it separates itself from its old customary life, and enters on a newer way of conversation, and will clearly teach those acquainted with it that it has become something different from its former self, bearing in it no token by which the old self was recognized. This, if you be persuaded by me, and keep my words as a law, is the mode of the transformation. The man that was before Baptism was wanton, covetous, grasping at the goods of others, a reviler, a liar, a slanderer, and all that is kindred with these things, and consequent from them. Let him now become orderly, sober, content with his own possessions, and imparting from them to those in poverty, truthful, courteous, affable— in a word, following every laudable course of conduct. For as darkness is dispelled by light, and black disappears as whiteness is spread over it, so the old man also disappears when adorned with the works of righteousness. You see how Zacchæus also by the change of his life slew the publican, making fourfold restitution to those whom he had unjustly damaged, and the rest he divided with the poor— the treasure which he had before got by ill means from the poor whom he oppressed. The Evangelist Matthew, another publican, of the same business with Zacchæus, at once after his call changed his life as if it had been a mask. Paul was a persecutor, but after the grace bestowed on him an Apostle, bearing the weight of his fetters for Christ's sake, as an act of amends and repentance for those unjust bonds which he once received from the Law, and bore for use against the Gospel. Such ought you to be in your regeneration: so ought you to blot out your habits that tend to sin; so ought the sons of God to have their conversation: for after the grace bestowed we are called His children.

And therefore we ought narrowly to scrutinize our Father's characteristics, that by fashioning and framing ourselves to the likeness of our Father, we may appear true children of Him Who calls us to the adoption according to grace. For the bastard and the supposititious son, who belies his father's nobility in his deeds, is a sad reproach. Therefore also, methinks, it is that the Lord Himself, laying down for us in the Gospels the rules of our life, uses these words to His disciples, *"Do good to them that hate you, pray for them that despitefully use you and persecute you; that you may be the children of your Father which is in heaven: for He makes His sun to rise on the evil and on the good, and sends rain on the just and on the unjust."* For then He says they are sons when in their own modes of thought they are fashioned in loving kindness towards their kindred, after the likeness of the Father's goodness.

Therefore, also, it is that after the dignity of adoption the devil plots more vehemently against us, pining away with envious glance, when he beholds the beauty of the new-born man, earnestly tending towards that heavenly city, from which he fell: and he raises up against us fiery temptations, seeking earnestly to despoil us of that second adornment, as he did of our former array. But when we are aware of his attacks, we ought to repeat to ourselves the apostolic words, *"As many of us as were baptized into Christ were baptized into His death* Romans 6:3 *."* Now if we have been conformed to His death, sin henceforth in us is surely a corpse, pierced through by the javelin of Baptism, as that fornicator was thrust through by the zealous Phinehas. Numbers 25:7-8 Flee therefore from us, ill-omened one! For it is a corpse you seek to despoil, one long ago joined to you, one who long since lost his senses for pleasures. A corpse is not enamoured of bodies, a corpse is not captivated by wealth, a corpse slanders not, a corpse lies not, snatches not at what is not its own, reviles not those who encounter it. My way of living is regulated for another life: I have learned to despise the things that are in the world, to pass by the things of earth, to hasten to the things of heaven, even as Paul expressly testifies, that the world is crucified to him, and he to the world. These are the words of a soul truly regenerated: these are the utterances of the newly-baptized man, who remembers his own profession, which he made to God when the sacrament was administered to him, promising that he would despise for the sake of love towards Him all torment and all pleasure alike.

And now we have spoken sufficiently for the holy subject of the day, which the circling year brings to us at appointed periods. We shall do well in what remains to end our discourse by turning it to the loving Giver of so great a boon, offering to Him a few words as the requital of great things. For You verily, O Lord, are the pure and eternal fount of goodness, Who justly turned away from us, and in loving kindness had mercy upon us. You hated, and were reconciled; You cursed, and blessed; You banished us from Paradise, and recalled us; You stripped off the fig-tree leaves, an unseemly covering, and put upon us a costly garment; You opened the prison, and released the condemned; You sprinkled us with clean water, and cleanse us from our filthiness. No longer shall Adam be confounded when called by You, nor hide himself, convicted by his conscience, cowering in the thicket of Paradise. Nor shall the flaming sword encircle Paradise around, and make the entrance inaccessible to those that draw near; but all is turned to joy for us that were the heirs of sin: Paradise, yea, heaven itself may be trodden by man: and the creation, in the world and above the world, that once was at variance with itself, is knit together in friendship: and we men are made to join in the angels' song, offering the worship of their praise to God. For all these things then let us sing to God that hymn of joy, which lips touched by the Spirit long ago sang loudly: *"Let my soul be joyful in the Lord: for He has clothed me with a garment of salvation, and has put upon me a robe of gladness: as on a bridegroom He has set a mitre upon me, and as a bride has He adorned me with fair array."* And verily the Adorner of the bride is Christ, Who is, and was, and shall be, blessed now and for evermore. Amen.

To Eusebius

To Eusebius

When the length of the day begins to expand in winter-time, as the sun mounts to the upper part of his course, we keep the feast of the appearing of the true Light divine, that through the veil of flesh has cast its bright beams upon the life of men: but now when that luminary has traversed half the heaven in his course, so that night and day are of equal length, the upward return of human nature from death to life is the theme of this great and universal festival, which all the life of those who have embraced the mystery of the Resurrection unites in celebrating. What is the meaning of the subject thus suggested for my letter to you? Why, since it is the custom in these general holidays for us to take every way to show the affection harboured in our hearts, and some, as you know, give proof of their good will by presents of their own, we thought it only right not to leave you without the homage of our gifts, but to lay before your lofty and high-minded soul the scanty offerings of our poverty. Now our offering which is tendered for your acceptance in this letter is the letter itself, in which there is not a single word wreathed with the flowers of rhetoric or adorned with the graces of composition, to make it to be deemed a gift at all in literary circles, but the mystical gold, which is wrapped up in the faith of Christians, as in a packet, must be my present to you, after being unwrapped, as far as possible, by these lines, and showing its hidden brilliancy. Accordingly we must return to our prelude. Why is it that then only, when the night has attained its utmost length, so that no further addition is possible, that He appears in flesh to us, Who holds the Universe in His grasp, and controls the same Universe by His own power, Who cannot be contained even by all intelligible things, but includes the whole, even at the time that He enters the narrow dwelling of a fleshly tabernacle, while His mighty power thus keeps pace with His beneficent purpose, and shows itself even as a shadow wherever the will inclines, so that neither in the creation of the world was the power found weaker than the will, nor when He was eager to stoop down to the lowliness of our mortal nature did He lack power to that very end, but actually did come to be in that condition, yet without leaving the universe unpiloted? Since, then, there is some account to be given of both those seasons, how it is that it is winter-time when He appears in the flesh, but it is when the days are as long as the nights that He restores to life man, who because of his sins returned to the earth from whence he came—by explaining the reason of this, as well as I can in few words, I will make my letter my present to you. Has your own sagacity, as of course it has, already divined the mystery hinted at by these coincidences; that the advance of night is stopped by the accessions to the light, and the period of darkness begins to be shortened, as the length of the day is increased by the successive additions? For thus much perhaps would be plain enough even to the uninitiated, that sin is near akin to darkness; and in fact evil is so termed by the Scripture. Accordingly the season in which our mystery of godliness begins is a kind of exposition of the Divine dispensation on behalf of our souls. For meet and right it was that, when vice was shed abroad without bounds, [upon this night of evil the Sun of righteousness should rise, and that in us who have before walked in darkness] the day which we receive from Him Who placed that light in our hearts should increase more and more; so that the life which is in the light should be extended to the greatest length possible, being constantly augmented by additions of good; and that the life in vice should by gradual subtraction be reduced to the smallest possible compass; for the increase of things good comes to the same thing as the diminution of things evil. But the feast of the Resurrection; occurring when the days are of equal length, of itself gives us this interpretation of the coincidence, namely, that we shall no longer fight with evils only upon equal terms, vice grappling with virtue in indecisive strife, but that the life of light will prevail, the gloom of idolatry melting as the day waxes stronger. For this reason also, after the moon has run her course for fourteen days, Easter exhibits her exactly opposite to the rays of the sun, full with all the wealth of his brightness, and not permitting any interval of darkness to take place in its turn : for, after taking the place of the sun at its setting, she does not herself set before she mingles her own beams with the genuine rays of the sun, so that one light remains continuously, throughout the whole space of the earth's course by day and night, without any break whatsoever being caused by the interposition of darkness. This discussion, dear one, we contribute by way of a gift from our poor and needy hand; and may your whole life be a continual festival and a high day, never dimmed by a single stain of nightly gloom.

To the City of Sebasteia

To the City of Sebasteia

Some of the brethren whose heart is as our heart told us of the slanders that were being propagated to our detriment by those who hate peace, and privily backbite their neighbour; and have no fear of the great and terrible judgment-seat of Him Who has declared that account will be required even of idle words in that trial of our life which we must all look for: they say that the charges which are being circulated against us are such as these; that we entertain opinions opposed to those who at Nicæa set forth the right and sound faith, and that without due discrimination and inquiry we received into the communion of the Catholic Church those who formerly assembled at Ancyra under the name of Marcellus. Therefore, that falsehood may not overpower the truth, in another letter we made a sufficient defence against the charges levelled at us, and before the Lord we protested that we had neither departed from the faith of the Holy Fathers, nor had we done anything without due discrimination and inquiry in the case of those who came over from the communion of Marcellus to that of the Church: but all that we did we did only after the orthodox in the East, and our brethren in the ministry had entrusted to us the consideration of the case of these persons, and had approved our action. But inasmuch as, since we composed that written defence of our conduct, again some of the brethren who are of one mind with us begged us to make separately with our own lips a profession of our faith, which we entertain with full conviction , following as we do the utterances of inspiration and the tradition of the Fathers, we deemed it necessary to discourse briefly of these heads as well. We confess that the doctrine of the Lord, which He taught His disciples, when He delivered to them the mystery of godliness, is the foundation and root of right and sound faith, nor do we believe that there is anything else loftier or safer than that tradition. Now the doctrine of the Lord is this: *"Go,"* He said, *"teach all nations, baptizing them in the name of the Father, and of the Son, and of the Holy Ghost."* Since, then, in the case of those who are regenerate from death to eternal life, it is through the Holy Trinity that the life-giving power is bestowed on those who with faith are deemed worthy of the grace, and in like manner the grace is imperfect, if any one, whichever it be, of the names of the Holy Trinity be omitted in the saving baptism— for the sacrament of regeneration is not completed in the Son and the

Father alone without the Spirit: nor is the perfect boon of life imparted to Baptism in the Father and the Spirit, if the name of the Son be suppressed: nor is the grace of that Resurrection accomplished in the Father and the Son, if the Spirit be left out :— for this reason we rest all our hope, and the persuasion of the salvation of our souls, upon the three Persons, recognized by these names; and we believe in the Father of our Lord Jesus Christ, Who is the Fountain of life, and in the Only-begotten Son of the Father, Who is the Author of life, as says the Apostle, and in the Holy Spirit of God, concerning Whom the Lord has spoken, *"It is the Spirit that quickens"*. And since on us who have been redeemed from death the grace of immortality is bestowed, as we have said, through faith in the Father, and the Son, and the Holy Spirit, guided by these we believe that nothing servile, nothing created, nothing unworthy of the majesty of the Father is to be associated in thought with the Holy Trinity; since, I say, our life is one which comes to us by faith in the Holy Trinity, taking its rise from the God of all, flowing through the Son, and working in us by the Holy Spirit. Having, then, this full assurance, we are baptized as we were commanded, and we believe as we are baptized, and we hold as we believe; so that with one accord our baptism, our faith, and our ascription of praise are to the Father, and to the Son, and to the Holy Ghost. But if any one makes mention of two or three Gods, or of three God-heads, let him be accursed. And if any, following the perversion of Arius, says that the Son or the Holy Spirit were produced from things that are not, let him be accursed. But as many as walk by the rule of truth and acknowledge the three Persons, devoutly recognized in Their several properties, and believe that there is one Godhead, one goodness, one rule, one authority and power, and neither make void the supremacy of the Sole-sovereignty , nor fall away into polytheism, nor confound the Persons, nor make up the Holy Trinity of heterogeneous and unlike elements, but in simplicity receive the doctrine of the faith, grounding all their hope of salvation upon the Father, the Son, and the Holy Spirit—these according to our judgment are of the same mind as we, and with them we also trust to have part in the Lord.

To Ablabius

To Ablabius

The Lord, as was meet and right, brought us safe through, accompanied as we had been by your prayers, and I will tell you a manifest token of His loving kindness. For when the sun was just over the spot which we left behind Earsus , suddenly the clouds gathered thick, and there was a change from clear sky to deep gloom. Then a chilly breeze blowing through the clouds, bringing a drizzling with it, and striking upon us with a very damp feeling, threatened such rain as had never yet been known, and on the left there were continuous claps of thunder, and keen flashes of lightning alternated with the thunder, following one crash and preceding the next, and all the mountains before, behind, and on each side were shrouded in clouds. And already a heavy cloud hung over our heads, caught by a strong wind and big with rain, and yet we, like the Israelites of old in their miraculous passage of the Red Sea, though surrounded on all sides by rain, arrived unwetted at Vestena. And when we had already found shelter there, and our mules had got a rest, then the signal for the down-pour was given by God to the air. And when we had spent some three or four hours there, and had rested enough, again God stayed the down-fall, and our conveyance moved along more briskly than before, as the wheel easily slid through the mud just moist and on the surface. Now the road from that point to our little town is all along the river side, going down stream with the water, and there is a continuous string of villages along the banks, all close upon the road, and with very short distances between them. In consequence of this unbroken line of habitations all the road was full of people, some coming to meet us, and others escorting us, mingling tears in abundance with their joy. Now there was a little drizzle, not unpleasant, just enough to moisten the air; but a little way before we got home the cloud that overhung us was condensed into a more violent shower, so that our entrance was quite quiet, as no one was aware beforehand of our coming. But just as we got inside our portico, as the sound of our carriage wheels along the dry hard ground was heard, the people turned up in shoals, as though by some mechanical contrivance, I know not whence nor how, flocking round us so closely that it was not easy to get down from our conveyance, for there was not a foot of clear space. But after we had persuaded them with difficulty to allow us to get down, and to let our mules pass, we were crushed on every side by folks crowding round, insomuch that their excessive kindness all but made us faint. And when we were near the inside of the portico, we see a stream of fire flowing into the church; for the choir of virgins, carrying their wax torches in their hands, were just marching in file along the entrance of the church, kindling the whole into splendour with their blaze. And when I was within and had rejoiced and wept with my people— for I experienced both emotions from witnessing both in the multitude—as soon as I had finished the prayers, I wrote off this letter to your Holiness as fast as possible, under the pressure of extreme thirst, so that I might when it was done attend to my bodily wants.

To Cynegius

We have a law that bids us *"rejoice with them that rejoice, and weep with them that weep"*: but of these commandments it often seems that it is in our power to put only one into practice. For there is a great scarcity in the world of *"them that rejoice,"* so that it is not easy to find with whom we may share our blessings, but there are plenty who are in the opposite case. I write thus much by way of preface, because of the sad tragedy which some spiteful power has been playing among people of long-standing nobility. A young man of good family, Synesius by name, not unconnected with myself, in the full flush of youth, who has scarcely begun to live yet, is in great dangers, from which God alone has power to rescue him, and next to God, you, who are entrusted with the decisions of all questions of life and death. An involuntary mishap has taken place. Indeed, what mishap is voluntary? And now those who have made up this suit against him, carrying with it the penalty of death, have turned his mishap into matter of accusation. However, I will try by private letters to soften their resentment and incline them to pity; but I beseech your kindliness to side with justice and with us, that your benevolence may prevail over the wretched plight of the youth, hunting up any and every device by which the young man may be placed out of the reach of danger, having conquered the spiteful power which assails him by the help of your alliance. I have said all that I want in brief; but to go into details, in order that my endeavour may be successful, would be to say what I have no business to say, nor you to hear from me.

A Testimonial

That for which the king of the Macedonians is most admired by people of understanding—for he is admired not so much for his famous victories over the Persians and Indians, and his penetrating as far the Ocean, as for his saying that he had his treasure in his friends—in this respect I dare to compare myself with his marvellous exploits, and it will be right for me to utter such a sentiment too. Now because I am rich in friendships, perhaps I surpass in that kind of property even that great man who plumed himself upon that very thing. For who was such a friend to him as you are to me, perpetually endeavouring to surpass yourself in every kind of excellence? For assuredly no one would ever charge me with flattery, when I say this, if he were to look at my age and your life: for grey hairs are out of season for flattery, and old age is ill-suited for complaisance, and as for you, even if you are ever in season for flattery, yet praise would not fall under the suspicion of flattery, as your life shows forth your praise before words. But since, when men are rich in blessings, it is a special gift to know how to use what one has, and the best use of superfluities is to let one's friends share them with one, and since my beloved son Alexander is most of all a friend united to me in all sincerity, be persuaded to show him my treasure, and not only to show it to him, but also to put it at his disposal to enjoy abundantly, by extending to him your protection in those matters about which he has come to you, begging you to be his patron. He will tell you all with his own lips. For it is better so than that I should go into details in a letter.

To Stagirius

They say that conjurors in theatres contrive some such marvel as this which I am going to describe. Having taken some historical narrative, or some old story as the ground-plot of their sleight of hand, they relate the story to the spectators in action. And it is in this way that they make their representations of the narrative. They put on their dresses and masks, and rig up something to resemble a town on the stage with hangings, and then so associate the bare scene with their life-like imitation of action that they are a marvel to the spectators—both the actors themselves of the incidents of the play, and the hangings, or rather their imaginary city. What do I mean, do you think, by this allegory? Since we must needs show to those who are coming together that which is not a city as though it were one, do you let yourself be persuaded to become for the nonce the founder of our city , by just putting in an appearance there; I will make the desert-place seem to be a city; now it is no great distance for you, and the favour which you will confer is very great; for we wish to show ourselves more splendid to our companions here, which we shall do if, in place of any other ornament, we are adorned with the splendour of your party.

To a Friend

What flower in spring is so bright, what voices of singing birds are so sweet, what breezes that soothe the calm sea are so light and mild, what glebe is so fragrant to the husbandman— whether it be teeming with green blades, or waving with fruitful ears as is the spring of the soul, lit up with your peaceful beams, from the radiance which shone in your letter, which raised our life from despondency to gladness? For thus, perhaps, it will not be unfitting to adapt the word of the prophet to our present blessings: *"In the multitude of the sorrows which I had in my heart, the comforts of God,"* by your kindness, *"have refreshed my soul,"* like sunbeams, cheering and warming our life nipped by frost. For both reached the highest pitch— the severity of my troubles, I mean, on the one side, and the sweetness of your favours on the other. And if you have so gladdened us, by only sending us the joyful tidings of your coming, that everything changed for us from extremest woe to a bright condition, what will your precious and benign coming, even the sight of it, do? What consolation will the sound of your sweet voice in our ears afford our soul? May this speedily come to pass, by the good help of God, Who gives respite from pain to the fainting, and rest to the afflicted. But be assured, that when we look at our own case we grieve exceedingly at the present state of things, and men cease not to tear us in pieces : but when we turn our eyes to your excellence, we own that we have great cause for thankfulness to the dispensation of Divine Providence, that we are able to enjoy in your neighbourhood your sweetness and good-will towards us, and feast at will on such food to satiety, if indeed there is such a thing as satiety of blessings like these.

To a Student of the Classics

When I was looking for some suitable and proper exordium, I mean of course from Holy Scripture, to put at the head of my letter, according to my usual custom, I did not know which to choose, not from inability to find what was suitable, but because I deemed it superfluous to write such things to those who knew nothing about the matter. For your eager pursuit of profane literature proved incontestably to us that you did not care about sacred. Accordingly I will say nothing about Bible texts, but will select a prelude adapted to your literary tastes taken from the poets you love so well. By the great master of your education there is introduced one, showing all an old man's joy, when after long affliction he once more beheld his son, and his son's son as well. And the special theme of his exultation is the rivalry between the two, Ulysses and Telemachus, for the highest meed of valour, though it is true that the recollection of his own exploits against the Cephallenians adds to the point of his speech. For you and your admirable father, when you welcomed me, as they did Laertes, in your affection, contended in most honourable rivalry for the prize of virtue, by showing us all possible respect and kindness; he in numerous ways which I need not here mention, and you by pelting me with your letters from Cappadocia. What, then, of me the aged one? I count that day one to be blessed, in which I witness such a competition between father and son. May you, then, never cease from accomplishing the rightful prayer of an excellent and admirable father, and surpassing in your readiness to all good works the renown which from him you inherit. I shall be a judge acceptable to both of you, as I shall award you the first prize against your father, and the same to your father against you. And we will put up with rough Ithaca, rough not so much with stones as with the manners of the inhabitants, an island in which there are many suitors, who are suitors most of all for the possessions of her whom they woo, and insult their intended bride by this very fact, that they threaten her chastity with marriage, acting in a way worthy of a Melantho, one might say, or some other such person; for nowhere is there a Ulysses to bring them to their senses with his bow. You see how in an old man's fashion I go maundering off into matters with which you have no concern. But pray let indulgence be readily extended to me in consideration of my grey hairs; for garrulity is just as characteristic of old age as to be blear-eyed, or for the limbs to fail. But you by entertaining us with your brisk and lively language, like a bold young man as you are, will make our old age young again, supporting the feebleness of our length of days with this kind attention which so well becomes you.

An Invitation

An Invitation

It is not the natural wont of spring to shine forth in its radiant beauty all at once, but there come as preludes of spring the sunbeam gently warming earth's frozen surface, and the bud half hidden beneath the clod, and breezes blowing over the earth, so that the fertilizing and generative power of the air penetrates deeply into it. One may see the fresh and tender grass, and the return of birds which winter had banished, and many such tokens, which are rather signs of spring, not spring itself. Not but that these are sweet, because they are indications of what is sweetest. What is the meaning of all that I have been saying? Why, since the expression of your kindness which reached us in your letters, as a forerunner of the treasures contained in you, with a goodly prelude brings the glad tidings of the blessing which we expect at your hands, we both welcome the boon which those letters convey, like some first-appearing flower of spring, and pray that we may soon enjoy in you the full beauty of the season. For, be well assured, we have been deeply, deeply distressed by the passions and spite of the people here, and their ways; and just as ice forms in cottages after the rains that come in— for I will draw my comparison from the weather of our part of the world —and so moisture, when it gets in, if it spreads over the surface that is already frozen, becomes congealed about the ice, and an addition is made to the mass already existing, even so one may notice much the same kind of thing in the character of most of the people in this neighbourhood, how they are always plotting and inventing something spiteful, and a fresh mischief is congealed on the top of that which has been wrought before, and another one on the top of that, and then again another, and this goes on without intermission, and there is no limit to their hatred and to the increase of evils; so that we have great need of many prayers that the grace of the Spirit may speedily breathe upon them, and thaw the bitterness of their hatred, and melt the frost that is hardening upon them from their malice. For this cause the spring, sweet as it is by nature, becomes yet more to be desired than ever to those who after such storms look for you. Let not the boon, then, linger. Especially as our great holiday is approaching, it would be more reasonable that the land which bare you should exult in her own treasures than that Pontus should in ours. Come then, dear one, bringing us a multitude of blessings, even yourself; for this will fill up the measure of our beatitude.

To Libanius

To Libanius

I once heard a medical man tell of a wonderful freak of nature. And this was his story. A man was ill of an unmanageable complaint, and began to find fault with the medical faculty, as being able to do far less than it professed; for everything that was devised for his cure was ineffectual. Afterwards when some good news beyond his hopes was brought him, the occurrence did the work of the healing art, by putting an end to his disease. Whether it were that the soul by the overflowing sense of release from anxiety, and by a sudden rebound, disposed the body to be in the same condition as itself, or in some other way, I cannot say: for I have no leisure to enter upon such disquisitions, and the person who told me did not specify the cause. But I have just called to mind the story very seasonably, as I think: for when I was not as well as I could wish— now I need not tell you exactly the causes of all the worries which befell me from the time I was with you to the present—after some one told me all at once of the letter which had arrived from your unparalleled Erudition, as soon as I got the epistle and ran over what you had written, immediately, first my soul was affected in the same way as though I had been proclaimed before all the world as the hero of most glorious achievements— so highly did I value the testimony which you favoured me with in your letter—and then also my bodily health immediately began to improve: and I afford an example of the same marvel as the story which I told you just now, in that I was ill when I read one half of the letter, and well when I read the other half of the same. Thus much for those matters. But now, since Cynegius was the occasion of that favour, you are able, in the overflowing abundance of your ability to do good, not only to benefit us, but also our benefactors; and he is a benefactor of ours, as has been said before, by having been the cause and occasion of our having a letter from you; and for this reason he well deserves both our good offices. But if you ask who are our teachers—if indeed we are thought to have learned anything—you will find that they are Paul and John, and the rest of the Apostles and Prophets; if I do not seem to speak too boldly in claiming any knowledge of that art in which you so excel, that competent judges declare that the rules of oratory stream down from you, as from an overflowing spring, upon all who have any pretensions to excellence in that department. This I have heard the admirable Basil say to everybody, Basil, who was your disciple, but my father and teacher. But be assured, first, that I found no rich nourishment in the precepts of my teachers , inasmuch as I enjoyed my brother's society only for a short time, and got only just enough polish from his diviner tongue to be able to discern the ignorance of those who are uninitiated in oratory; next, however, that whenever I had leisure, I devoted my time and energies to this study, and so became enamoured of your beauty, though I never yet obtained the object of my passion. If, then, on the one side we never had a teacher, which I deem to have been our case, and if on the other it is improper to suppose that the opinion which you entertain of us is other than the true one— nay, you are correct in your statement, and we are not quite contemptible in your judgment,— give me leave to presume to attribute to you the cause of such proficiency as we may have attained. For if Basil was the author of our oratory, and if his wealth came from your treasures, then what we possess is yours, even though we received it through others. But if our attainments are scanty, so is the water in a jar; still it comes from the Nile.

To Libanius (2)

To Libanius

It was a custom with the Romans to celebrate a feast in winter-time, after the custom of their fathers, when the length of the days begins to draw out, as the sun climbs to the upper regions of the sky. Now the beginning of the month is esteemed holy, and by this day auguring the character of the whole year, they devote themselves to forecasting lucky accidents, gladness, and wealth. What is my object in beginning my letter in this way? Why, I do so because I too kept this feast, having got my present of gold as well as any of them; for then there came into my hands as well as theirs gold, not like that vulgar gold, which potentates treasure and which those that have it give—that heavy, vile, and soulless possession,— but that which is loftier than all wealth, as Pindar says, in the eyes of those that have sense, being the fairest presentation, I mean your letter, and the vast wealth which it contained. For thus it happened; that on that day, as I was going to the metropolis of the Cappadocians, I met an acquaintance, who handed me this present, your letter, as a new year's gift. And I, being overjoyed at the occurrence, threw open my treasure to all who were present; and all shared in it, each getting the whole of it, without any rivalry, and I was none the worse off. For the letter by passing through the hands of all, like a ticket for a feast, is the private wealth of each, some by steady continuous reading engraving the words upon their memory, and others taking an impression of them upon tablets; and it was again in my hands, giving me more pleasure than the hard metal does to the eyes of the rich. Since, then, even to husbandmen— to use a homely comparison — approbation of the labours which they have already accomplished is a strong stimulus to those which follow, bear with us if we treat what you have yourself given as so much seed, and if we write that we may provoke you to write back. But I beg of you a public and general boon for our life; that you will no longer entertain the purpose which you expressed to us in a dark hint at the end of your letter. For I do not think that it is at all a fair decision to come to, that—because there are some who disgrace themselves by deserting from the Greek language to the barbarian, becoming mercenary soldiers and choosing a soldier's rations instead of the renown of eloquence—you should therefore condemn oratory altogether, and sentence human life to be as voiceless as that of beasts. For who is he who will open his lips, if you carry into effect this severe sentence against oratory? But perhaps it will be well to remind you of a passage in our Scriptures. For our Word bids those that can to do good, not looking at the tempers of those who receive the benefit, so as to be eager to benefit only those who are sensible of kindness, while we close our beneficence to the unthankful, but rather to imitate the Disposer of all, Who distributes the good things of His creation alike to all, to the good and to the evil. Having regard to this, admirable Sir, show yourself in your way of life such an one as the time past has displayed you. For those who do not see the sun do not thereby hinder the sun's existence. Even so neither is it right that the beams of your eloquence should be dimmed, because of those who are purblind as to the perceptions of the soul. But as for Cynegius, I pray that he may be as far as possible from the common malady, which now has seized upon young men; and that he will devote himself of his own accord to the study of rhetoric. But if he is otherwise disposed, it is only right, even if he be unwilling, he should be forced to it; so as to avoid the unhappy and discreditable plight in which they now are, who have previously abandoned the pursuit of oratory.

Selected Works

On His Work Against Eunomius

On his work against Eunomius

We Cappadocians are poor in nearly all things that make the possessors of them happy, but above all we are badly off for people who are able to write. This, be sure, is the reason why I am so slow about sending you a letter: for, though my reply to the heresy (of Eunomius) had been long ago completed, there was no one to transcribe it. Such a dearth of writers it was that brought upon us the suspicion of sluggishness or of inability to frame an answer. But since now at any rate, thank God, the writer and reviser have come, I have sent this treatise to you; not, as Isocrates says , as a present, for I do not reckon it to be such that it should be received in lieu of something of substantial value, but that it may be in our power to cheer on those who are in the full vigour of youth to do battle with the enemy, by stirring up the naturally sanguine temperament of early life. But if any portion of the treatise should appear worthy of serious consideration, after examining some parts, especially those prefatory to the *"trials,"* and those which are of the same cast, and perhaps also some of the doctrinal parts of the book, you will think them not ungratefully composed. But to whatever conclusion you come, you will of course read them, as to a teacher and corrector, to those who do not act like the players at ball , when they stand in three different places and throw it from one to the other, aiming it exactly and catching one ball from one and one from another, and they baffle the player who is in the middle, as he jumps up to catch it, pretending that they are going to throw with a made-up expression of face, and such and such a motion of the hand to left or right, and whichever way they see him hurrying, they send the ball just the contrary way, and cheat his expectation by a trick. This holds even now in the case of most of us, who, dropping all serious purpose, play at being good-natured , as if at ball, with men, instead of realizing the favourable hope which we hold out, beguiling to sinister issues the souls of those who repose confidence in us. Letters of reconciliation, caresses, tokens, presents, affectionate embrace by letters— these are the making as if to throw with the ball to the right. But instead of the pleasure which one expects therefrom, one gets accusations, plots, slanders, disparagement, charges brought against one, bits of a sentence torn from their context, caught up, and turned to one's hurt. Blessed in your hopes are you, who through all such trials exercise confidence towards God. But we beseech you not to look at our words, but to the teaching of our Lord in the Gospel. For what consolation to one in anguish can another be, who surpasses him in the extremity of his own anguish, to help his luckless fortunes to obtain their proper issue? As He says, *"Vengeance is Mine; I will repay, says the Lord."* But do you, best of men, go on in a manner worthy of yourself, and trust in God, and do not be hindered by the spectacle of our misfortunes from being good and true, but commit to God that judges righteously the suitable and just issue of events, and act as Divine wisdom guides you. Assuredly Joseph had in the result no reason to grieve at the envy of his brethren, inasmuch as the malice of his own kith and kin became to him the road to empire.

To the Bishop of Melitene

To the Bishop of Melitene

How beautiful are the likenesses of beautiful objects, when they preserve in all its clearness the impress of the original beauty! For of your soul, so truly beautiful, I saw a most clear image in the sweetness of your letter, which, as the Gospel says, *"out of the abundance of the heart"* you filled with honey. And for this reason I fancied I saw you in person, and enjoyed your cheering company, from the affection expressed in your letter; and often taking your letter into my hands and going over it again from beginning to end, I only came more vehemently to crave for the enjoyment, and there was no sense of satiety. Such a feeling can no more put an end to my pleasure, than it can to that derived from anything that is by nature beautiful and precious. For neither has our constant participation of the benefit blunted the edge of our longing to behold the sun, nor does the unbroken enjoyment of health prevent our desiring its continuance; and we are persuaded that it is equally impossible for our enjoyment of your goodness, which we have often experienced face to face and now by letter, ever to reach the point of satiety. But our case is like that of those who from some circumstance are afflicted with unquenchable thirst; for just in the same way, the more we taste your kindness, the more thirsty we become. But unless you suppose our language to be mere blandishment and unreal flattery— and assuredly you will not so suppose, being what you are in all else, and to us especially good and staunch, if any one ever was—you will certainly believe what I say; that the favour of your letter, applied to my eyes like some medical prescription, stayed my ever-flowing *"fountain of tears,"* and that fixing our hopes on the medicine of your holy prayers, we expect that soon and completely the disease of our soul will be healed: though, for the present at any rate, we are in such a case, that we spare the ears of one who is fond of us, and bury the truth in silence, that we may not drag those who loyally love us into partnership with our troubles. For when we consider that, bereft of what is dearest to us, we are involved in wars, and that it is our children that we were compelled to leave behind, our children whom we were counted worthy to bear to God in spiritual pangs, closely joined to us by the law of love, who at the time of their own trials amid their afflictions extended their affection to us; and over and above these, a fondly-loved home, brethren, kinsmen, companions, intimate associates, friends, hearth, table, cellar, bed, seat, sack, converse, tears— and how sweet these are, and how dearly prized from long habit, I need not write to you who know full well— but not to weary you further, consider for yourself what I have in exchange for those blessings. Now that I am at the end of my life, I begin to live again, and am compelled to learn the graceful versatility of character which is now in vogue: but we are late learners in the shifty school of knavery; so that we are constantly constrained to blush at our awkwardness and inaptitude for this new study. But our adversaries, equipped with all the training of this wisdom, are well able to keep what they have learned, and to invent what they have not learned. Their method of warfare accordingly is to skirmish at a distance, and then at a preconcerted signal to form their phalanx in solid order; they utter by way of prelude whatever suits their interests, they execute surprises by means of exaggerations, they surround themselves with allies from every quarter. But a vast amount of cunning invincible in power accompanies them, advanced before them to lead their host, like some right-and-left-handed combatant, fighting with both hands in front of his army, on one side levying tribute upon his subjects, on the other smiting those who come in his way. But if you care to inquire into the state of our internal affairs, you will find other troubles to match; a stifling hut, abundant in cold, gloom, confinement, and all such advantages; a life the mark of every one's censorious observation, the voice, the look, the way of wearing one's cloak, the movement of the hands, the position of one's feet, and everything else, all a subject for busy-bodies. And unless one from time to time emits a deep breathing, and unless a continuous groaning is uttered with the breathing, and unless the tunic passes gracefully through the girdle (not to mention the very disuse of the girdle itself), and unless our cloak flows aslant down our backs— the omission of anyone of these niceties is a pretext for war against us. And on such grounds as these, they gather together to battle against us, man by man, township by township, even down to all sorts of out-of-the-way places. Well, one cannot be always faring well or always ill, for every one's life is made up of contraries. But if by God's grace your help should stand by us steadily, we will bear the abundance of annoyances, in the hope of being always a sharer in your goodness. May you, then, never cease bestowing on us such favours, that by them you may refresh us, and prepare for yourself in ampler measure the reward promised to them that keep the commandments.

To Adelphius the Lawyer
To Adelphius the Lawyer

I write you this letter from the sacred Vanota, if I do not do the place injustice by giving it its local title:— do it injustice, I say, because in its name it shows no polish. At the same time the beauty of the place, great as it is, is not conveyed by this Galatian epithet: eyes are needed to interpret its beauty. For I, though I have before this seen much, and that in many places, and have also observed many things by means of verbal description in the accounts of old writers, think both all I have seen, and all of which I have heard, of no account in comparison with the loveliness that is to be found here. Your Helicon is nothing: the Islands of the Blest are a fable: the Sicyonian plain is a trifle: the accounts of the Peneus are another case of poetic exaggeration— that river which they say by overflowing with its rich current the banks which flank its course makes for the Thessalians their far-famed Tempe. Why, what beauty is there in any one of these places I have mentioned, such as Vanota can show us of its own? For if one seeks for natural beauty in the place, it needs none of the adornments of art: and if one considers what has been done for it by artificial aid, there has been so much done, and that so well, as might overcome even natural disadvantages. The gifts bestowed upon the spot by Nature who beautifies the earth with unstudied grace are such as these: below, the river Halys makes the place fair to look upon with his banks, and gleams like a golden ribbon through their deep purple, reddening his current with the soil he washes down. Above, a mountain densely overgrown with wood stretches with its long ridge, covered at all points with the foliage of oaks, worthy of finding some Homer to sing its praises more than that Ithacan Neritus, which the poet calls *"far-seen with quivering leaves."* But the natural growth of wood, as it comes down the hill-side, meets at the foot the planting of men's husbandry. For immediately vines, spread out over the slopes, and swellings, and hollows at the mountain's base, cover with their colour, like a green mantle, all the lower ground: and the season at this time even added to their beauty, displaying its grape-clusters wonderful to behold. Indeed this caused me yet more surprise, that while the neighbouring country shows fruit still unripe, one might here enjoy the full clusters, and be sated with their perfection. Then, far off, like a watch-fire from some great beacon, there shone before our eyes the fair beauty of the buildings. On the left as we entered was the chapel built for the martyrs, not yet complete in its structure, but still lacking the roof, yet making a good show notwithstanding. Straight before us in the way were the beauties of the house, where one part is marked out from another by some delicate invention. There were projecting towers, and preparations for banqueting among the wide and high-arched rows of trees crowning the entrance before the gates. Then about the buildings are the Phaeacian gardens; rather, let not the beauties of Vanota be insulted by comparison with those. Homer never saw *"the apple with bright fruit "* as we have it here, approaching to the hue of its own blossom in the exceeding brilliancy of its colouring: he never saw the pear whiter than new-polished ivory. And what can one say of the varieties of the peach, diverse and multiform, yet blended and compounded out of different species? For just as with those who paint *"goat-stags,"* and *"centaurs,"* and the like, commingling things of different kind, and making themselves wiser than Nature, so it is in the case of this fruit: Nature, under the despotism of art, turns one to an almond, another to a walnut, yet another to a *"Doracinus ,"* mingled alike in name and in flavour. And in all these the number of single trees is more noted than their beauty; yet they display tasteful arrangement in their planting, and that harmonious form of drawing— drawing, I call it, for the marvel belongs rather to the painter's art than to the gardener's. So readily does Nature fall in with the design of those who arrange these devices, that it seems impossible to express this by words. Who could find words worthily to describe the road under the climbing vines, and the sweet shade of their cluster, and that novel wall-structure where roses with their shoots, and vines with their trailers, twist themselves together and make a fortification that serves as a wall against a flank attack, and the pond at the summit of this path, and the fish that are bred there? As regards all these, the people who have charge of your Nobility's house were ready to act as our guides with a certain ingenuous kindliness, and pointed them out to us, showing us each of the things you had taken pains about, as if it were yourself to whom, by our means, they were showing courtesy. There too, one of the lads, like a conjuror, showed us such a wonder as one does not very often find in nature: for he went down to the deep water and brought up at will such of the fish as he selected; and they seemed no strangers to the fisherman's touch, being tame and submissive under the artist's hands, like well-trained dogs. Then they led me to a house as if to rest— a house, I call it, for such the entrance betokened, but, when we came inside, it was not a house but a portico which received us. The portico was raised up aloft to a great height over a deep pool: the basement supporting the portico of triangular shape, like a gateway leading to the delights within, was washed by the water. Straight before us in the interior a sort of house occupied the vertex of the triangle, with lofty roof, lit on all sides by the sun's rays, and decked with varied paintings; so that this spot almost made us forget what had preceded it. The house attracted us to itself; and again, the portico on the pool was a unique sight. For the excellent fish would swim up from the depths to the surface, leaping up into the very air like winged things, as though purposely mocking us creatures of the dry land. For showing half their form and tumbling through the air, they plunged once more into the depth. Others, again, in shoals, following one another in order, were a sight for unaccustomed eyes: while in another place one might see another shoal packed in a cluster round a morsel of bread, pushed aside one by another, and here one leaping up, there another diving downwards. But even this we were made to forget by the grapes that were brought us in baskets of twisted shoots, by the varied bounty of the season's fruit, the preparation for breakfast, the varied dainties, and savoury dishes, and sweetmeats, and drinking of healths, and wine-cups. So now since I was sated and inclined to sleep, I got a scribe posted beside me, and sent to your Eloquence, as if it were a dream, this chattering letter. But I hope to recount in full to yourself and your friends, not with paper and ink, but with my own voice and tongue, the beauties of your home.

To Amphilochius

To Amphilochius

I am well persuaded that by God's grace the business of the Church of the Martyrs is in a fair way. Would that you were willing in the matter. The task we have in hand will find its end by the power of God, Who is able, wherever He speaks, to turn word into deed. Seeing that, as the Apostle says, *"He Who has begun a good work will also perform it "*, I would exhort you in this also to be an imitator of the great Paul, and to advance our hope to actual fulfilment, and send us so many workmen as may suffice for the work we have in hand.

Your Perfection might perhaps be informed by calculation of the dimensions to which the total work will attain: and to this end I will endeavour to explain the whole structure by a verbal description. The form of the chapel is a cross, which has its figure completed throughout, as you would expect, by four structures. The junctions of the buildings intercept one another, as we see everywhere in the cruciform pattern. But within the cross there lies a circle, divided by eight angles (I call the octagonal figure a circle in view of its circumference), in such wise that the two pairs of sides of the octagon which are diametrically opposed to one another, unite by means of arches the central circle to the adjoining blocks of building; while the other four sides of the octagon, which lie between the quadrilateral buildings, will not themselves be carried to meet the buildings, but upon each of them will be described a semicircle like a shell , terminating in an arch above: so that the arches will be eight in all, and by their means the quadrilateral and semicircular buildings will be connected, side by side, with the central structure. In the blocks of masonry formed by the angles there will be an equal number of pillars, at once for ornament and for strength, and these again will carry arches built of equal size to correspond with those within. And above these eight arches, with the symmetry of an upper range of windows, the octagonal building will be raised to the height of four cubits: the part rising from it will be a cone shaped like a top, as the vaulting narrows the figure of the roof from its full width to a pointed wedge. The dimensions below will be—the width of each of the quadrilateral buildings, eight cubits, the length of them half as much again, the height as much as the proportion of the width allows. It will be as much in the semicircles also. The whole length between the piers extends in the same way to eight cubits, and the depth will be as much as will be given by the sweep of the compasses with the fixed point placed in the middle of the side and extending to the end. The height will be determined in this case too by the proportion to the width. And the thickness of the wall, an interval of three feet from inside these spaces, which are measured internally, will run round the whole building.

I have troubled your Excellency with this serious trifling, with this intention, that by the thickness of the walls, and by the intermediate spaces, you may accurately ascertain what sum the number of feet gives as the measurement; because your intellect is exceedingly quick in all matters, and makes its way, by God's grace, in whatever subject you will, and it is possible for you, by subtle calculation, to ascertain the sum made up by all the parts, so as to send us masons neither more nor fewer than our need requires. And I beg you to direct your attention specially to this point, that some of them may be skilled in making vaulting without supports: for I am informed that when built in this way it is more durable than what is made to rest on props. It is the scarcity of wood that brings us to this device of roofing the whole fabric with stone; because the place supplies no timber for roofing. Let your unerring mind be persuaded, because some of the people here contract with me to furnish thirty workmen for a stater, for the dressed stonework, of course with a specified ration along with the stater. But the material of our masonry is not of this sort , but brick made of clay and chance stones, so that they do not need to spend time in fitting the faces of the stones accurately together. I know that so far as skill and fairness in the matter of wages are concerned, the workmen in your neighbourhood are better for our purpose than those who follow the trade here. The sculptor's work lies not only in the eight pillars, which must themselves be improved and beautified, but the work requires altar-like base-mouldings , and capitals carved in the Corinthian style. The porch, too, will be of marbles wrought with appropriate ornaments. The doors set upon these will be adorned with some such designs as are usually employed by way of embellishment at the projection of the cornice. Of all these, of course, we shall furnish the materials; the form to be impressed on the materials art will bestow. Besides these there will be in the colonnade not less than forty pillars: these also will be of wrought stone. Now if my account has explained the work in detail, I hope it may be possible for your Sanctity, on perceiving what is needed, to relieve us completely from anxiety so far as the workmen are concerned. If, however, the workman were inclined to make a bargain favourable to us, let a distinct measure of work, if possible, be fixed for the day, so that he may not pass his time doing nothing, and then, though he has no work to show for it, as having worked for us so many days, demand payment for them. I know that we shall appear to most people to be higglers, in being so particular about the contracts. But I beg you to pardon me; for that Mammon about whom I have so often said such hard things, has at last departed from me as far as he can possibly go, being disgusted, I suppose, at the nonsense that is constantly talked against him, and has fortified himself against me by an impassable gulf— to wit, poverty— so that neither can he come to me, nor can I pass to him. This is why I make a point of the fairness of the workmen, to the end that we may be able to fulfil the task before us, and not be hindered by poverty— that laudable and desirable evil. Well, in all this there is a certain admixture of jest. But do you, man of God, in such ways as are possible and legitimate, boldly promise in bargaining with the men that they will all meet with fair treatment at our hands, and full payment of their wages: for we shall give all and keep back nothing, as God also opens to us, by your prayers, His hand of blessing.

To Eustathis, Ambrosia and Basilissa

To Eustathia, Ambrosia, and Basilissa.

To the most discreet and devout Sisters, Eustathia and Ambrosia, and to the most discreet and noble Daughter, Basilissa, Gregory sends greeting in the Lord.

The meeting with the good and the beloved, and the memorials of the immense love of the Lord for us men, which are shown in your localities, have been the source to me of the most intense joy and gladness. Doubly indeed have these shone upon divinely festal days; both in beholding the saving tokens of the God who gave us life, and in meeting with souls in whom the tokens of the Lord's grace are to be discerned spiritually in such clearness, that one can believe that Bethlehem and Golgotha, and Olivet, and the scene of the Resurrection are really in the God-containing heart. For when through a good conscience Christ has been formed in any, when any has by dint of godly fear nailed down the promptings of the flesh and become crucified to Christ, when any has rolled away from himself the heavy stone of this world's illusions, and coming forth from the grave of the body has begun to walk as it were in a newness of life, abandoning this low-lying valley of human life, and mounting with a soaring desire to that heavenly country with all its elevated thoughts, where Christ is, no longer feeling the body's burden, but lifting it by chastity, so that the flesh with cloud-like lightness accompanies the ascending soul— such an one, in my opinion, is to be counted in the number of those famous ones in whom the memorials of the Lord's love for us men are to be seen. When, then, I not only saw with the sense of sight those Sacred Places, but I saw the tokens of places like them, plain in yourselves as well, I was filled with joy so great that the description of its blessing is beyond the power of utterance. But because it is a difficult, not to say an impossible thing for a human being to enjoy unmixed with evil any blessing, therefore something of bitterness was mingled with the sweets I tasted: and by this, after the enjoyment of those blessings, I was saddened in my journey back to my native land, estimating now the truth of the Lord's words, that *"the whole world lies in wickedness,"* 1 John 5:19 so that no single part of the inhabited earth is without its share of degeneracy. For if the spot itself that has received the footprints of the very Life is not clear of the wicked thorns, what are we to think of other places where communion with the Blessing has been inculcated by hearing and preaching alone. With what view I say this, need not be explained more fully in words; facts themselves proclaim more loudly than any speech, however intelligible, the melancholy truth.

The Lawgiver of our life has enjoined upon us one single hatred. I mean, that of the Serpent: for no other purpose has He bidden us exercise this faculty of hatred, but as a resource against wickedness. *"I will put enmity,"* He says, *"between you and him."* Since wickedness is a complicated and multifarious thing, the Word allegorizes it by the Serpent, the dense array of whose scales is symbolic of this multiformity of evil. And we by working the will of our Adversary make an alliance with this serpent, and so turn this hatred against one another , and perhaps not against ourselves alone, but against Him Who gave the commandment; for He says, *"You shall love your neighbour and hate your enemy,"* commanding us to hold the foe to our humanity as our only enemy, and declaring that all who share that humanity are the neighbours of each one of us. But this gross-hearted age has disunited us from our neighbour, and has made us welcome the serpent, and revel in his spotted scales. I affirm, then, that it is a lawful thing to hate God's enemies, and that this kind of hatred is pleasing to our Lord: and by God's enemies I mean those who deny the glory of our Lord, be they Jews, or downright idolaters, or those who through Arius' teaching idolize the creature, and so adopt the error of the Jews. Now when the Father, the Son, and the Holy Ghost, are with orthodox devotion being glorified and adored by those who believe that in a distinct and unconfused Trinity there is One Substance, Glory, Kingship, Power, and Universal Rule, in such a case as this what good excuse for fighting can there be? At the time, certainly, when the heretical views prevailed, to try issues with the authorities, by whom the adversaries' cause was seen to be strengthened, was well; there was fear then lest our saving Doctrine should be over-ruled by human rulers. But now, when over the whole world from one end of heaven to the other the orthodox Faith is being preached, the man who fights with them who preach it, fights not with them, but with Him Who is thus preached. What other aim, indeed, ought that man's to be, who has the zeal for God, than in every possible way to announce the glory of God? As long, then, as the Only-begotten is adored with all the heart and soul and mind, believed to be in everything that which the Father is, and in like manner the Holy Ghost is glorified with an equal amount of adoration, what plausible excuse for fighting is left these over-refined disputants, who are rending the seamless robe, and parting the Lord's name between Paul and Cephas, and undisguisedly abhorring contact with those who worship Christ, all but exclaiming in so many words, *"Away from me, I am holy"*?

Granting that the knowledge which they believe themselves to have acquired is somewhat greater than that of others: yet can they possess more than the belief that the Son of the Very God is Very God, seeing that in that article of the Very God every idea that is orthodox, every idea that is our salvation, is included? It includes the idea of His Goodness, His Justice, His Omnipotence: that He admits of no variableness nor alteration, but is always the same; incapable of changing to worse or changing to better, because the first is not His nature, the second He does not admit of; for what can be higher than the Highest, what can be better than the Best? In fact, He is thus associated with all perfection, and, as to every form of alteration, is unalterable; He did not on occasions display this attribute, but was always so, both before the Dispensation that made Him man, and during it, and after it; and in all His activities in our behalf He never lowered any part of that changeless and unvarying character to that which was out of keeping with it. What is essentially imperishable and changeless is always such; it does not follow the variation of a lower order of things, when it comes by dispensation to be there; just as the sun, for example, when he plunges his beam into the gloom, does not dim the brightness of that beam; but instead, the dark is changed by the beam into light; thus also the True Light, shining in our gloom, was not itself overshadowed with that shade, but enlightened it by means of itself. Well, seeing that our humanity was in darkness, as it is written, *"They know not, neither will they understand, they walk on in darkness,"* the Illuminator of this darkened world darted the beam of His Divinity through the whole compound of our nature, through soul, I say, and body too, and so appropriated humanity entire by means of His own light, and took it up and made it just that thing which He is Himself. And as this Divinity was not made perishable, though it inhabited a perishable body, so neither did it alter in the direction of any change, though it healed the changeful in our soul: in medicine, too, the physician of the body, when he takes hold of his patient, so far from himself contracting the disease, thereby perfects the cure of the suffering part.

Let no one, either, putting a wrong interpretation on the words of the Gospel, suppose that our human nature in Christ was transformed to something more divine by any gradations and advance: for the increasing in stature and in wisdom and in favour, is recorded in Holy Writ only to prove that Christ really was present in the human compound, and so to leave no room for their surmise, who propound that a phantom, or form in human outline, and not a real Divine Manifestation, was there. It is for this reason that Holy Writ records unabashed with regard to Him all the accidents of our nature, even eating, drinking, sleeping, weariness, nurture, increase in bodily stature, growing up— everything that marks humanity, except the tendency to sin. Sin, indeed, is a miscarriage, not a quality of human nature: just as disease and deformity are not congenital to it in the first instance, but are its unnatural accretions, so activity in the direction of sin is to be thought of as a mere mutilation of the goodness innate in us; it is not found to be itself a real thing, but we see it only in the absence of that goodness. Therefore He Who transformed the elements of our nature into His divine abilities, rendered it secure from mutilation and disease, because He admitted not in Himself the deformity which sin works in the will. *"He did no sin,"* it says, *"neither was guile found in his mouth* 1 Peter 2:22 *."* And this in Him is not to be regarded in connection with any interval of time: for at once the man in Mary (where Wisdom built her house), though naturally part of our sensuous compound, along with the coming upon her of the Holy Ghost, and her overshadowing with the power of the Highest, became that which that overshadowing power in essence was: for, without controversy, it is the Less that is blest by the Greater. Seeing, then, that the power of the Godhead is an immense and immeasurable thing, while man is a weak atom, at the moment when the Holy Ghost came upon the Virgin, and the power of the Highest overshadowed her, the tabernacle formed by such an impulse was not clothed with anything of human corruption; but, just as it was first constituted, so it remained, even though it was man, Spirit nevertheless, and Grace, and Power; and the special attributes of our humanity derived lustre from this abundance of Divine Power.

There are indeed two limits of human life: the one we start from, and the one we end in: and so it was necessary that the Physician of our being should enfold us at both these extremities, and grasp not only the end, but the beginning too, in order to secure in both the raising of the sufferer. That, then, which we find to have happened on the side of the finish we conclude also as to the beginning. As at the end He caused by virtue of the Incarnation that, though the body was disunited from the soul, yet the indivisible Godhead which had been blended once for all with the subject (who possessed them) was not stripped from that body any more than it was from that soul, but while it was in Paradise along with the soul, and paved an entrance there in the person of the Thief for all humanity, it remained by means of the body in the heart of the earth, and therein destroyed him that had the power of Death (wherefore His *body* too is called *"the Lord"* on account of that inherent Godhead)— so also, at the beginning, we conclude that the power of the Highest, coalescing with our entire nature by that coming upon (the Virgin) of the Holy Ghost, both resides in our soul, so far as reason sees it possible that it should reside there, and is blended with our body, so that our salvation throughout every element may be perfect, that heavenly passionlessness which is peculiar to the Deity being nevertheless preserved both in the beginning and in the end of this life as Man. Thus the beginning was not as our beginning, nor the end as our end. Both in the one and in the other He evinced His Divine independence; the beginning had no stain of pleasure upon it, the end was not the end in dissolution.

Now if we loudly preach all this, and testify to all this, namely that Christ is the power of God and the wisdom of God, always changeless, always imperishable, though He comes in the changeable and the perishable; never stained Himself, but making clean that which is stained; what is the crime that we commit, and wherefore are we hated? And what means this opposing array of new Altars? Do we announce another Jesus? Do we hint at another? Do we produce other scriptures? Have any of ourselves dared to say *"Mother of Man"* of the Holy Virgin, the Mother of God : which is what we hear that some of them say without restraint? Do we romance about three Resurrections ? Do we promise the gluttony of the Millennium? Do we declare that the Jewish animal-sacrifices shall be restored? Do we lower men's hopes again to the Jerusalem below, imagining its rebuilding with stones of a more brilliant material? What charge like these can be brought against us, that our company should be reckoned a thing to be avoided, and that in some places another altar should be erected in opposition to us, as if we should defile their sanctuaries? My heart was in a state of burning indignation about this: and now that I have set foot in the City again, I am eager to unburden my soul of its bitterness, by appealing, in a letter, to your love. Do ye, wherever the Holy Spirit shall lead you, there remain; walk with God before you; confer not with flesh and blood; lend no occasion to any of them for glorying, that they may not glory in you, enlarging their ambition by anything in your lives. Remember the Holy Fathers, into whose hands you were commended by your Father now in bliss , and to whom we by God's grace were deemed worthy to succeed and remove not the boundaries which our Fathers have laid down, nor put aside in any way the plainness of our simpler proclamation in favour of their subtler school. Walk by the primitive rule of the Faith: and the God of peace shall be with you, and you shall be strong in mind and body. May God keep you uncorrupted, is our prayer.

To Flavian

To Flavian

Things with us, O man of God, are not in a good way. The development of the bad feeling existing among certain persons who have conceived a most groundless and unaccountable hatred of us is no longer a matter of mere conjecture; it is now evinced with an earnestness and openness worthy only of some holy work. You meanwhile, who have hitherto been beyond the reach of such annoyance, are too remiss in stifling the devouring conflagration on your neighbour's land; yet those who are well-advised for their own interests really do take pains to check a fire close to them, securing themselves, by this help given to a neighbour, against ever needing help in like circumstances. Well, you will ask, what do I complain of? Piety has vanished from the world; Truth has fled from our midst; as for Peace, we used to have the name at all events going the round upon men's lips; but now not only does she herself cease to exist, but we do not even retain the word that expresses her. But that you may know more exactly the things that move our indignation, I will briefly detail to you the whole tragic story.

Certain persons had informed me that the Right Reverend Helladius had unfriendly feelings towards me, and that he enlarged in conversation to every one upon the troubles that I had brought upon him. I did not at first believe what they said, judging only from myself, and the actual truth of the matter. But when every one kept bringing to us a tale of the same strain, and facts besides corroborated their report, I thought it my duty not to continue to overlook this ill-feeling, while it was still without root and development. I therefore wrote by letter to your piety, and to many others who could help me in my intention, and stimulated your zeal in this matter. At last, after I had concluded the services at Sebasteia in commemoration of Peter of most blessed memory, and of the holy martyrs, who had lived in his times, and whom the people were accustomed to commemorate with him, I was returning to my own See, when some one told me that Helladius himself was in the neighbouring mountain district, holding martyrs' memorial services. At first I held on my journey, judging it more proper that our meeting should take place in the metropolis itself. But when one of his relations took the trouble to meet me, and to assure me that he was sick, I left my carriage at the spot where this news arrested me; I performed on horseback the intervening journey over a road that was like a precipice, and nearly impassable with its rocky ascents. Fifteen milestones measured the distance we had to traverse. Painfully travelling, now on foot, now mounted, in the early morning, and even employing some part of the night, I arrived between twelve and one o'clock at Andumocina; for that was the name of the place where, with two other bishops, he was holding his conference. From a shoulder of the hill overhanging this village, we looked down, while still at a distance, upon this outdoor assemblage of the Church. Slowly, and on foot, and leading the horses, I and my company passed over the intervening ground, and we arrived at the chapel just as he had retired to his residence.

Without any delay a messenger was dispatched to inform him of our being there; and a very short while after, the deacon in attendance on him met us, and we requested him to tell Helladius at once, so that we might spend as much time as possible with him, and so have an opportunity of leaving nothing in the misunderstanding between us unhealed. As for myself, I then remained sitting, still in the open air, and waited for the invitation indoors; and at a most inopportune time I became, as I sat there, a gazing stock to all the visitors at the conference. The time was long; drowsiness came on, and languor, intensified by the fatigue of the journey and the excessive heat of the day; and all these things, with people staring at me, and pointing me out to others, were so very distressing that in me the words of the prophet were realized: *"My spirit within me was desolate."* I was kept in this state till noon, and heartily did I repent of this visit, and that I had brought upon myself this piece of discourtesy; and my own reflection vexed me worse than this injury done me by my enemies , warring as it did against itself, and changing into a regret that I had made the venture. At last the approach to the Altars was thrown open, and we were admitted to the sanctuary; the crowd, however, were excluded, though my deacon entered along with me, supporting with his arm my exhausted frame. I addressed his Lordship, and stood for a moment, expecting from him an invitation to be seated; but when nothing of the kind was heard from him, I turned towards one of the distant seats, and rested myself upon it, still expecting that he would utter something that was friendly, or at all events kind; or at least give one nod of recognition.

Any hopes I had were doomed to complete disappointment. There ensued a silence dead as night, and looks as downcast as in tragedy, and daze, and dumbfoundedness, and perfect dumbness. A long interval of time it was, dragged out as if it were in the blackness of night. So struck down was I by this reception, in which he did not deign to accord me the merest utterance even of those common salutations by which you discharge the courtesies of a chance meeting — *"welcome,"* for instance, or *"where do you come from?"* or *"to what am I indebted for this pleasure?"* or *"on what important business are you here?"*— that I was inclined to make this spell of silence into a picture of the life led in the underworld. Nay, I condemn the similitude as inadequate. For in that underworld the equality of conditions is complete, and none of the things that cause the tragedies of life on earth disturb existence. Their glory, as the Prophet says, does not follow men down there; each individual soul, abandoning the things so eagerly clung to by the majority here, his petulance, and pride, and conceit, enters that lower world in simple unencumbered nakedness; so that none of the miseries of this life are to be found among them. Still, notwithstanding this reservation, my condition then did appear to me like an underworld, a murky dungeon, a gloomy torture-chamber; the more so, when I reflected what treasures of social courtesies we have inherited from our fathers, and what recorded deeds of it we shall leave to our descendants. Why, indeed, should I speak at all of that affectionate disposition of our fathers towards each other? No wonder that, being all naturally equal, they wished for no advantage over one another, but thought to exceed each other only in humility. But my mind was penetrated most of all with this thought; that the Lord of all creation, the Only-begotten Son, Who was in the bosom of the Father, Who was in the beginning, Who was in the form of God, Who upholds all things by the word of His power, humbled Himself not only in this respect, that in the flesh He sojourned among men, but also that He welcomed even Judas His own betrayer, when he drew near to kiss Him, on His blessed lips; and that when He had entered into the house of Simon the leper He, as loving all men, upbraided his host, that He had not been kissed by him: whereas I was not reckoned by him as equal even to that leper; and yet what was I, and what was he? I cannot discover any difference between us. If one looks at it from the mundane point of view, where was the height from which he had descended, where was the dust in which I lay? If, indeed, one must regard things of this fleshly life, thus much perhaps it will hurt no one's feelings to assert that, looking at our lineage, whether as noble or as free, our position was about on a par; though, if one looked in either for the true freedom and nobility, *i.e.* that of the soul, each of us will be found equally a bondsman of Sin; each equally needs One Who will take away his sins; it was Another Who ransomed us both from Death and Sin with His own blood, Who redeemed us, and yet showed no contempt of those whom He has redeemed, calling them though He does from deadness to life, and healing every infirmity of their souls and bodies.

Seeing, then, that the amount of this conceit and overweening pride was so great, that even the height of heaven was almost too narrow limits for it (and yet I could see no cause or occasion whatever for this diseased state of mind, such as might make it excusable in the case of some who in certain circumstances contract it; when, for instance, rank or education, or pre-eminence in dignities of office may have happened to inflate the vainer minds), I had no means whereby to advise myself to keep quiet: for my heart within me was swelling with indignation at the absurdity of the whole proceeding, and was rejecting all the reasons for enduring it. Then, if ever, did I feel admiration for that divine Apostle who so vividly depicts the civil war that rages within us, declaring that there is a certain *"law of sin in the members, warring against the law of the mind,"* and often making the mind a captive, and a slave as well, to itself. This was the very array, in opposition, of two contending feelings that I saw within myself: the one, of anger at the insult caused by pride, the other prompting to appease the rising storm. When by God's grace, the worse inclination had failed to get the mastery, I at last said to him, *"But is it, then, that some one of the things required for your personal comfort is being hindered by our presence, and is it time that we withdrew?"* On his declaring that he had no bodily needs, I spoke to him some words calculated to heal, so far as in me lay, his ill-feeling. When he had, in a very few words, declared that the anger he felt towards me was owing to many injuries done him, I for my part answered him thus: *"Lies possess an immense power among mankind to deceive: but in the Divine Judgment there will be no place for the misunderstandings thus arising. In my relations towards yourself, my conscience is bold enough to prompt me to hope that I may obtain forgiveness for all my other sins, but that, if I have acted in any way to harm you, this may remain for ever unforgiven."* He was indignant at this speech, and did not suffer the proofs of what I had said to be added.

It was now past six o'clock, and the bath had been well prepared, and the banquet was being spread, and the day was the sabbath , and a martyr's commemoration. Again observe how this disciple of the Gospel imitates the Lord of the Gospel: He, when eating and drinking with publicans and sinners, answered to those who found fault with Him that He did it for love of mankind: this disciple considers it a sin and a pollution to have us at his board, even after all that fatigue which we underwent on the journey, after all that excessive heat out of doors, in which we were baked while sitting at his gates; after all that gloomy sullenness with which he treated us to the bitter end, when we had come into his presence. He sends us off to toil painfully, with a frame now thoroughly exhausted with the over-fatigue, over the same distance, the same route: so that we scarcely reached our travelling company at sunset, after we had suffered many mishaps on the way. For a storm-cloud, gathered into a mass in the clear air by an eddy of wind, drenched us to the skin with its floods of rain; for owing to the excessive sultriness, we had made no preparation against any shower. However, by God's grace we escaped, though in the plight of shipwrecked sailors from the waves: and right glad were we to reach our company.

Having joined our forces we rested there that night, and at last arrived alive in our own district; having reaped in addition this result of our meeting him, that the memory of all that had happened before was revived by this last insult offered to us; and, you see, we are positively compelled to take measures, for the future, on our own behalf, or rather on his behalf; for it was because his designs were not checked on former occasions that he has proceeded to this unmeasured display of vanity. Something, therefore, I think, must be done on our part, in order that he may improve upon himself, and may be taught that he is human, and has no authority to insult and to disgrace those who possess the same beliefs and the same rank as himself. For just consider; suppose we granted for a moment, for the sake of argument, that it is true that I have done something that has annoyed him, what trial was instituted against us, to judge either of the fact or the hearsay? What proofs were given of this supposed injury? What Canons were cited against us? What legitimate episcopal decision confirmed any verdict passed upon us? And supposing any of these processes had taken place, and that in the proper way, my standing in the Church might certainly have been at stake, but what Canons could have sanctioned insults offered to a free-born person, and disgrace inflicted on one of equal rank with himself? *"Judge righteous judgment,"* you who look to God's law in this matter; say wherein you deem this disgrace put upon us to be excusable. If our dignity is to be estimated on the ground of priestly jurisdiction, the privilege of each recorded by the Council is one and the same; or rather the oversight of Catholic correction , from the fact that we possess an equal share of it, is so. But if some are inclined to regard each of us by himself, divested of any priestly dignity, in what respect has one any advantage over the other; in education for instance, or in birth connecting with the noblest and most illustrious lineage, or in theology? These things will be found either equal, or at all events not inferior, in me. *"But what about revenue?"* he will say. I would rather not be obliged to speak of this in his case; thus much only it will suffice to say, that our own was so much at the beginning, and is so much now; and to leave it to others to enquire into the causes of this increase of our revenue , nursed as it is up till now, and growing almost daily by means of noble undertakings. What licence, then, has he to put an insult upon us, seeing that he has neither superiority of birth to show, nor a rank exalted above all others, nor a commanding power of speech, nor any previous kindness done to me? While, even if he had all this to show, the fault of having slighted those of gentle birth would still be inexcusable. But he has not got it; and therefore I deem it right to see that this malady of puffed-up pride is not left without a cure; and it will be its cure to put it down to its proper level, and reduce its inflated dimensions, by letting off a little of the conceit with which he is bursting. The manner of effecting this we leave to God.

Made in the USA
Middletown, DE
16 September 2023